Kundalin

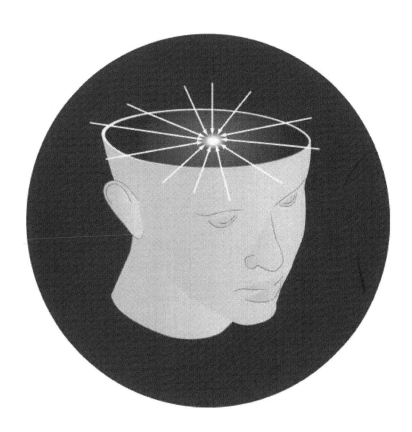

Michael Beloved

Shiva Art:	Sir Paul Castagna
Illustrations:	Author
Proofreader:	Tobe Terrell

Correspondence:
Michael Beloved
19311 SW 30th Street
Miramar FL 33029
USA
Email: axisnexus@gmail.com
         michaelbelovedbooks@gmail.com

Paperback ISBN: 9781942887065
eBook ISBN: 9781942887058

LCCN:
2016919026

Table of Contents

How to use this book:

Make a casual reading page for page without becoming stressed about the concepts and ideas. Read to become familiar with the language style and presentation. If you read something of particular interest make a mental note. Read on to get through the entire book.

Make a second reading pausing at areas of interest, where you feel you can grasp the material. Here and there, you may not follow the meanings but read on nevertheless.

Make a third reading with intent to grasp the concepts and methods given.

Finally, make an indepth study of this information.

Introduction

Read this book if you are interested in researching the mystery of sexual facility in a physical/subtle body system. If you ever considered being celibate, read this book. If you ever realize that celibacy is impossible because of the potential developments of nature, then read this book. If you ever wanted to practice tantric yoga which is defined as sexual self-exploration, read this book.

I picked up this body in the year 1951 from ordinary parents, non-yogis, persons who in their lifetime did not practice any form of yoga and had not even a whimsical interest in it. My purpose in subjecting myself to the development of this body was to practice yoga and write about my discoveries. In the past life, I saw the need for more literary elaboration about yoga techniques. There were yogis of worth but most of these had little or no interest in jotting down their meditation experiences and observations about the various valid and invalid yogic methods.

There was a tradition in India where in seclusion one learned from a worthy teacher. It was the procedure that until the teacher passed on that technique, a disciple would not discuss what he learnt from the teacher, and then only in the same way which the teacher instructed. This greatly restricted the transmission of method.

In the past birth, I decided to break this rule and to divulge techniques openly to one and all. In this body, I fulfill this desire to expound yoga in books. However the risk of misuse of this information is reduced by the very fact that unless one practices ardently one cannot use the information to make psychological progress in the relationship between the core-self and its adjuncts. I can give techniques because even if you read of them, you will not be able to practice unless you develop yourself psychologically. That decreases the danger of anyone exploiting this.

I am not alone in this task because several spiritual masters of repute, yogis who are long departed, use my literary skill to express themselves, to divulge techniques which they mastered. This assistance which I render, aids them in continuing their austerities on the astral planes. It prevents the assumption of a new embryo just for the reason of having to teach students who use material bodies.

The whole subject of brahmacharya or celibacy will be discussed in this book in a comprehensive and final way, without superficiality. Traditionally celibacy meant that a person did not have sexual intercourse during juvenile years or did not have it during adult age. This meant that a person whose body did not reach sexual maturity displayed no interest in sexual intercourse, and a man who did reach sexual maturity also had no sexual contact.

However the fallacy in this definition is that it did not take into account the situation of the subtle body. Celibacy or brahmacharya was traditionally a description of a lack of sexual interest in physical behavior. It has to do with moral values on the social plane where the person's lack of sexual interest was observed. In this book however, we uproot that definition and include the behavior of the subtle form.

Chapter 1
Questions regarding Birth Process

Sex Pleasure Analyzed

Before we can understand what celibacy is, we must first check to see what nature intends when it manifests celibacy, irrespective of the human need to forego sexual experience. Whatever we say which does not entail nature's view is futile because nature is in a position to upset human aspirations.

Before a human body develops sexual maturity, the gender of it is limited because of the lack of reproductive fluids, but this proves that nature itself produces the non-sexual interest condition in bodies. Nature does this for its own reason. From a biological viewpoint mammals are without sexual interest in the time of a body's development in its early appearance when it is first produced. Even though initially sexual organs are produced, these do not have the pleasure possibly which later becomes obvious in a sexually-mature form.

If a pre-pubescent human engages in sexual interplay, there will be no pleasure feelings tied to the activity. The attraction to sex will not be impetuous. This happens by nature's arrangement rather than by human choice.

It appears that at the onset of a body, nature cannot produce a mammalian form with sex pleasure. It requires some time in development after the form is born, for the production of sex expression.

The obvious feature of sexual maturity is not the pleasure which is felt during sexual arousal but rather the body's ability to reproduce an infant form. Nature's result of a sexual intercourse between one fertile male and a female one, is the development of an embryo. The infant represents responsibility. Sexual interplay in nature, invariably results in progeny with the responsibility for nurture.

The more advanced the species, the more responsibility is placed on the parent(s). In some mammals, the females are left with most of the responsibility but in the human form, many males voluntarily support progeny.

The individual involved in a sexual liaison may be focused on the pleasure derived but it is obvious that nature is not concerned with that, except in its use of that pleasure in causing the mixture of sexual fluids from each party involved.

How then is it possible to be celibate if one uses a body which has sexual maturity?

Please include the subtle body in this consideration. A living physical body is inclusive of a subtle form. A dead physical body is immobile because it is not interspaced with a subtle form. Any discussion we make should include the subtle body. For actions to be complete, both bodies must be consistent with the ideals. If for instance only the physical body is celibate while the subtle one is deviant, our definition of sexual expression or restraint needs to be clarified with clear statements about the participation or lack of it by each form.

Reason for Desiring Celibacy

Motive must be regarded as well. The motive may support or undermine the achievement. It is not what we attain but for how long we attain it and for how long will nature permit the skill. Nature is in a position to undermine any alteration or reform. With the support of nature in any venture, a human being can achieve much but with nature's objections, the human is left with less than desired.

Why would anyone want to be celibate?

There are many reasons. Here we are concerned with spiritual achievement. If celibacy can assist that, if nature supports the effort, we should do it. Suppose someone wants to be celibate because of having unpalatable experiences during sexual intercourse? Will that serve the purpose to cause celibacy? Suppose another person wants to be celibate because he can acquire great respect from human society if he exhibits sexual disinterest, will that serve the purpose to cause celibacy?

Suppose I wish to be celibate for moral reasons. Suppose I feel that if I am not duly married, I should be exempt from sexual intercourse. Suppose, otherwise, I wish to be celibate because I feel that the conservation of sexual fluids will cause me to be healthier? Will any of these motives serve the purpose for celibacy?

Suppose I noticed that during sexual intercourse my psyche becomes highly energized but after climax it becomes depressed. Should I then develop a desire for celibacy in the hope of conserving vitality?

Since nature's use of sexual intercourse is for begetting progeny, should I conclude that I should always beget a child when I have sexual intercourse and otherwise I should not indulge?

Is it possible to fully restrain the physical and astral bodies?

One who advocates celibacy may not regard nature's position. He may not understand the limits of his power. A monk may assume a celibate posture for reasons of status in the monk and lay community. Especially in Asia, anyone who joins a monastery is respected by that very act, irrespective of if his subtle body is compliant. In fact so long as his celibate claims are not breached publicly, he gets the respect intended. But is that celibacy? Or is that social manipulation?

Besides the monks and nuns, we have the situation of persons who have no access to sexual intercourse because of not having a partner to indulge. Any of these persons if they aspire for celibacy, may either starve their bodies of indulgence or self-indulge. In cases where the person starves the physical system from indulgence, what happens to the sexual fluids which the body produces? If such liquids are not used in indulgence how does nature accommodate it? Is it reabsorbed into the body? Is it squirted from the body in urine?

What about sexual dormancy, where the physical body and/or the subtle one, appears to lose sexual interest but only for a time? Is sexual dormancy a form of celibacy? Suppose a monk is successful and has no sexual intercourse physically, how can we know if his subtle body is compliant? Does he know even?

What about a monk who is successful physically with celibacy and who is sincere in the aspiration, what can he tell us about what will happen to him when he transmigrates to another embryo? Will that new body be celibate?

How does the power of the subtle person who survives a physical body, match up to the genetic attitude of a new body which he assumes from new parents who are sexually involved? Unless we can clarify these issues, the idea of celibacy is left undefined.

Push for Indulgence

One opinion is that sexual indulgence is driven by the urge for pleasure. However that view is questionable. Even before a youth understands that there will be sex pleasure, that person is urged to indulge. What therefore is impetus for indulgence, something in which the pleasure feelings arrive after the impetus operated?

It is the sense of incompletion which arises suddenly in youth which drives the youngster to come in contact with someone else for sexual relation. In fact youths who never heard of sexual indulgence, who never saw any other human engaged in it, regularly indulge after they are motivated by a sense of incompletion which causes their lifeforms to copulate for completion.

Of course soon after a climax, such youths find themselves without the incompletion motive, back to being as they were before it manifested in their feelings. Pleasure however is not to be disregarded. When it forms a memory it is an important auxiliary reason for intercourse. With that memory, the person may crave sexual indulgent to such an extent that the initial incompletion urge is no longer experienced all by itself as it did at the onset of sexual maturity.

Memory as Motivation

Many humans rely on memory as the prime motivator for sexual stimulation. This stimulation in turn generates pleasure which demands completion through climax during intercourse or masturbation. The exercise of memory is a hidden feature but it is effective as it mobilizes the physical and subtle bodies to complete sexual acts singly or with a partner.

Even if the individual is unwilling to invoke memories of indulgence, still the memories have their own presentation power, through which they appear in the mind. Once visualized, these reminiscent energies push the individual to procure sexual opportunities.

Memories of indulgence are also transmitted from one mind to another, and from media (literature, art or video) to the mind. Any impression may trigger an urge to pursue sexual opportunities.

Since nature intended to generate progeny through sexual coupling, what is the situation of human beings who engage but who do not produce children? Some fail to reproduce because of infertility. Others fail because of contraceptive means.

We observed that in nature, there might be excessive progeny produced by either animal or vegetation parents, whereby the progeny starves to death soon after birth? What does nature intend for this? A mango tree may produce hundreds of fruit with a high percentage of fertile seeds which fall to the ground, sprout for a time and then die from one cause or another. Why does nature overproduce?

We also observed that able human beings who can be parents use contraceptive methods to avoid pregnancy. Some remain single and masturbate. What is the basis of this behavior?

Reproduction Complexities

Some human females become pregnant against their wills. Some do so without understanding that the sexual act may result in pregnancy. In the animal kingdom many females become pregnant with no understanding that they have to nurture progeny for weeks, months or years. Why is this enforced in their lifestyles?

Nature's reproduction schemes seems to be random and haphazard to say the least, with both successes and failures in both small and large quantities. Some species produce hundreds or thousands of offspring with no guarantee for their welfare.

In the bee kingdom most females in a hive are either the sisters or daughters of the queen who is the only one who ever had sexual intercourse. She is the sole mother for hundreds of bees who live side by side with her sisters.

As for the drones only one or two of these brothers of the queen get the opportunity to mate with her. The others have no companion just as their sisters and nieces pass through their entire lifetimes without ever realizing anything about sexual intercourse. Are these bees, who never had an inkling of sex pleasure, celibate?

Genetic Influence

The social environment in which one assumes an embryo becomes part of the psychology of one's mind and body, such that even if one was a confirmed celibate in the past life, the new environment may have a sexually-permissive influence which erases the previous accomplishment. This is the cultural power of the ancestors of one's new body, as well as the genetic influence which is in material nature, and which is a force to recon with. A successful celibate in one life may become aware of himself (herself) in a new body but without the celibate tendency. With enough effort this lost tendency may be retrieved. In as much as sexual expression may become dormant and may again resurface and force the body into indulgence, so the celibate tendency may also become dormant and may surface to cause a reverse in sexual behavior.

Taking a new body even from well-to-do pious people is risky because one cannot be sure that everything will happen which will be positive towards whatever spiritual progress one made in the past life. Once departed, it is best one should continue making spiritual progress on the astral planes because there one does not have to assume an infant body. One is not reliant on parents for nurture and support through infancy and adolescence.

If however one has to take an embryo, one should set the attitude in a come-what-may submission, so that if one is neglected by parents and society one does not harbor resentments. The attitude should be that nature owes one nothing. The other entities owe one nothing. Whatever little one gets one should be grateful for. Whatever goes to the contrary, one should overlook as being an integral part of this mundane reality.

Why do seeds get abundant rainfall to encourage sprouting?

Obviously it is because nature wants them to sprout?

Why do the same seeds get a drought season as soon as they are sprouted?

Obviously because nature intended for them to sprout profusely so that it could, in turn, kill them.

These are experiences in nature which should be appreciated. The ascetic should not harbor resentments. His expectations should be nil. His egocentricity about himself being at the center of welfare should be ignored. Nature gave the sense of possession but it should not be taken seriously.

Sexually Involved Ascetics

Some ascetics will discover their new adolescent bodies with a craving for sexual intercourse. This is due to genetics and social pressures. It does not matter if one was a full celibate in the immediate past life. If one takes a body from parents who are sexually-permissive or who are sexually-addicted, it is likely that the body one received will have the parental tendency. This means that in practice one will be unable to desist from being sexual involved.

Meeting a yoga-guru cannot erase the need for sexual intercourse which is embedded in such a body. However one can try to change that body by doing yoga austerities. In the meantime however until one is successful in that, one will be involved in sexual behaviors.

The practical method is to find a way to reduce the sexual conduct of the sex-prone body which one derived from the new parents. Becoming a sannyasi or celibate monk or nun is hardly a solution, because even though that may seem to solve the problem it will in fact increase the complexity.

As soon as one takes birth in a certain family, one takes along with the body certain obligations to the ancestors of that family. No amount of guru-grace of any kind can waiver or delete that obligation. The easily way out is to recognize the obligation and service it to the best of one's ability. However one should do so without losing one's footing in the yoga austerities.

One has to live a dual life, one where one fulfills ancestral obligations and proceeds with the yoga austerities. A careful study of the Bhagavad Gita discourse of Krishna will help considerably in this effort because Arjuna was perplexed when Krishna asked Arjuna to be a yogi on one hand and to be a social compliant member of the Kuru dynasty on the other hand. How is it that one can be an ascetic and simultaneously be involved with materialistic relatives?

Krishna established in the Bhagavad Gita, that it is only he, Krishna, who can teach the science of the application of yoga austerities to the involved cultural life (karma yoga). Those ascetics who do not have much cultural obligation to fulfill, should consider themselves to be lucky. They should immediately escape from the social environment in which they will be drawn into numerous schemes for the status upgrade of the relatives and friends. Those who are not so lucky should service duties to one and all while simultaneously practicing the austerities. It is best to be private when doing yoga so as not to draw the ire of relatives and friends who feel threatened by the practice.

Liberation from material existence, also includes liberation from nature's psychic influence. This applies to the individual not the family, nor the friends, nor the society. It is not a church, temple or mosque affair. It is a singular accomplishment. It must be pursued introspectively.

Negative Parental Influence

Regardless of one's celibate accomplishment in a previous birth, the new birth may foreshadow what one previously achieved. An ascetic who takes an embryo is fool number one if he thinks that material nature will recognize and support his previous achievement.

It is highly unlikely that material nature will lean towards asceticism. The probabilities for support from material nature is towards indulgence. This means sensual indulgence. Sexual expression is only one of the methods of such habits. Even the kundalini lifeforce energy which is particular to the ascetic, will if it is empowered by material nature, ruin his asceticism.

Thus it is only a foolish yogi or yogini who thinks that there will be support in the new life for yoga austerities. Sane ascetics realize that whatever was achieved before may be erased by material nature and must be re-earned by hard endeavor in the new life.

Despite the fact that there will be little or no support for true asceticism in the new life, the yogi (yogini) should not be resentful towards nature or towards those family members and friends who are hostile to yoga, or who are superficially favorable to it.

A negative parental influence will impact the yogi. He should change his attitude. He should not indulge in resentments. Again and again the yogi should remind himself that nature owes him nothing. He should not think that he can change nature to suit his fancy. He should not feel that nature must support yogic efforts. It is up to the ascetic to service responsibilities which appear to be mandatory for him. But while doing this, he should complete the yoga austerities.

Societal Influences

Apart from the parents and relatives, there will be a societal influence which will afflict the ascetic in the new birth. This will come from people who are not related. In schools the ascetic will be subjected to adverse influences which cause him to do things which are counterproductive to yoga.

Due to losing contact with the qualities of behavior which were cultivated in the previous life, the yogi will act in a way which is harmful to yoga practice. He will do this because of the prevailing influences. However if the yogi is graced by fate, he will realize the situation and may be inspired to extricate himself. This identifies two negative environments. The first is the relatives. The second is people who are not related.

When a yogi realizes these negative factors, he should not alert people about his knowledge but should instead be secretive so as not to let anyone know that he changed his mind about how he should behave and what he should regard as a priority.

If the yogi makes the mistake of alerting others, he will absorb resentment energies. There will be increased pressure for him to participate in the family and society. Thus a smart yogi should keep the realizations to himself. He should practice secretly.

Study of Yoga Books

A yogi should take help from books which were written by accomplished ascetics. One should also take help from any current teacher who achieved resistance to the materialistic way of life and who studied and developed a method of escape from sensual pleasure addiction and dominance.

It is not enough to become a monk, because that might lead the ascetic into the path of sexual hypocrisy where he poses as a celibate on the external level, while on the subtle plane he is indulgent. There are enough stories of false ascetics in regards to celibacy, such that no one needs to add his name to the list of phonies.

It is best to be a parent with limited sexual indulgence, than to be a dishonest or perverted ascetic. Some monks have homosexual tendencies and are forced to express this with other male ascetics. Hence the monk status which appears to be a safe haven for aspiring celibates may become a degrading avenue for them.

Books like *Bhagavad Gita, Yoga Sutras of Patanjali, and Hatha Yoga Pradipika* should be studied. Whatever assistance we may derive from that literature would be to our benefit, provided we do not have intentions to misuse the information.

The societies of forest ascetics (vanaprastha) which existed in the time of the Upanishads are described in the Vedic literature in part. It is good to read books like the *Mahabharata* so that we may get some idea of the lifestyle of the master yogis. But we must also honestly gage our current status and realize that what was possible for the ancient yogis is hardly achievable today.

And yet, we should not be discouraged. The mere fact that we are in a much more negative environment is reason why we should spur on with practice to secure for ourselves whatever little advancement we can garnish.

There were social rules of conduct in the times of the Upanishads and the Mahabharata. These are described in the various texts of the period. Books like the *Manu-Samhita, Manu Smriti,* and *Vishnu-Smriti,* are about the prescribed conduct. Sexual regulation is prescribed therein for the people of that time, those who were in the social setting under which the Upanishads was composed.

The information in these books do more to give us ideas about the structure of those societies, then it does for giving us practical means of sociology for our time. In the Manu Samhita, there is advice about celibacy and rules for sexual indulgence for those people which were indoctrinated in the methods prescribed. Just as today there are acceptable standards of sexual relation, so at that time there was approved conduct. For instance, a couple was prohibited from sexual intercourse during the female's menstrual cycle. They were given approved days for intercourse. Sexual love was to be regarded as a function of procreation.

Today, this is different. The approvals for sexual acts today are vastly different to that in the time of the Upanishads. Of course when we say the time of the Upanishads we also mean for specific societies of the time. In the Vedic literature there are stories about societies which clashed with the Vedic methods. In the time of Rama for instance, there are stories of encounters with forest people who had more permissive licenses for sexual behavior.

When all is said and done, we are left to examine the current standards. Once we cull out the self-destructive approvals, we may work for reformation which will cause our spiritual progress to accelerate. It is an individual quest requiring individual austerity within the psyche. If the ascetic determines that a specific habit is counterproductive, he should restrict it. Gradually over time, he should if he can, eliminate it. If he cannot because nature totally supports that tendency, he should reduce it to a minimum.

Sex Desire / a Composite Energy

Sex desire is a composite energy. It is composite not only in terms of energy contributions but self-donations. One person's sex desire is actually the desire of many other persons, but it passes conventionally as the desire of one person, the self which has the material and/or subtle body. Because we are innately selfish, we cannot realize that our sex pleasure is a composite and is a fund to which others contributed. With sex, if we check ourselves, it is all about me, me, me, with no objectivity to know that it is composite.

Sorting sex desire into its constituent parts is a mystic feat which only a few advanced yogis can perform. Still, unless we sort it, we cannot detach from its grasp. However, freedom from its grasp does not mean that one's material and/or subtle body will be exempt from sexual acts.

Sorting the psychic components of sexual desire is a difficult feat. The energies are abstract to the self. Even though there is enjoyment in sex pleasure, still it is for the most part abstract and difficult to dissect. To make matters worse, our innate selfishness prevents clarity.

However one may begin the sort by considering that sexual desire is reinforced by ancestors and by people who are alive today. Ancestors are people who require new material bodies. To perceive them one must have astral awareness which begins by being conscious during dreams. In dreams one makes contact with departed souls who are in the astral dimension which the astral body enters when the physical one sleeps.

The ancestors are present with us even when we are awake physically but our focus on the physical matter causes a reduction in psychic perception. We can however through meditation increase that perception so that we can sense and even identify ancestors who are present when we are physically awake. The value of this is that we could be aware of the ancestral influence during the physical waking hours, so that at the very least, we will know who motivates a sexual encounter.

If when aspiring for celibacy, a person can be completely isolated from the ancestral influence, there would be no need to track their influence. However most persons who aspire for celibacy are not isolated even physically.

What would you do if you were a monk and found yourself with sex desires which developed in your psyche because of an ancestral influence which you could not repel?

Would you renounce the monk status?

Would you masturbate to expel the energy?

Would you keep the monastic status but privately secure a partner to indulge?

Suppose unknown to you, the food at the monastery caused excess sexually fluids to be created in your sexual organs. How would you deal with that increased sex urge?

Realization of the Sex Composition

To begin the process of segregation between the primary person and others who are involved in a sexual encounter, we may first accept that reincarnation is a fact, an unseen fact, but fact nevertheless. This would mean that the soul who is to take birth as the son or daughter of the couple involved, is present during the sexual act which initiates that departed soul's embryo.

Some mystics say that the soul takes possession of the embryo just before its birth, before expulsion from the mother's passage. Others say that the soul takes possession of the infant body immediately after the expulsion. Others claim that it is at conception, meaning at the time that the sperm particle from the father's fluids embeds itself into the mother's egg.

For this book, we present the premise that the ancestor who is to become the son or daughter of the sexual engaged persons, is present even before the liaison of the parents. He or she is present with either the mother or father or a relative or close acquaintance of the same before the sexual act.

This departed soul's presence is felt as sexual urge, as a romantic feeling of one or both of the parents before a sexual coupling occurs or before in the case of artificial insemination, when the male fluids are placed in proximity of the would-be mother's uterus.

While physically we consider the penetration of the male into the female parent as the beginning of the embryo, the psychic penetration occurs when the departed soul enters the emotional energy of the mother or father to-be. The astral body of the departed soul, who will be a live-birth some months after, penetrates the emotions of the mother or father. That is the abstract beginning of the embryo. It is an emotional not a physical penetration.

Once the departed soul is fused into the emotions of one of the parents to-be, it is only a matter of time when that person will become the experience of the parent's sexual emotions. When a child is born it identifies itself as a small human body, but before that physical identity, it was an emotional identity in the body of the mother or father.

If the departed soul fused into the mother's emotion, it would have to be transferred into the father's emotions for development as a sperm particle. But if the departed soul fused into the father's emotion, it will remain there, become a sperm and then be expelled into the mother's body for being an embryo.

The father or mother for his or her part, will rarely know that such a person-transfer occurred, where he or she was possessed by another entity who is the child to be. As nature would have it, there is an abject ignorance regarding this, where the would-be parent cannot realize that the emotional energy he or she feels is composite. Parents will usually be emphatic about identifying any emotional they feel as their energy. The child-to-be for its part is just as ignorant of the procedure of nature in causing it to have a new body as the son or daughter of this male and that female.

This is the Sequences of Events:

In the past life in an old or young body, the departed soul was among the living and was not regarded as an ancestor. It passed from that previous body when that form proved to be non-responsive to its astral presence. Then on the physical side, the person was regarded as being dead. It was however still existing on the psychic plane but with no physical presence.

Immediately after death of its physical form, that departed soul remained in the vicinity of its physical residence and stayed close to the minds and emotions of those relatives and friends who still used physical bodies. It pestered these people for responses but it got nowhere because those on the physical side were for the most part psychically insensitive. This experience of not coherently communicating with living friends and relatives, caused mental frustration and emotional anguish.

After some time, this departed soul discovered itself being attracted to people who were having sexual intercourse. It was also attracted to people who were sexually aroused but who were not having sexual connections. This occurred frequently until it was particularly and irresistibly attracted to a couple who either had a sexual relationship or did not have one. It became compulsively attracted to the male or female and merged into that person's feelings.

Once it entered the feelings of that would-be parent, it lost self-objectivity. For all practical purposes, it became that person's emotion and no longer was aware of itself as an individual. Even though it experienced itself as a subjective feeling of that would-be parent, its need for rebirth remained embedded in the energy of that person. This surfaced in that person's emotion as a need to be with the would-be father or mother.

The parent who was possessed in this way, was unaware of the presence of this departed person who would be its child. However the child-to-be was felt as an urge to be sexually unified with the other would-be parent.

If the possessed parent is the female in the relationship, then in the proximity of the person who is to be the father, the emotional energy will flash across and enter the emotions of the father. It will fuse into the father who will experience that addition to his nature as a loving feeling of desire coming to him from the mother, where he will feel that the woman loves him dearly. This is a form of conceit but it is natural.

If the possessed parent is the male in the relationship, then there would be only one transfer which will occur when the sperm particle which is the departed soul is expelled from the male organ and travels into the uterus of the mother.

In cases where the possessed parent is the female, the emotional energy which is the departed soul will move into the father-to-be's body. There it will become a sperm which will be transferred into the mother's uterus.

In all respects, the female is the terminal of this process because from the female body only, the baby is delivered. The male may or may not be the initiation but his body creates the sperm particle always.

The duration of time when a departed soul waits on the astral planes for a birth opportunity, varies from person to person. It depends on many factors which are not controlled by the person requiring a body. In a society where there is widespread use of contraceptives, the wait for a body may be longer.

In summary, the lusty energy of sexually-inclined people is an embodied emotional force which comprise ancestors who require rebirth. However on the physical side, this energy is interpreted as romantic experience only. Nature reveals the enjoyment energy in the lust-force but it does not give insight into the person-content.

Many departed people reside as sperm particles in the body of would-be fathers but neither they nor those potential fathers are aware that this force is possessed of actually persons who were adults in previous lives. The process of transmigration is a natural psychic procedure which ignores the entities who are involved in it and disables their observational perception during phases of the transfers. This is why reincarnation is not evident to the average human.

Each sperm particle has a potential human in it but that does not mean that each one will become an embryo. The probability is higher in other species of life, for instance in vegetation it is likely that from one plant, hundreds of seeds may sprout into viable plants but in the more sophisticated species, it is hardly likely because of the amount of nurture which is required to bring an embryo to adult stage.

Contraceptive Actions

Contraceptives methods are ways of blocking ancestral access. It does not matter if it is a chemical or physical. The result is the same which is that an ancestor is prevented embryo access. Masturbation in its result is a contraceptive procedure because it prevents ancestors from taking birth. There are several stories in the Puranas, where an advanced yogi who was sexually-aroused and did not have a physical partner, passed semen but he collected it and made sure that it developed into an embryo.

Yogis did this because of their awareness of the person-content of semen. If they felt that life of a body begins at conception when the sperm fused into the ova, they would not have collected their ejected semen with the feeling that they were preserving the opportunity of an ancestor.

This book is not a text on morality. We are not here passing judgment on sexual acts as being moral or immoral. It is a fact however that there is a backlog of souls awaiting rebirth as infants. Hence, any contraception blocks birth access. In addition if a male or female has an infertile body through chemical manipulation or because of gland malfunction, that also blocks entities from becoming infants.

Jesus Christ gave the advice to regard others as one would prefer to be regarded. If this is applied to reincarnation, then one should be careful to afford an ancestor opportunity, to have an embryo, in consideration that hereafter one will be in a similar predicament and will be reliant on relatives and friends to allow access as an infant.

There is however the objection raised which is that if one were to become a parent, it is a never-ending obligation with on-going complications with a spouse and relatives. Hence it is best to avoid any sexual involvement for the sake of achieving liberation from material existence. This proposal sounds good at first hearing but it is flawed when examined in detail.

In the first place no ascetic is here because of not beginning the present life as sexual fluid. Every human body we see began its history in that way. Actually it began as emotions. These emotions in the parent body took possession of sexual hormones, which were developed under genetic influence to form sperm, which fused with ovum, which resulted in an embryo. That is the history of every human being, ascetic or non-ascetic.

Sexual intercourse has that exalted purpose of providing embryos. It condemnation is irrational if we do not first appreciate that it is the sole act which resulted in anyone having a material body. What is the value of that body to an ascetic?

If having progeny will bog me down spiritually, then I have every reason to be hesitant about it. At least I should know why something which is responsible for my being here, is such a handicap.

Is it the pleasure which I may become addicted to?

Is it the responsibility of a prolonged relationship with the partner who shares parenting duties?

What is it?

Why is something which is so useful such a scare for an ascetic?

Monk Status Obsolete

On March 5, 2016, just after typing the above paragraph, I did some pranayama breath-infusion practice. This was in the afternoon in the State of Florida, USA. During the meditation which followed I had an astral visitor who was known as Śrī Swāmī Rāma (1925–1996). Being aware that I was composing this book, he said this:

One should not take the sannyasa monk status in the Shankaracharya lineage. It is no longer supported socially anywhere on the planet. My sannyasa was taken in a conducive society but once I went west it was no longer supported. In the West, opportunities opened to me to be with desirous women. I had secret relationships. I had a child who was hidden on my behalf because of the fear of disgrace as a sannyasi monk.

In the West and even in the East now, no one should take sannyasa. That needs a support which society can no longer afford. I was private with the woman who is the mother of my child. That was all which was required to create a pregnancy. It was so easy, so natural, so accommodating.

As sons of Shiva what have we to do with women? There is Shiva. There may or may not be his woman, who knows?

Who saw her?

Books mention her.

Who actually said he saw her?

To whom did she appear?

She is not our concern. Like Skanda in the North, we are his sons. That is all we know. We have nothing to do with women.

Does Shiva have a woman?

Who knows?

Even if he does, we are his boys only. The instrument, if anything, you urinate with it.

As boys there is no urge to use it in any other way.

Remember that!

Otherwise it is a bad dream. Wake from it. Be his son only!

Contraceptives

Contraceptives as chemicals, herbs and mechanical devices are effective in preventing pregnancies but we cannot be sure that there will be no unwanted consequences. If a departed soul is bared entry into a family in which he or she performed many uplifting social acts, nature may take offense. It may give a reaction which is worse than having that person as an infant in the family.

There is always the flip side of a contraceptive act, which is that in the future when one needs a body, one may be similarly inconvenienced just as one hampered an ancestor who needed a body which one could have provided.

What would it be like to wait years, say ten, or one hundred years, on the astral side, to acquire an embryo because one's living relatives successful blocked access by using contraceptives?

Abortion

Abortion means the removal of an embryo from the body of the would-be mother. There are many reasons for taking such an action. Some are considered to be justified, for instance in cases of rape or even marital violent abuse. There might be the acknowledgement of incapacitating disease in the embryo, where medical professionals show that the child would be born with a handicapped body. Some reasons for abortion may be unjustified. For instance in cases where the parents are well-off and can easily afford to sponsor a live birth.

In an abortion, the consciousness of the person who otherwise would be that child, is in a trance state due to the development of the embryo. When the event occurs, that soul finds itself to be again in the astral existence, being disrupted from the trance condition. There might be pain felt according to the means used to cause the abortion. The main hassle with this is the resentment which will arise in that departed soul. That resentment will surface somewhere but a portion of it will lodge in the psyche of the would-be parents.

Nowadays the medical professionals provide many means of sure contraception and abortion. Thus they too are implicated in this regard. It is to be seen how material nature will sort the liabilities and spread the resentments which comes from those departed souls who are disenfranchised. However one should always consider what it would be like to be an aborted embryo. Since we usually do not remember our uterine condition, we should meditate to get the insight.

Abstinence as Birth Control

One method of birth control which is approved by some religious groups is abstinence. This is not always free from bad energies. It is a more approved method than contraceptives and abortion but it is a form of blocking ancestors nevertheless. Many religious groups tout abstinence as if it is heaven-sent.

Abstinence means that one will not be involved in helping any departed ancestor as the biological parent, which means that one will not be held responsible by society for the welfare of that infant. It also means that one turns that person away and forces that person to seek a parent elsewhere.

The Mahabharata begins with the abstinence of Jarat Karu, an ascetic monk. His ancestors, who were imperiled hereafter, appealed to him to have sexual intercourse because that was their only hope for acquiring embryos.

As a religious act, abstinence means that there is no sexual involvement but does it mean that there might be masturbation because in masturbation ancestors who merged into the emotions of the potential parent are ejected through the climax experience. These ancestors find themselves reentering into the emotions of that would-be parent, which in turn may cause repeats of masturbation with repeated ejection of the departed soul in successive sexual climaxes.

Abstinence, even though it is extoled as being the honorable way to avoid family responsibility, is itself a method of baring others from getting the bodies which they so much desire and which they deserve because of social services committed to the family in a past life.

The ideal and seemingly faultless type of abstinence occurs when the person has no sexual intercourse and does no masturbation. But in some cases like this, the sexual energy in the form of the abstainer produces obesity which results in other problems like diabetes, laziness, grasping for political or social power, becoming ambitious to run social institutions as a head monk or manager. The only way abstinence would be faultless is if there is no sexual charge in the form of the person concerned, where that one is never possessed by any ancestor.

Sexual Intercourse as a Compulsive Habit

If one finds that sexual intercourse is a compulsive habit, one should research the reason. We know that it is not an addiction for every human being but some humans become so inclined that they continue it even in elderly bodies. Any behavior which remains as a compulsion for the whole life of the body may be regarded as a vice or as an unwanted compulsion which does not promote the desirable lifestyle.

The nature of sexual intercourse is that it is a compulsion from day one, from the time the body becomes sexually-mature. No human being can make a valid claim about creating sex desire in his or her body. Nature creates the sex desire in every human body at a certain age. Some experience the development sooner than others but it happens in nearly every case. It is also present in other mammals where it manifests in a similar way. It is a natural urge.

At the height of youth, the desire for sex is experienced as being compulsive but that initial strength of the urge decreases when the body is in middle age. If at that time one finds that one is still compelled for it, one may meditate to discover the cause.

Is it supported by association of another person?
Is it because of diet?
Is it because of viewing sexual media?
Is it because of reminiscing about past indulgences?

Best Way to Avoid Parental Responsibility

The best way to avoid parental responsibility is abstinence. It is the least involved method but this abstinence has to be without masturbation and without the power grasping tendency manifesting as it does in the lives of so many monks and nuns. First one must determine if it is possible for one to do this. One must have sufficient self-honesty to make the assessment.

History shows that leading monks and nuns may be power hungry people in the guise of saints. There is no question that masturbation is a fault which is present in many people who say that they abstain from sexual contact. The problem is that material nature constructed these human forms to beget progeny. Refusal to comply with this natural plan is not likely to be successful.

As Swami Rama indicated to me in the astral conversation which I mentioned previously, there was a time when society supported abstinence for priests.

That was done by shielding the priest from sexual influences and by allowing the priest to serve families in which that priest's ancestors took birth. In that way the priest got opportunities to discharge their obligations without become parents of the said ancestors.

I feel that the best way to avoid parental duties is to accept those duties, to become a dutiful parent but in a very limited way with a strict steady spiritual discipline through the child nurturing years. This is the type of life which was defined for rishis or householder ascetics in the time of the Upanishads. Such yogis had families but they reserved the right to continue spiritual practice daily. They did not postpone it for the elderly years. They were partially focused on social life, not fully as non-ascetics are.

Becoming a so called celibate monk and avoiding parental duties is risky because one will have to find a way to deal with the sexual energy which accumulates in one's body. This will, more than likely, lead to masturbation or to secret sexual liaison with male or female partners. That will breach the celibacy even though the public may never discover it. Material nature will know of it and will react accordingly either now or hereafter.

Physical/Subtle Pleasure Compared

In all respects what we experience as pleasure in a physical body has a subtle counterpart. Despite that, physical and subtle may be sorted. It is necessary for the ascetic to gain insight into the partition between physical and subtle. Sex pleasure is sensational. Hence it was singled out. However for a detailed study, the ascetic should regard every type of sensation, sorting each into physical and subtle parts, and knowing what will remain after the death of the material body.

It is clear that nature intended to use physical sex pleasure primarily for creating new material bodies. Even a simple and routine task of nature which is eating and digesting, was designed to create sexual fluids. Ultimately the perpetual continuation of a life form is not possible except in any indirect way, which is that the form has to create new forms, which it can influence in the future to accommodate it as an embryo.

If we do not create new forms, we will have no opportunity for physical life in the future. If we cease creating new forms, our eating and digesting will allow the present forms to survive for a time, for say one hundred years for the most. Then we will only have subtle bodies as our total opportunity.

With this insight, we can understand that the kundalini lifeforce psychic mechanism is involved with these life systems in a selfish way. Each person is involved in this selfish behavior for self-continuation both in the current physical body and by the generation of new physical forms by its descendants.

Nature continues its drive for reproducing bodies, as many bodies as the environment can support. All the while, we humans remained focused on acquiring the sex pleasure which is really an electric sensation which is necessary for the generation of progeny. Since we interpret that energy as a pleasure, we become addicted to it. We prejudicially regard it as something apart from reproduction.

When a child is born, it has no idea about sex pleasure. This is because even though it was aware of that pleasure in previous bodies and in the astral existence, still those memories are off-limits to it. A child however is aware of gender and differentiates its mother or father. The child has instincts which can identify females or males. Pleasure with females at that time, has to do with the mother's willingness to breast-feed and give affection.

After sexual maturity, the juvenile becomes aware of the sexual urge. This causes the young body to pursue sexual opportunities with the result of sexual intercourse in which sexual climax experience is interpreted as a super-pleasure. Once the individual gets sexual climax experience, it hankers after that repeatedly. It does so on the basis of memory of previous events. While rating this pleasure as the highest experience, the individual unwittingly sets a precedence of making sex pleasure the highest priority. This attitude did not begin with sexual relations. It is there at the onset when the embryo first suckle the mother's breast.

The same attitude he or she had while nursing, is carried over into sexual experiences which is an exploitation of the sense of touch. However sexual experience gives a more demanding focus because of the pleasure intensity. An ascetic should strive to be positioned in nature's sense of importance. Then he or she will shift away from seeing sex pleasure in its own right, and will perceive it as a necessary energy in the creation of new life forms.

Suggestion from the Physical Body

The suggestion from the physical body is that sex pleasure is available at its prime in the young adult years. Then it tails off to nil in the elderly years. For a body, sex pleasure is absent at its beginning, then it develops over time as the appropriate glands develop full functioning in the juvenile and young adult years. In the end however if the body survives to the elderly years, a noticeable reduction in sexual capacity is observed.

Human beings because of memory access may counteract nature's dumbing down of the sex urge. They can do this by invoking memories of sex indulgence in the body's prime years or by subjecting their visual and other senses to sexual stimulation. The body itself as a whole may be subjected to hormonal treatments and electric stimulations which may reverse nature's reduction plan for the elderly.

Just after middle age an ascetic should study the reduction of sex fluids production as well as the loss of sexual memories.

Should the ascetic willingly go along with nature's reduction plan?

Should he, otherwise, buck against it by using hormone boosts and other sex-reviving methods?

Sex Pleasure as an Interpretation

Is sex pleasure an interpretation of the human mind?

Is it a warped view?

Is the actual fact that the pleasurable feelings endured during sexual interplay are not pleasure but are merely energy movements which register to the persons involved as pleasure?

What is the result of eating a sweet beverage?

Is the result the pleasure which is experienced through the taste buds?

Should a person eat merely to taste sweet food?

Should we have sex just for the pleasure of it?

Is sex pleasure or any pleasure for that matter, something other than pleasure?

Is it an energy flow which is interpreted by the person as pleasure but which is the movement of energy with a purpose which is different to pleasure?

System of Pleasure Conditioning

As nature would have it whenever there is a pleasure yield, the mind makes special note of it. This is retained as a memory impression. Again and again this memory is requisitioned where it is enjoyed through reminiscence. Then the self feels the needs to recreate that experience physically. That happens and another memory impression which reinforces the original one is created.

This is how pleasure conditioning is formatted. The indication is that there is a strategy which a person can use to break from the process of experiencing a pleasure, remembering it, and then physically re-enacting it. Of course the question remains as to why anyone would voluntarily deprive the self of pleasure.

One should consider curtailing a pleasure influence if one finds that one develops an inordinate uncontrollable impulse for it. For self-tantric yoga, one should research any pleasure which the psyche develops an addiction towards. One should dissect the experience to determine its formulation and reinforcement. It is not sufficient for the observer to be entertained by pleasurable or unpleasant experiences. It should know how the experience is formulated and how the observer becomes the object of pleasures.

Subtle Body Considered

Pleasure experience has a subtle counterpart which is so interlaced with what we experience physically, that it is not easy to cull the subtle portion. This confusion reinforces our lack of insight. If the subtle body has a sexual need and can fulfill that with its corresponding pleasurable energy flow, then efforts at physical celibacy are useful only if they effectively rein in sex desire on the subtle plane.

What, if any, does a physical action impact the subtle in a more than superficial way? In existence the subtle precedes the physical just as in construction, the building plan is completed before the physical construction begins. Does the physical project affect the building plan?

Generally a physical construction mimics what was drawn in the plan. But on occasion a physical construction causes the architect to significantly change the plan. Can the reduction or elimination of physical sex desire terminate the need for sex in the subtle body? To what extent is there feedback between the physical sex attitude and the psychological indulgence?

There is also a question about reincarnation. If the person leaves his or her body in the elderly years after the sex indulgence needs of the body was diminished to nil, would the subtle body retain that abstinence forever or would it be present in a dormancy.

Memory Support for Indulgence

The memories are the special assistants in the continuation of the quest to extract sex pleasure. To sabotage the sexual indulgence compulsion, the memories are the first aspect of the psyche which must be tackled. The key to overcoming the memories, is the realization that pleasure is re-enacted from memory replay.

Memories are not physical actions but they yield a subtle pleasure which is similar to that acquired by the physical actions which produce them. In addition subtle actions creates memories which are replayed in the mind just as physically-created memories can be re-enacted.

Favorable memories have a compulsion energy. Unless one can ignore or disengaged from it, one cannot turn off the display of a memory. The ascetic must evaluate a memory to recognize its desirable part. He must then make a decision if he will abandon or attempt to delete that impression even though it has desirable content.

To enjoy a pleasurable incidence, sexual or otherwise, which was enacted but which can be access through a stored memory, the individual is required to access that memory or to be induced by the mind to give permission for its display. Once the memory is displayed, the individual is usually enthralled by it. This fascination disempowers the person, so that he or she must comply with the display and must relive the memory once or twice or more frequently according to the desire energy in the mind.

If the ascetic shuts down his or her interest in a memory, there will be a call in the mind for the release of the memory but the ascetic should firmly ignore even that request, even when that gives a preview of the excitement which would be enjoyed if the memory is viewed.

Regular shut down of a memory as soon as it arises, results in its elimination over time, over a long period of time, or the memory acquires a discouragement energy which makes it near impossible for the mind to reveal it at any future time.

Format of Sex Pleasure

Sex pleasure like much else has a specific format which can be adjusted by using moods, herbs, chemicals, sounds, visuals or odors. It begins with an incidence of some type which causes arousal. The incidence may be psychic however. For that matter the person involved may have no idea of how it was initiated. Once an arousal begins it may fade to nothing. Or it may increase to a peak which is known as the climax or highest intensity of the experience.

In males it is generally the case that there is one climax to be experienced out of one arousal but in females this may or may not be the case. Females have reported multiple climaxes like in a musical piece with a series of rushes to peaks.

From the point of view of physiology, each climax expends a quantity of hormonal energy of which the body has a limited supply. Thus if there is one or many climaxes in one arousal there will come a point in which the system will become depressed and will be unable to create any other climaxes due to the lack of hormonal energy.

This insufficiency is rectified by the body's production and accumulation of hormonal energy from digested food. One can still have desire for sex pleasure even if the body is unable to produce the intense pleasure of climax. To be practical it is best that one not desire sexual indulgence when the body has insufficient hormonal energy but the mind and emotions do not always comply with this logic.

Cultural Influences

Depending on the cultural environment, one may or may not be needful of excessive sex pleasure. There will always be some who are without sexual urge. There will always be those who seem to need much of it. But there is an additional factor which is the cultural influence which prevails.

In kundalini self-tantric, the aim is to discover the situation of one's gender and determine how best to be whatever it is. Am I male? Am I female? Am I bi-sexual? Am I neuter?

What is the best way to express gender?

What cultural influence promotes my individuality?

What cultural influence reduces me?

Self-Esteem

Am I dependent on the look of my body, such that if my body is not rated as being beautiful or handsome, I become depressed if I cannot transform it to the current standard? In one country a person with a broad nose may be rated as being beautiful, while elsewhere one with a narrow nostril might be appreciated.

Do I feel neglected when I am in an environment where my body is considered to be ugly?

Is my body obese?

Am I unable to control food intake such that my body grows bigger and bigger even though I do not desire for it be?

The situation of the type of body one derived from the parents is an ongoing challenge because there is this comparison habit which demands that one prepare oneself to be prominent in life. For each of us this preparation is different. One person likes red clothing while the other likes the blue type.

What causes this differentiation?

Cosmetic adjustments are done by humans in their effort to adjust the format of the body received from nature but it is done on the basis of personal and social demands for this type of nose, with this type of mouth, with this shape of eyebrows, with this color hair and so on.

Much of this is focused on sexual attraction, which develops into sexual indulgence, the means of acquiring sex pleasure. It seems that sex pleasure is the objective of much human enterprise. From a biological view point, a portion of what one eats in a sexually-mature body converts into sex hormone energy which is used in sexual intercourse which provides intense pleasure in the body.

Even juvenile bodies may be said to use food for ultimately producing sex hormone energy because the growth of such bodies is for the development of sexual maturity which yields sexual attraction and interaction.

Domestic Life and Asceticism

We know that physically, if there is a sexual intercourse between a fertile male and female, at the proper time of the woman's menstrual cycle, there is likely to be the development of an embryo. This is provided there is no contraceptive interruption.

This method of nature to produce progeny merely on the basis of sexual intercourse between a male and female caused human beings to initiate contraceptive methods to interrupt and frustrate nature's intentions.

Self-tantric practice requires an investigation into the need to participate in nature's system of reproduction. It makes sense to invest in it because if one requires another physical body, one can get that only through sexual reproduction. In addition, from the angle of ancestors who are now departed souls, they require opportunities to get embryos. One may render an ancestor, a service by parenting a body.

Since domestic life is time consuming and is filled with social complications, some ascetics feel that one should avoid participating in family life and focus only on developing one's individuality in way which frees one from social involvement. This however does not make sense in every case. Some ascetics should invest in family life but in a way which does not undermine their efforts at spiritual practice. These persons have a task before them, a balancing act between involvement in social life and detachment for the same.

If an ascetic decides to do the domestic duties, he or she will have to be in partner with a person of the opposite sex. There will be a question of how involved to become. Should one have one, two, three or more children?

How should one curtail sexual involvement so as to limit the number of progeny?

Should one use contraceptive methods instead of curtailing sexual acts?

What if either partner is discovered to be infertile but that person still has sexual needs?

Is it possible to limit the number of sexual acts to the number of progeny planned?

In other words can a human being have absolute control over his or her sex desire so that there is involvement only when one intends to assist an ancestor by providing an embryo?

Sensual Dominance

From a sensual perspective, one circumstance is desired and another is not. The senses act according to their prejudiced notions. A greater percentage of the time they are correct but their choices do on occasion lead to disaster. Suppose for instance the senses of a woman tell her that a certain man is sexually desirable. Then when she develops a relationship with him, it results in her being battered and bruised. She will have to correct the perception, take the injury and try to use the adjusted prejudice to choose a better partner.

The senses are dominant because that is the way the psyche was created but the sensual judgement may be flawed. In sexual matters one should not fully trust the senses. They do not see the angles. Their method is to locate one choice feature and make the selection based on that, ignoring or denying other features which may be harmful to the self in the short or long term.

It is not the condition of his or her senses but that of my senses. How do my senses influence my opinions? Is there a resistance between me and my senses whereby I can analyze what my senses prefer, consider that as only part of the information, and then get the rest of the report from the same sense or from other senses, then make an independent decision which may or may not be consistent with what the senses initially proposed?

For doing sexual self-exploration, the ascetic must explore the relationship between the core-self and the senses. Due to heavy reliance on the senses, it came to be that the senses not only collect information but make decisions because the core-self relaxed itself and surrendered fully to the fact that it cannot perceive anything without taking help from the senses. The core-self made a costly mistake which is to let the senses form the conclusions about what is desirable and what may be unpleasant. This means that the core-self has less work to do and is entertained more by the senses but at the core-self's expense when the senses make the wrong selection.

Sex Energy Composition

A sexual action is more than hormones and pleasure. It has within it a potential personality. Otherwise there would be no possibility of an embryo. There is a lack of insight regarding this. During sexual intercourse the overwhelming feature is the pleasure surges. Being forced to focus on that, the partners cannot consider anything else. They certainly cannot see a potential embryo as being a component of the act.

When we consider personality, failure to develop an embryo in a sexual act really means that some person, or some potential person, lost an opportunity to become a human.

Was the deprived person frustrated?

Is that person or potential person aware of the lost opportunity?

Result of a Contraceptive Action

For *inSelf Yoga™* and self-tantric accomplishment, the term contraceptive is defined in an irregular way. While people think of contraceptives as chemicals which ruin the sperm or ovum, and they regard celibate actions as not being related to contraception; here contraception includes both chemical actions, and any other method which prevents sperm from fusing into ovum, as well as any other type of action which prevents a sexual action from taking place. Blocking sexual actions and blocking non-sexual actions may both frustrate the development of an embryo.

In this respect even a monk or nun, a so called celibate, is involved in contraception. Abstinence is a form of contraception. It does the same depriving course towards a potential embryo. For this practice one must regard that and not think that abstinence is free from casualty. Merely being a monk or nun does not free a person from the fault of depriving someone of a body. The idea that being a single ascetic is grand, and is free from sexual fault, must be abandoned.

Sannyasins, sexually mature brahmacharis, monks, nuns and ascetics of all types who are not creating progeny and whose psyches have other entities living in their subtle energies, are involved in contraception. This changes the argument completely. We can now proceed with self-tantric, the investigation as to self-gender and its uses and abuses.

What is the result of a monk's life for his ancestors?

Unless he breaks the celibacy vow, the result is that he will deprive ancestors of getting embryos from his body. They will have to beg elsewhere for rebirth opportunities. In that sense there is no difference between a monk's celibate action and a sexually involved person's contraceptive action, or even an infertile couple's sexual action.

This does not mean that there is a faultless person as a monk or as a sexually involved individual. The issue here is not the fault but rather the research into self-gender to understand the feature of gender and its spread as sexual polarity which leads to family involvement. The involvement carries liabilities for which the individual is held responsible.

Liabilities Any Which Way

No matter how it is viewed, any time a departed soul is deprived of an embryo, there will be repercussions. This is because usually the departed souls hold resentments for not having fruitful opportunities for rebirth. If I am a monk with vows for celibacy, my action not to be sexually involved will result on ancestors being turned away from a birth opportunity. Suppose however as a monk I masturbate to relieve myself of sexual energy, then again the result will be the same, that of an ancestor being entombed in my ejaculated fluids.

If on the other hand, I became sexually involved in a marital or unofficial relationship and I used a contraceptive substance or my partner did so, then again an ancestor would be turned away from a birth opportunity.

Can we say that because the person was a monk, the ancestor will not be resentful and because the person was sexually permissive, the ancestor was depressed? That would make no sense because the fact is that for the departed soul, the result will be the same which is that no embryo would be acquired. That departed soul would have to go elsewhere to apply for a body, or will have to repossess sexual fluids and make a renewed effort to influence someone to create an embryo.

Reactionary Psychic Nature

Regardless of human moral standards, acceptable social behavior, religious tenets, supposed religious authorities in the afterlife, there is one thing which is above question and that is the reactionary power of psychic material nature.

In one country, an action is recommended while in some other country, the same action is condemned. One religion says that after death a man will be punished for his irreligious acts. Another belief is that there is no supernatural agency.

For self-tantric discovery, the ascetic needs to accurately gage the reaction he will get from the psychic material nature. What will be the return if he takes a contraceptive action as compared to if he indulges?

Nothing is completed with mere agency. In fact agency may be the beginning of series of unfavorable returns. What will happen in my afterlife when I try to get the next embryo? Will I be subjected to the same contraceptive means which I subjected my ancestors to?

A question arises as to if it will matter because if there was a past life, I cannot remember it. Most humans have no recall of making an effort to get an embryo before birth. If I will become a stress energy and lose my personality format in the afterlife, why should it matter if I am blocked from becoming an embryo?

Urges are repeat demands occurring in the minds and emotions of a human being. Hence if I were to become a sexual urge in the afterlife, I would be a repeat impulse in the sexual nature of my future parent (s). I would become that format of anxiety for him and her.

Affection as Relational Currency

The ascetic should take the task of understanding affection energy. What is it? How is it best used?

It is involved in sexual exchanges between lovers but is affection, a sexual energy?

What is the different between the affection between one person and his or her sex partner and that same person as his mother or father? Why does sexual affection carry emphasis?

If sexual energy is different to affection, it is a task to sort it because in sexual affairs, the energies are merged whereby there is no way to differentiate one from the other.

One way to test this would be to take one life as the lover of a person. Then take another life as the son or daughter of the same person. Then take another life as the parent of that person, then take a life as an authority figure over that person.

When comparing these experiences we may derive an understanding as to what love really is. The love for that person should be constant in each role played. That core of affection would be different to the sexual energy attraction which is experienced between the lovers.

Natural Reduction of Sex Desire

As the body grows older, especially after middle age (50 years), there is a reduction in the lusty impetus. This is due to aging of the organs which produce sex hormones. An ascetic should take advantage of this reduction but he or she should not think that this diminished libido is permanent.

The moon has no prominence on a dark moon night but that does not mean that there will never be another full moon. The full glitter is sure to return. The reduction of sex desire in one life is no sign of its elimination. For that matter a person who in one life has little or no desire cannot guarantee that he or she may never become sex-crazed in some other life? The potential for full-blown sex impulse is always present.

It depends on the birth one gets in what type of body, with what amount of lusty impetus in that form. In terms of meditative insight it depends on the condition of the subtle body when it is interspaced in a physical form and what it has as content when it is without the physical casing.

One would do well to realize the contents of the subtle form. One should study its adaptability to various life forms and its accommodation or resistance to sex energy in various conditions. How much does sex expression rely on circumstance rather than on the individual's willpower? In this usage circumstance includes but is not limited to the environment. The condition of mental and emotional energy in the psyche of the individual and his or her partner(s) is also part of the environment. How much of that can the core-self truly control?

External Environmental Exposure

There is the internal mental environment. There are the external physical and subtle worlds. Generally we feel that the external environment is the physical world but on a close inspection, we should admit that there is also an external subtle environment around the subtle body.

This means that there are at least two sources for sex stimulation. One is from the external physical or subtle world. The other is from within the mind, from within the psyche.

Of these the external concern two ranges, the physical and subtle ones. The physical is one dimension while the subtle are multiple frequencies with mostly abstract occurrences.

The internal is one range with multi levels of varying control by the core-self.

To tackle the external exposures, we need to sort between physical and subtle. We should bear in mind that whatever is physical has a subtle counterpart, even though what is subtle may or may not have a corresponding physical format.

How is the ascetic affected by sexually-suggestive forms and media?

Does it make sense to be exposed to sexual formats if that sensual information will increase sex desire or cause stimulation of sexual organs which might lead to masturbation or sexual intercourse?

What about sexual forms in dreams and astral projection? Can the ascetic avoid these? If so, what is the method of ceasing those abstract perceptions?

Exposure to Sex Stimuli

The effort at celibacy requires that the ascetic should reduce exposure to sex stimuli to the minimum. This is because sex exposure causes stimulation of sex impulse which automatically causes an increase in sex desire which culminates either in masturbation or sexual intercourse.

If however the effort is not for celibacy or more precisely is not for full-blown celibacy, then still the question remains as to if the exposure is helpful or harmful. In other words if one intends to have sexual intercourse even for the purpose of producing an embryo, why not increase sex desire by exposing oneself to sex stimuli?

Self-tantric is an efficient personal process which does not include extraneous stimuli. It does not include increases in sexual desire which come from the external environment. It is a study about the gender potential of the individual. If anything it includes a very limited access to what is external. Hence for the most part external stimuli is not a part of the practice.

Irrespective of if the ascetic has or does not have a partner, he or she should curtail all access to external stimuli because that is the only method to observe the self-gender. Any access to the external environment either in the physical or astral terrains would ruin the research.

External Stimuli Reduction Methods

If you are serious about doing self-tantric, you may begin by restricting access to external physical and astral sex stimuli. You must restrict the mind's use of sexual memories. Do this:

- As soon as you become aware of sexual memories, cease mental indulgence.
- Avoid seeing photos, illustrations, videos or movies which portray sexual activities
- Avoid listening to lyrics which describe or suggest sexual activities.
- Avoid associating with persons who are addicted to physical or astral sex stimuli.

Excessive Sexual Expression

To complete the self-tantric research, the ascetic should identify and if possible eliminate all excessive sexual expression. Some of this cannot be eliminated because of being enforced by fate. The ascetic should identify the excess, label it and take steps to eliminate, or quarantine it. The ascetic should observe it and study how it became a mandatory incidence.

There are simple steps for reducing excess. These include the following:

- Monitor thinking to identify and cease thoughts about sexuality.

- Monitor thinking to stamp out the revival of memories related to sexually promises and pleasures.
- Control vision to reduce visual contact with sexually related forms and images.
- Recognize mandatory contact with sexually related forms and images. Study nature's enforcement of these encounters.

Chapter 2
Sensual Expression

Sensual Struggle with Interpretation of Objects

The mind relies on the senses for information about the available of threatening objects. Essentially the senses locate three types of objects in the environment. These are:

- consumable objects
- detested objects
- neutrally attractive objects

The senses are by their very nature pleasure-seekers. It may be that the core-self, the observant I-factor, is not interested in pleasure, but that is of little significance because that self has to rely on the senses for information about objects. As influenced the core-self gives permission for the procurement of consumable objects.

To be realistic the ascetic must realize that he is formatted to accept consumable objects. He must hunt for these in the environment because the form requires these consumptions for its survival. Beyond just survival is the need to hoard energy for hard-times, to secure a stockpile. That is also a feature of this existence. It is not enough to live on subsistence. Excess is required, not just for sexual needs but in every other area of sensual consumption. Obesity in humans is the sure indication that there is some strong impulse to acquire more than is required for the present. This may develop into outright greed but nevertheless it is natural. The ascetic should come to terms with this.

Consumable Objects

Sex pleasure is a consumable object. Obviously so is rice or potatoes, so is meat or fish, so is spinach or bananas. Pleasing sounds are a consumable object. To procure an object, the core-self relies on the senses to detect, identify, sample and then acquire the item. There are visuals which are consumable merely by sight even without smelling, tasting, touching or hearing. Whatever could increase sex desire through sensual contact should be avoided if possible. This is to conserve the interest energy of the core-self. For self-tantric, it is the energy of the core-self which is investigated not additional types which are generated in contact with other psyches or objects.

Detested Objects

Some objects including sexual objects, are detestable to a person's senses. The ascetic should quell any strongly feelings about such objects. If possible he should assume a neutral stance. Energy is expended for desirable objects. It is the same for the detestable kind. To conserve the energy neutrality should be induced.

Neutrally Attractive Objects

Neutrally attractive objects should be inspected to understand why the senses are indifferent to them. An object which is very attractive on one occasion may invoke a neutral response at another time. What is the difference? What in the psyche determines how it should relate to the same object at different times and under different or the same circumstances?

The senses are prejudiced. They will remain so forever and will never be completely reformed. To be realistic the ascetic should be detached from sensual bias. This applies to all forms of sensuality which include sexuality.

Whatever one can gain a neutral posture towards, should be altered so that it does not resume a desirable aspect, but all the same for those objects which the senses remain favored towards, one should realize that if one is to gain neutrality, one would have to change to another environment or form where the natural response is one of indifference.

Details of Sensual Compulsion

Some details about sensual compulsion are given by Lord Krishna in the Bhagavad Gita discourse:

ध्यायतो विषयान्पुंसः

सङ्गस्तेषूपजायते ।

सङ्गात्संजायते कामः

कामात्क्रोधोऽभिजायते ॥ २.६२ ॥

dhyāyato viṣayānpuṁsaḥ
saṅgasteṣūpajāyate
saṅgātsaṁjāyate kāmaḥ
kāmātkrodho'bhijāyate (2.62)

dhyāyato = dhyāyataḥ — considering; viṣayān — sensual objects; puṁsaḥ — a person; saṅgas — attachment; teṣūpajāyate = teṣu — in them + upajāyate — is born, is created; saṅgāt — from attachment; saṁjāyate — is born; kāmaḥ — craving; kāmāt — from craving; krodho = krodhaḥ — anger; 'bhijāyate = abhijāyate — is derived

The act of considering sensual objects, creates in a person, an attachment to them. From attachment comes craving. From this craving anger is derived. (Bhagavad Gita 2.62)

क्रोधाद्भवति संमोहः

संमोहात्स्मृतिविभ्रमः ।

स्मृतिभ्रंशाद्बुद्धिनाशो

बुद्धिनाशात्प्रणश्यति ॥ २.६३ ॥

krodhādbhavati sammohaḥ
sammohātsmṛtivibhramaḥ
smṛtibhraṁśādbuddhināśo
buddhināśātpraṇaśyati (2.63)

krodhād = krodhāt — from anger; bhavati — becomes (comes); sammohaḥ — delusion; sammohāt — from delusion; smṛti — conscience + vibhramaḥ — vanish; smṛtibhraṁśād = smṛtibhraṁśāt = smṛti — memory, judgement + bhraṁśāt — from fading away; buddhināśo = buddhināśaḥ = buddhi — discerning power + nāśaḥ — lose, affected; buddhināśāt = buddhi — discernment + nāśāt — from loss, from being affected; praṇaśyati — is ruined

From anger, comes delusion. From this delusion, the conscience vanishes. When he loses judgment, his discerning power fades away. Once the discernment is affected, he is ruined. (Bhagavad Gita 2.63)

It does not matter if the object is physically present or not, the very act of considering the animate or inanimate object, creates in a person an attachment. The physical presence of the object or the mental representation (memory) of the object are both sufficient for the development of attachment. Even if there is no evident attachment, even if the person feels that there is no longing for the item, still if it is considered, an attachment energy is deposited in the psyche in relation to it.

Once the attachment is deposited in the mind, it may act to motivate the person to procure the object. Or it may remain as a dormant energy which will later produce the compelling motivation. A series of sensual contacts to a particular object will in time cause an accumulation of so much incremental attachment energy, that eventually this will form into a compulsion or craving. Sex indulgence is just one such energy.

If the craving is not fulfilled for any reason, then anger develops in the mind as a matter of course, because sufficient craving will convert into anger automatically. At first this anger will be felt as frustration merely but if the accumulation of attachment was large, it will manifested as ripe frustration or anger.

The value of anger is that it gives the individual the opportunity to be obnoxious which in turn causes that person to vent some of the attachment energy which causes stress release. This anger may produce violence to others but if it does that or does not produce that, it serves to vent some of the accumulated attachment.

Subtle World Sensuality Compared

Subtle world sensuality when it is unconnected to physical world reality, is more intense and potent than physical pleasure. We are familiar with physical experience but for the purpose of self-tantric, subtle experience is more important. There are two types of subtle world sexual intercourse. One leads back to taking a physical body. The other secures the person to remain in subtle existence with resistance to taking a physical form.

This all depends on the nature of the subtle body used by the ascetic. If the subtle form does not have resistance to physical rebirth, sexual acts on the subtle plane will invariably cause a deposit of energy in the fate of the person such that he or she will take a physical body to play out sexual activities which exhaust the accumulated sexual deposits.

An ascetic should if he or she can, avoid those subtle planes in which resistant to physical rebirth is absent. Otherwise any sexual activity, or any attraction to the sexual activity of others, will guarantee a physical rebirth. It may not occur in a matter of days or weeks, or even years or centuries but it will occur as soon as a physical environment is available somehow somewhere.

When one takes a physical form as a human being or some other species, one becomes mentally and emotionally isolated from every other reality. It is likely that one will become so preoccupied as that new physical body, that one will completely forget every other reality and will become more and more involved in that type of psychology. This will guarantee that one will continue transmigrating in that physical type of existence.

In the Mahabharata, there is the case of King Mahabhisha and Goddess Ganga, where the king viewed the panties of the Goddess and was sexually aroused. This happened in the Brahmaloka super-subtle world. Subsequently, Mahabhisha was dismissed from Brahma's world to assume his physical body with the arousal energy.

The Goddess for her part was predestined to take a physical body because she developed an attachment to some accursed supernatural beings who were condemned to take physical bodies. Her compassion to these beings converted into a compulsion for physical birth.

If one can do something to increase the resistance of the subtle body to physical rebirth, then that is the course of action. There are astral places where even if there is sexual intercourse it does not lead to physical rebirth. It does not imperil those involved in it. In such a dimension, one may if one is lucky study self-tantric even while associating with a sexual partner

Such ascetics have one fault however which is that they may become attached to the partner. This type of attachment causes a resistance to the deity or yoga-guru. That is undesirable. Both male and female ascetics may acquire a centric mentality which means that one or the other or both use the other as a *you-focus-only-on-me* object but this is against deity affiliation.

An ascetic who gets trapped in such a relationship with a partner is for all purposes doomed because he or she has no higher association which is more attractive than the partner or the sex pleasure derived in that partner's association. If one finds oneself in such a situation, one should refocus on the deity even if the partner is hostile to that process.

The means of fate are complicated. No limited being can be fate's master. However if one has a connection to a deity, one should divine the possibility of living in that deity's astral or spiritual province. This means that life with a partner has to be secondary. An ascetic should always be clear about his or her priorities which should be compliant with the deity's desire. No partner of a self-tantric should become so important as to supersede the wishes of the deity. No self-tantric should ever allow himself or herself to be so self-obsessed as to compete with the deity. There is exception in this only when the partner is the deity.

Physical/Spiritual Sexuality

It may be reasoned as to if it is possible to have physical sexual relationship which is spiritual in content. The answer is that it is not possible. The confusion about this arises because of mistaking what is subtle or psychic with what is spiritual. In this material existence it is natural to assume that what is subtle is spiritual. There are many religions on the earth which profess that the ghost or departed ancestor is a spiritual existence. This has value when we consider the physical to be the reference but still it is totally untrue.

All the same those who feel that they can jump from the physical to the spiritual, bypassing the subtle, are impractical. There are some religious sects which advocate that anyone who joins their Cult will at the time of death be translated to the spiritual and will not have to deal with challenges in the subtle existence which is between the two. That is religious hype.

For all practical purposes, from where we are located, the exclusive spiritual existence is non-existent. For us the higher subtle planes are just as valid as the spiritual world. Even though the practical achievement for us is to go to the highest subtle existence, still we should always know that it is not the spiritual world.

There is no direct transit between the spiritual and physical. Arjuna, the disciple-hero of the Bhagavad Gita took instructions from the Krishna deity but all the same this does not mean that what Arjuna did in applying martial discipline to others, is a correlation of something which occurs in the spiritual world.

There is no such correlation because there is no conflict in the spiritual existence. However there is a parallel in the subtle worlds. In fact in the Mahabharata, Arjuna, even before he fought at the Battle of Kurukshetra, went to the subtle world and defeated criminal sorcerers there.

Sexual activity in the physical existence may have a parallel in the subtle psychic material world but it is not related to anything in spiritual existence. Our minds however have this tendency to feel that there is.

Sexual Attraction to a Deity

It is possible to be sexually attracted to a deity. This however begs the question as to the accuracy of sensual perception. How can one be sure that the deity is actually there and that the attraction energy is of divine nature? How does one sort between subtle and spiritual energy? What is a highest level of subtle energy? How does one rate subtle energy to spiritual energy?

In most religions of the Western nations there is little conversation about sexual attraction to a deity. The Judaic tradition is that God is the father. There is nothing about conjugal love for that Father God. In the Christian religion there is a hint about the sexual attraction between Jesus and Mary Magdalene. Even though some people blow this out of proportion, the truth is that it is hardly mentioned in the New Testament. One has to read between the lines to even come up with an idea of a conjugal relation with Jesus Christ, Lord that he is.

In the East however there is mention about conjugal love with deities. One famous example is the gopis' love for Lord Krishna. This is used by devotees of Krishna as the prime example of a loving relationship with this deity.

For self-tantric any conjugal love for a deity must be put aside for the time being, until the ascetic realizes his or her gender potential and its safe sexual applications. There must be a shift to the highest level of the subtle body. From there one can examine relationships with the deity. There is no valid focus on relationship until the subtle body reaches its highest configuration.

In the meantime however the ascetic has to exist and may have to do so in several dimensions according to how he or she is shifted here and there by the whims of fate. Hence while aspiring for the highest subtle level, the ascetic must manage whatever happens. If perchance a deity appears and reveals or inspires a sexual relationship, the ascetic must handle that in most productive way according to the level of advancement and the inspiration given. The ascetic should be vigilant.

In the Mahabharata, there is the story of a woman named Kunti, who invoked several deities and was sexually involved with each of them. From this we know that it is possible but it is not likely for every ascetic. In the Puranas there are hardly any tales about male ascetics having conjugal relationships with female deities. There is the story about Pururava and Urvashi but Puru was ruined by his conjugal craving for the goddess. King Mahabhisha came to distress because of his conjugal compulsion for Goddess Ganga. Ravana wanted a sexual relationship with Goddess Sita and that desire ruined him and his country. This is why I hint that it requires detailed inspection as to the inspiration and the quality of attraction energy.

Deity means someone who is higher, a god, goddess, God or Goddess. Therefore if one finds that one feels to be the equal of the authority, one should examine the energy to be sure that there is no distortion.

Sexual Influence is Universal

Sexual influence is not to be ignored. It demands attention because it is at the heart of the reproduction of bodies. In this respect there are two aspects which have such importance. One is weapons. The other is sexual intercourse. Weapons threaten to terminate reproduction. Unhampered sexual intercourse subscribes to reproduction. It gives bodies while weapons kill them.

Sexual intercourse presses down on us from every side. It is just as potent as gravity but it is psychic oppression. Those who pretend that it is not there do so at their peril. That includes monks and nuns.

A legend has it that a king in India asked a yogi about the fading of sex desire. The yogi replied that sex desire never fades. The king however, based on observations, concluded that in old age sex desires fades gradually, where elderly people eventually lose interest. The yogi laughed when the king said this. The monarch was offended. He challenged the yogi to prove that sex desire does not reduce as the body goes through infirmity in old age.

The yogi made an arrangement such that the king, disguised as a peasant, would come to a hospice for the elderly. At the appointed time, the yogi met the disguised king when a scantily-clad buxom young woman walked through the hospice. Every old man in that place sat up and peered at the body of the woman. The king was convinced.

If anyone is interested in sex desire, it is the elderly and for good reason, for the purpose that soon such elderly people will be forced to transmigrate to the astral world hereafter with their desires for physical social life intact. Hereafter, an elderly person is motivated to become part of a sexual act through which an embryo would develop as a new social identity giving access to the physical world all over again.

There is no human being who is absolutely resistant to sex desire. This is because the nature of the material body is to reproduce and the means of that is sexual intercourse. It is built into the physiological and psychological energy of the material body. It is present in the subtle body.

Despite this, idealistic human beings are of the opinion that a monk or nun, should not have sex desire and should not be interested in sexual contact. This is a false expectation because the laws of nature do not support it except superficially.

Even if the person-self of the monk or nun has no interest in taking another material body, the body itself has interest in indirectly perpetuating itself and wants to reproduce more bodies. The kundalini lifeforce has that as its mission in every life form. Once a form begins as sperm, it wants to survive. Once it survives infancy and can fend for itself it wants to reproduce because new forms are its one and only means of projecting itself into the future.

Yes, someone may not be interested in sex pleasure but that does not mean that there is no interest in reproduction which is the way to invest in the future. It is not sex pleasure that is behind this. It is the urge for survival come what may. At every step we are pressured to reproduce.

Reduction of Sensual Stimulation

For self-tantric investigation all external stimuli should be reduced to a minimum. The ascetic should not willingly put himself or herself into environments where sexual stimulation is available.

If the ascetic is with a partner, both persons should observe the reduction in sex stimuli and continue the investigation in self-gender. We have five senses. We have an interest-energy which pursues sense objects either by itself or in liaison with the senses. These faculties should be reined in so that sexual stimuli is reduced. This is just on the physical side. Once the physical access is regulated, the problem of the subtle access can be investigated. That subtle access is very problematic and requires hours and hours of meditation to understand and curb.

- The ascetic should avoid being in places where the smells of sexual related substances are available.
- He or she should avoid tasting and/or speaking about sexually related subjects.

- He or she should avoid seeing sex related forms.
- He or she should avoid touching sex related persons or things.
- He or she should avoid hearing sex related sounds.
- He or she should avoid visualizing or thinking of sexual related instances.
- He or she should avoid considering sexual activities.
- He or she should avoid day-dreaming or dreaming of sexual related people or things.

Any sexual experience which one is exposed to may cause an increase in desire. This has nothing to do with one's celibate or permissive inclination. A monk or a debauchee, either will be affected if exposed to sexual stimuli. It is no respecter of persons. If one wants to have sexual intercourse, and one is exposed to addition stimuli, one's sex desire will increase. If one does not desire intercourse and wants to have none of it, still if one is exposed, the lack of desire will transformed into desire however small or miniscule it may be. Hence for the purpose of self-tantric investigation, one should avoid exposure and only be under it when one is fated. Then one should realize the invasion, own up to it and see how best one can manage.

Ancestral Influence

Most human beings are completely unaware of ancestral influence. They have no idea that most departed souls must take rebirth through an embryo. This ignorance of the human beings causes mass miscalculation and certain arrogance whereby we cannot understand what happens even in our minds and feelings. Being essentially ego-centric beings, we may break away from being self-centered if we could develop the insight into the psychic influences which penetrate and direct us.

The ancestral influences control much of what we do but due to self-obsession we assume those influences as our mental or emotional compositions. Over the years explaining this to students, it was rough and tumble as most students give lip service to the idea of reincarnation but fight in a rough and tumble when they are shown how reincarnation really operates.

People do not want to be confronted with the idea that their views are not their own and that their desires may be those of other persons who are long dead and gone. Many arrogant human beings assume a religious or spiritual path. These people are usually confident of their view even though they lack the mystic insight to really know how we are influenced. Religious people want to deny that they may be controlled by ancestors. They feel that the religious affiliation protects them from obeah.

People who underestimate the ancestral influence are being silly because that energy dominates human affairs. There is no such thing as human beings who are isolated from ancestors. The mere idea that we use bodies which are based on ancestral contribution, means that we cannot be entirely free from their influence. There are two aspects to this. One is that our bodies carry genetic material which will always remain loyal to the ancestors. The other is that the ancestors are present as invisible people, ghosts, in the astral atmosphere which surrounds us.

The energy of romance, affection or love, which we cherish so dearly and which to us is our expression, has in its content, ancestral feelings. We however rate all of it as being our very own. This self-tantric practice will clarify that, removing confusion. When two people are engaged in sexual intercourse, most of the energy may not be their own. Most of it may be the emotions of one or more ancestors.

Senses Promote Pleasure Excess

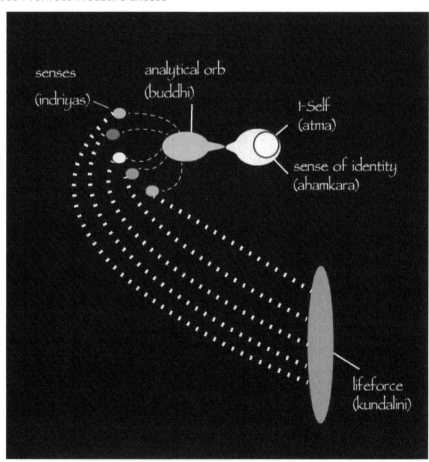

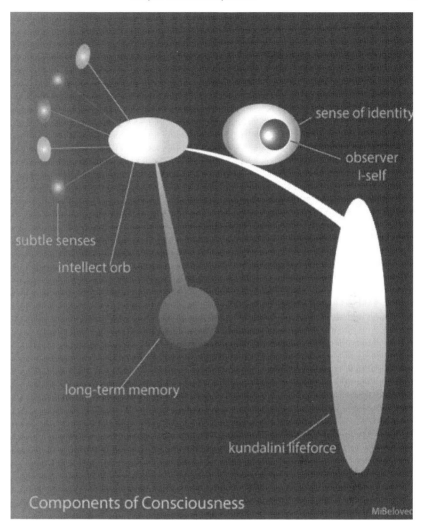

sense of identity

observer
I-self

subtle senses

intellect orb

long-term memory

kundalini lifeforce

Components of Consciousness

MiBeloved

The senses are more inclined to pleasure excess than they are to the welfare of the psyche. The senses act as either a friend or enemy to the psyche. They side with excess but their actions imperil the psyche. Vice means that there is excess of something which the senses like to procure. *inSelf Yoga™* concerns vice but not in terms of religion or morality. The interest in vice has to do with the relationship between the core-self and its adjuncts; the senses being conjointly the messengers of the kundalini lifeforce psychic mechanism.

The senses are loyal to the needs and request of the kundalini lifeforce. This is something that we must accept. The senses do not care about religious tenets, moral codes and human social conventions. The senses are not loyal to the core-self, the observer-I. To feel that the senses can be coerced or influenced into obeying the desire of the core-self or following religious or moral stipulations is a false expectation which does not take into account how the senses were created and formatted. The senses as experienced in a material human body are not offshoots of the core-self. They are direct productions and out-growths of the kundalini psychic lifeforce mechanism.

To influence the senses in real terms, dealing with them directly is a waste of time. If one really wants to curb the senses, one should change the behavior and tendencies of the lifeforce. Failure to do that will result in some compliance when the senses are socially-pressured or willpower-forced to do something, but as soon as they are able they will resume the old behaviors. Read this from Lord Krishna:

यततो ह्यपि कौन्तेय

पुरुषस्य विपश्चितः।

इन्द्रियाणि प्रमाथीनि

हरन्ति प्रसभं मनः ॥२.६०॥

yatato hyapi kaunteya
puruṣasya vipaścitaḥ
indriyāṇi pramāthīni
haranti prasabhaṁ manaḥ (2.60)

yatato = yatataḥ — concerning an aspiring seeker; hyapi = hi — indeed + api — also; kaunteya — son of Kuntī; puruṣasya — of the person; vipaścitaḥ — of the discerning educated; indriyāṇi — the senses; pramāthīni — tormenting; haranti — seize, adjust; prasabhaṁ — impulsively, by impulse; manaḥ — mentally

Concerning an aspiring seeker, O son of Kuntī, concerning a discerned educated person, the senses do torment him. By impulses, the senses do adjust his mentality. (Bhagavad Gita 2.60)

If the senses become attached to sex pleasure, they will do everything in their power to procure that. But if the individual deprives the senses of that pleasure when the senses seek a source for that, the senses will secretly summarize their desire and keep deposits of sexual urges until those energies pile up into a tsunami of energy which overpowers the core-self and forces the psyche to indulge. We have evidence of this tactic of the senses by the numerous sexual breaches of monks and nuns through history. Besides the known downfalls, there were many more which were never documented.

The truth is that the senses cannot be directly loyal to the core-self. They can only be loyal to it indirectly by being loyal first to the kundalini lifeforce. Hence if the core-self can change the tendencies of the lifeforce, the sensual treason would cease.

Senses are Hyperactive for Pleasures

The senses are electrically hyperactive for pleasures. This means that there need be no willful intention for the sense to crave an indulgence. It does not have to be sex pleasure. It can be any enjoyment. It can even be reverse-pleasure, pain. The senses can become attached to any pleasure or pain. It will then accept any information, even the slightest, which is illustrated in the mind based on recent memory or instinct.

The more intense the pleasure, the more sensitive the senses will be in their procurement of anything which the mind can related to that enjoyment. Sex pleasures happens to be one of the intense feelings which the mind can never forget.

In animals like deer, we observed that the smell of the female sexual secretions causes the sexual urge in the males to be aroused significantly. This means that once the olfactory gland passes the information to the brain, there arises a strong urge to copulate. We can assume that these animals are not thinking of sex deliberately, and yet they develop a strong urge merely on the basis of scent.

The core-self has little to do with this except that it is influenced to give permission for the indulgence. The smelling sense sends information to the kundalini lifeforce, which instantly checks its memory to match the input information with what was experienced before. If there were no similar experiences, it checks to see if there is an instinct which is related, then it acts according to a previous memory or instinct.

This confidence of the kundalini lifeforce, is transmitted to the analyzing faculty in the head of the subtle body. That in turn may produce supportive arguments for aggressive procurement of the object which emitted the smell. That process influences the core-self to be interested in the decision of the analytical faculty. With the interest of the core-self flowing through the mind to the analytical faculty, the psyche is commanded by the kundalini to procure the pleasure.

Sensual Objects as Hair-Triggers

There are many objects which if the senses contact them, the mind will drum-up memories of experiences which are or are not related. It will then use those memories to force the psyche to procure select pleasures. It will do this even if such pleasures ruin the person.

Once a pleasure becomes a compulsion, the senses become tasked with using the related sensual object to procure that pleasure at all cost. The being will then risk itself to procure the enjoyment. This applies to sexual intercourse as it does to any other addiction.

I give the example of body sweat. If the nose catches a whiff of a stranger's sweat, the mind might convert that impression into a sexual need. It may suggest to the self that the body should go near to someone else with whom sexual intercourse could be shared.

As soon as the psyche develops an attachment to a certain pleasure, it is likely that it will become anxious for that enjoyment. It may use any sensual contact which is or is not related, to justify acquiring more of the pleasure.

Psychic Sensual Objects as Super-Hair-Triggers

Psychic objects affect everything we do in the world of the physical living. Yet, most of us ignore the psychic phenomena or dismiss it as irrelevant. The yogi cannot be successful if he or she does not develop acute psychic perception. The psyche detects psychic occurrences from moment to moment but it is unconscious to this activity. The psyche is impelled to act by psychic influences but the psyche interprets such actions as its very own. This must change in the life of a yogi.

Sensitivity and conscious interpretation of subtle movements and motivations comes to the yogi through meditation practice. There is no other way to develop this. The yogi must have meditation as a priority and must fit it into his daily routine.

Self-Discipline

Self-tantric includes self-discipline, which is an agreement with oneself to take restrictive measures in certain habits. It has nothing to do with controlling others. It is fully involved with studying the core-self and its relationship with the adjuncts. The ascetic should determine where the core-self can increase command over the psyche. The authority of the adjuncts should be consistently reduced.

In this practice, teachers are helpful if they can show the student how to differentiate the core-self from the adjuncts. A few psychological geniuses like Gautam Buddha, for instance, mastered their psyches with little assistance from teachers but the majority of humans need to take help from teachers who perfected a method of release.

Even if a student has the best teacher, the major endeavor must be done by the student. Each core-self is unique. Each is in a peculiar position in relationship to its adjuncts. Each must work with itself to gain mastery.

A yogi should not be naïve. He should not be a person who lives on pipe-dreams and imaginative schemes. He should not be addicted to believing in plans or in thinking that he can create reality. He should always observe what nature does and did, so as to get a valid assessment of what is required for an objective.

Resentment is a real force to content with. There is resentment from others, even from students of a yogi, even from relatives, even from lovers. This is because resentment is an intrinsic part of this creation.

A yogi should forget everything he learnt about resentment being a negative energy which comes from others or which is self-generated due to frustration. He should change his outlook and consider that resentment is an integral part of creation, an energy that is here to stay.

The technique is to avoid being influenced by this energy. Any time someone is disciplined, resentment arises as the flip side. Even when there is self-discipline resentment arises from the self to itself. It is an energy we should get accustomed to. We should neither panic nor be alarmed of it. Someone has to resent someone else because the stockpile of resentment energy on earth has to surface somewhere somehow. A yogi should hold nothing against those who are resentful but should instead understand that they are victims of the energy.

Self-Tantric Morality

Self-tantric morality is not a group effort. It is not reliant on social props. It is not part of what the government wants its citizens to do. It is not designed to promote anything except the advancement of the ascetic and the requirements given by the yoga-guru.

A yogi must have moral values but these concern the yoga practice, particularly the stage of the practice. At one stage, this is the requirement. At another stage this or that may be acceptable. It is flexible and not stereo-typed. All the same as far as possible a yogi should be segregated from the general public and from other ascetics because the yogi may do things which irritate others, which in turn would cause the flow of unwanted relationship energies to enter the yogi's mind.

A yogi should not interfere with the moral views of others. He should not object to the rules of social behavior which are recommended by the government. But all the same, he or she should do whatever is necessary to advance the progress in the self-investigation of gender and sexuality. This concerns inner behavior between the core-self and the adjuncts. It is not a plan for external social interaction with others. The least complicated course is for the yogi or yogini to be single with quelled sex desire on the physical level and carefully document sexual interaction, if any, on the subtle plane. However if the yogi or yogini has a partner(s), he or she should manage that complication so that all concerned gain more understanding of the gender aspect and its sexual expression needs.

Demands of the Sexual Organs

A yogi must face up to the demands of the sex organs. The genitals of males or females have their own needs. The breasts of a female ascetic has its own way of satisfaction. Females who bear children get direct understanding of their breast needs for suckling.

Most of the compulsion we feel for using the sexual organs comes into play after arousal of sexual feelings in the organs. This arousal is usually triggered by sensual contact with sex objects or with sensual items which the mind interprets to be relational to sex.

Each ascetic should study his or her sexual nature to understand how it is stimulated. What are the triggers which cause arousal? How can arousal be quelled or avoided? What is the best way to complete sexual acts once arousal becomes compulsive? How best to accommodate and take responsibility for pregnancies which arise even from non-deliberate sexual acts?

Women in astral heavens also have breasts. These persons do not carry pregnancies. Rarely do they yield milk from the nipples. We may question as to why they have breast in the first place. If breasts are there for nurturing infants primarily, why do women in the heavenly world have breasts? It is an interesting question.

There are stories in the Puranas about heavenly goddess or nymphs who descended into physical or astral bodies, which causes advanced yogis, even celibate ones, to get instant erections and sexual discharge merely by seeing the bodies of such women. And yet, when these women were in the heavenly world, the males there were not stimulated by their voluptuous forms.

But they are heavenly worlds in which denizens are preoccupied with sexual intercourse where one session may last for one, ten, one hundred or one thousand years in earth time. Does this degrade these individuals?

Tagging Pleasure, Responsibility and Gender Identity

The ascetic must in time sort what is pleasure, what is responsibility and what is unapplied isolated gender identity.

Is the person-self genderless or gender-variable?

In the Puranas there are cases of persons who took birth as one gender in one life, and then as the opposite gender in another life. Does this mean that the person-self has adjustable gender in which it may swing one way or the other or even manifest both genders simultaneously?

How much pleasure should be consumed?

How much responsibility should be assumed?

How much should the self segregate its gender from the sex pleasure needs of its body?

In some heavenly astral regions there is sexual intercourse with no possibility of responsibility for nurturing infants. What then is the purpose of such sex pleasure? Is it for coupling pleasure observation?

On the earth, there is sex pleasure which may be followed by a pregnancy which carries with it the responsibility to nurture infants. Is sexual intercourse on earth only for producing progeny responsibility? What should human do with the pleasure surges they feel during intercourse? How much of that should be enjoyed? How much should be suppressed?

Whether on earth or in heaven should the self focus on its gender and not on the application of gender to sex pleasure?

Family Roles

Family life is important in terms of creating embryos and nurturing infants. Without that there would be no physical bodies for humans. Even if one has no interest in taking another physical body, still one should understand that for most people, family life is important and should be tendered.

Family life, however, in so far as it is a social situation for creating material bodies, has little to do with the self-tantric practice. This does not mean that the ascetic should avoid family life. He may function in it but it should not be his main focus. It should be done as a matter of routine but the focus should be on gender research and the ins and outs of sexual participation.

In the heavenly world, there is no begetting of embryos. Birth by being squeezed through a woman's passage does not occur. Life on earth is not the standard, but all the same it should not be neglected. The ascetic should be willing to play the father or mother role efficiently but should not make family life on earth, the priority.

Trail of Sensuality

An ascetic must see to it that he studies the sensual trail of events which leads to pleasure enjoyment. What is the beginning event? How are a series of activities developed in the physical, mental and emotional parts of the psyche? How is the event concluded? The mystery of the beginning is just as revealing as that of how an event ends either gradually or abruptly.

The ascetic has the task to study the sensual method. Those who are single and have no access to sexual intercourse, may research on the astral planes. Those who are single and who can avoid partnering on the astral level, may study other compelling sensual events.

What is the sequence from the start of an event until the mind exhausts its interest in the same?

What is the course from a memory of an event which the mind's re-enacts until it again becomes exhausted from indulgence in that pursuit?

Composition of Lust

In most religions, lust is regarded negatively. When lust becomes impulsive, it is regarded as a social risk. Laws were created to restrict lusty expression. What is its composition? Is there a way to know its constituent parts? Is lust one homogenous energy which is uniform in potency and effect?

Lust may be regarded as identical to sex attraction. This is obvious or so it seems. Lust however is in every passionate or forceful urge. It is not restricted to matters of sexual interest. Pinning down sex as the most common medium for lust may cause the ascetic to be lax, resulting in him or her being overtaken by lust when it saturates other sensual access. The ascetic should recognize lust in any sensual pursuit, not just the sexual one.

For instance a person may condemn a monk or nun for a proven breach of celibate vows. But the critic may do this under the influence of lust. Who then is better the monk or critic? Sexual expression is the vulgar manifestation of lust, its obvious expression, but all forms of lust especially its abstract formats are just as potent and self-destructive. Because an individual has a critical streak which is designed to focus on others, he or she is apt to see lust in others but is disinclined to discover it in the self.

Sex Media Avoidance

For self-tantric there should be a reduction in viewing sex media. Pornographic images and theatre should be avoided. When the ascetic is circumstantially forced to view it, he or she should be analytical and observant to study its effects. One should make use of every occasion even the unavoidable sexual ones, so that these experiences serve the purpose of discovering self-gender and its relationship to sexual involvement.

Terminal of Sexual Lust

Regarding the creation of an embryo, the terminal of sexual lust is the womb of a woman. That is where a sexual expression which went through its unimpeded course, met its biological conclusion. A male serves as a beginning for the creation of the sperm particle but he does not have to carry the development of the embryo.

This stresses a female for the expense of infant nurture. Modern medicine gave females a way out in the form of effective contraceptives. These disable ovum or impede any viable sperms which enter the uterus. At the moment there may be little consideration of fly back reactions from the psychic material nature but if we consider reincarnation and if we get insight into ancestors who are part of the lust energy, the advantage of having contraceptives can be seen as a short term fix for a long term complication.

Due to short-sightedness, a man may not grasp the liability. He may focus on the physiological fact that the female is the terminal. After sexual enjoyment, the woman only has the risk of carrying an embryo. On the surface it seems that the man is spared the liability.

Interplay ~ Rational Faculty / Emotions

There is a continuous interplay between the rational faculty and the emotions. By convention the emotions dominate, with the rational faculty serving emotional behests. This means that feelings rule the psyche with analysis operating to facilitate and justify sensations. In self-tantric practice this is listed as the kundalini lifeforce and the sensual energies commanding the psyche for the most part, with the buddhi intellect kowtowing and supporting the sensuality.

Is there something amiss in this natural way?

Can it be adjusted if need be?

In *inSelf Yoga™* jargon, the kundalini lifeforce, using the senses which are its inquisitive daughters, influences the buddhi intellect analysis faculty to acquire justifications for sensual activities. Once these are secured, the core-self is confronted. In fear of being overpowered, that core-self complies with the requests presented to it. These are illustrated as ideas in the mind.

This is the pitiful situation of the core-self or atma as it is termed in the Sanskrit language.

If we put aside the yoga jargon, it is that the sense of reason is influenced by the feelings which uses the sense of reason to muster intellectual supports for carrying out sensual activities which may be helpful to or detrimental to the psyche. The core-self, the observing-identity, is victimized by these operations such that it is afraid to make objections even when it realizes that the psyche will be imperiled by the activities.

Sensuality versus Sexuality

There is no contest between sexuality and sensuality. Sexuality is merely part of the range of sensual experience. An ascetic has to wake up to the fact that even though sexuality is a prominent and obvious sensual feature, a focus on sexuality as a solution to the problem will cause a sense of false progress and will lead to one's downfall when one least expects.

The study of gender and its sexual application is necessary for all ascetics but it is only the beginning. To remove sensual funding of sexuality means that there will be a great reduction of sensual activities but that may result in more covert sensual operations no matter how small. These in turn will accumulated, and will in time, degrade the ascetic even without causing him to breach celibacy.

In the history of monks, some breached the vows but others maintained celibacy at least physically. Still, they were condemned for other activities like misuse of finances, abuse of political or social power.

To feel that sexuality may be compared to sensuality signifies that one does not understand that the overarching feature is sensuality. We cannot come to terms with a tendency by studying and restricting only it's obvious or blatant manifestations. We have to tackle its covert, abstract and incremental means. When these are pinned down, the ascetic is sure to get the full understanding about the energy. In this respect sexuality even though it must be considered in detail is a distraction for any ascetic who feels that his (her) conquest of it, is the accomplishment even though that proficiency gives little insight into the abstract operation of the sensual energies.

Restraint versus Indulgence

Which of the two are more helpful, restraint or indulgence?

The usual answer is that restraint is the best choice.

Assuming that we are considering sexual activities, it would appear that it is best to restrain but how can one study the sexual nature of gender by restraining the feelings which are aroused in sexual attraction?

If it is possible to become liberated from sensuality merely by restraint then one would be foolish to indulge if one has the power to fully turn away from every sensual opportunity. However this is idealistic because hardly a person has that total control.

More important, is the fact that unless something is studied in detail, restraint of it, does nothing to develop resistance to it except in the short term and with the consequence of the tendency developing a great compulsion, which will overpower the ascetic at some other time.

If indulgence is necessary for studying how to control of a sensual feature, when would the ascetic flip that indulgence and apply the full restraint?

Patanjali Mahayogin, gave us an important hint where he spoke about the bhogas or sensual experiences which are offered by the psychic material nature. He said that such experiences continue for everyone beside the lone ascetic who already evolved through the sequences and developed a need not to be indulgent. Here is the verse:

कृतार्थं प्रति नष्टमप्यनष्टं तदन्यसाधारणत्वात्॥ २२ ॥

kṛtārthaṁ prati naṣṭam api
anaṣṭaṁ tadanya sādhāraṇatvāt

kṛt – fulfilled done; ārthaṁ – purpose; prati – toward; naṣṭam – destroyed, non-existent, non-effective; api – although, but; anaṣṭaṁ – not finished, still existing, effective; tat – that; anya – others; sādhāraṇatvāt – common, normal, universal.

It (the range of experiences) is not effective for one to whom its purpose is fulfilled, but it has a common effect on the others. (Yoga Sutras 2.22)

Indulgence is necessary for studying the experiences but the same indulgence discourages such study. Hence the problem. Study of both the obvious indulgences and the abstract type is necessary. Since such study involves indulgence which itself discourages objectivity, what should the ascetic do?

Can a yogi become freed from sensuality merely by restraint even if he does not fully comprehend the details of the sensual process?

Near Complete Sensual Restraint Success

Certainly there were ascetics who successfully applied the complete sensual restraint. For instance there was the person, Gautam Buddha. There is a history of the two persons Nara and Narayana who are mentioned in the Puranas. These individuals, exceptional as they were, applied the full restraint on all aspects of the sensuality, not just the obvious ones. The micro-aspects, the abstract portions, are where one has to really defeat the sensual urges, as exemplified in the practice of these mahayogin great ascetic persons.

It is believed that everyone can achieve ascetic control but before we repeat that, we should check to be sure that everyone has the same degree of willpower effectiveness. To be fair and honest, I do not have that degree of willpower control which Buddha demonstrated. Even practice to develop increased willpower application caused me to realize that I could not readily achieve the degree of control he established over the sensuality while using his last body. Perhaps somewhere else in some other dimension with a subtle body which is upgraded, I may exercise that control but for now, it is not true, at least in my case, thus I cannot claim to be on par.

Intellect versus Sensuality

In the tossup between the intellect and the sensual energies, the intellect will, the majority of times, be the loser. This is why it is necessary for the yogi (yogini) to study his (her) sensuality. The intellect is so designed that it is for the most part subservient to the sensual energy. Statements by leading ascetics which indicate that an intellectual decision or belief, is sufficient to stop an undesirable sensual behavior are for the most part hype.

The truth is that most of the time the sensual energies are dominant over the intellectual faculties. The misunderstanding occurs because in the mind compartment, the intellectual faculties can present their reasons or objections in a theoretically perfect way. The observing-self will then see these conclusions and become confident that what was visualized will play out physically or astrally. But this cast of events may not become reality. The reality will be that the sensually energies will make the entire psyche, intellect and all, obey its commands and procure whatever excitements it desires.

This is sad news for an ascetic but it is sobering. It could lead to a segregation between the observing-self and the intellect whereby that self no longer has so much confidence in the intellect and realizes that if anything, he or she needs to retract the sensual energies.

The first step is to understand the relationship between the observing self and the intellect. What does the intellect do which the observing-self relies on? How does the intellect keep the observing-self entertained or hypnotized?

Is the intellect influenced by the sensual energy? Does the intellect have more loyalty to the sensual energy than it does to the observing-self?

Design of the Psyche

The design of the psyche, how it really operates, its objectives, the observing-self's control or lack thereof, must be research by the ascetic. Taking the psyche for granted, living in it as it is, accepting its operations as being satisfactory, come what may, is not the way of a self-tantric.

All the same he (she) should never make convenient assumptions, and should never get into the game of rationalizing everything which happens. One should observe what the psyche does, how it does what it does, how it can be tampered with or adjusted in the short or long term. Then one may remove interest in a sensual quest what is undesirable.

Sooner or later, the realization will hit the core-self that the psyche is designed in a way which does not give autonomy to core-self. It is the sensual energies which for the most part dominate the psyche. The way out is to redesign it; to lessen the sway of the sensual energies and to intimidate the intellect so that it no longer has such loyalty to the sensual energies.

Human belief does not make anything valid. If something is true and a human being has a positive opinion or belief regarding it; that does not change the true nature of the event. It does not add or subtract from the event. If something is false, and a human being regards it to be true, the incidence does not change this way or that way because of the feelings.

We do however become confidence or feel depressed when our views are confirmed or denied. For self-tantric practice, one needs to get over the self-value of one's proven views. One must also get over the depression or disappointment which arises due to one's disproven ideas.

Sense Control

It is assumed that the self should control its sensuality and should not be cowered under by urges. However in the real world this reason is illogical. Many religious leaders, moral advocates and others find it convenient to hold the individual responsible for every bit of sensuality. The truth is that moral standards are breached even by the most ardent moralists.

Why is this?

Because nature does not care anything about human mores.

Sensuality expresses itself on the physical, emotional, rational, psychic and abstract levels. To confront it and upset it on any of those planes is challenging enough. The ascetic should study the formulation and application of the sensual energies in meditation. Then taking the least powerful lusts, he or she should manages these to limit their expression.

Sense Memory as Desire

Memory of a sensual event, becomes desire if such memory has enough force to induce the psyche into indulgence. If an urge has no memory support, it too can become desire if it has enough force to induce indulgence.

What then is desire?

When the memory of an event reaches a certain threshold, it exhibits an irresistible pressure under which the person is force to indulge. The person feels this as compulsion. The same threshold occurs even if there is no memory of any event. With a completely new urge, if it reaches a certain threshold, the person is compelled to indulge.

If the ascetic squelches the memory before it reaches the threshold, the desire does not develop an irresistible pressure and hence there is no indulgence. The same development may cease in cases where there is no memory to support a developing urge.

The subsiding of an urge or of the memory of an indulgence should be observed by the ascetic, so that he (she) can learn how to squelch it. However, he should know that this does not mean the elimination of the desire-force. When an urge or memory is squelched, that energy reverts to dormancy and will emerge again with less, the same or greater force. This may be termed as postponing the inevitable.

Indulgence and Observation

Indulgence does not mean astute observation. Those who feel that indulgence implies objective observation are not being realistic and do not understand how the psychic nature operates. Indulgence which means enjoyment and which is really indulgence for its own sake, does not help in the self-tantric practice. Total abstinence of any indulgence does not necessarily produce clarity. It all depends on the evolutionary integration of the person involved.

One ascetic can complete the research into self-gender without sexual involvements, while another just cannot. Those who require the observation of their sexual involvements must do so in a very careful way so as to procure the proper conclusions from the experience.

For this mastership, meditation is required. It is not particular to sex indulgence. It concerns sensual indulgence of all types, especially the very abstract experiences. Those who think that the study of sex gender and its outlays settles everything are mistaken. The settlement comes when the ascetic integrates the abstract pleasures and matures his psyche so that it does not require these. It is necessary to curtail and eventually stamp out vulgar sexual intercourse but that achievement is not the culmination of this practice. It is only the removal of one complication.

Observation of pleasurable occurrences, sensual treats, is difficult to make. In fact during the experiences, the individual is attentive but only to the perspective from which this can be regarded as pleasure. The ascetic needs to have these same experiences but shifted, so that the observations do not occur from the pleasure-absorbing perspective and moves to perceiving the various composite parts of the incidence.

The technique is to be in a sensual indulgence and to be objective to it simultaneously. This applies both to pleasurable and undesirable incidences. How is it possible to be in a sex pleasure experience and simultaneously be objective to it? The irresistible pleasure flows but the observing-self remains objective, monitoring it from a psychological distance, being other than it?

What about subtle pleasures in which the self is hardly aware that it was involved. How can the self realize these experiences and study their compulsions?

Sensuality Research

Sensuality research is a must but it should be done psychically not physically. Physical experience really means psychic experience which is attenuated because of physical interception. Ultimately, as an enjoyer, the person wants psychic experience. However, since what is psychic is subtle and hard to grasp, we are attracted to the physical side, because there, the psychic experiences are channeled through physical reality, which is easier to perceive.

Despite the convenience of using the physical to perceive the subtle or psychic, a yogi should gradually abandon the physical and develop direct access to subtle reality. Reliance on the physical means that one will be repeatedly drawn into material bodies, as a human being or some other life form. Hence a yogi should integrate physical experience, and then abandon the need for it.

In each life form a range of experiences is afforded. For instance in a cow's body there is limited facility for sexual intercourse and very little if any for exploratory sensual acts apart from smelling and tasting. The animal cannot enjoy sex pleasure in the variety of ways which a human being can indulge. This means that each body affords a certain range of pleasures. The ignorance about sexual intercourse before puberty is there both in the cow and human equally but after sexual maturity, the human may derive more carnal knowledge than the cow ever would.

This does not mean the person-self in the cow's body is forever limited to that. If that self transmigrated to a human body, it would discover the additional faculties which the selves using human forms enjoy.

There are two ways to consider this:

- The person-self is limited in experience by the faculties available in its current physical body.
- The person-self is relatively unlimited, such that it will experience a wide range of sense faculties, all depending on what is possible in any particular body.

This means that arrogance is inappropriate because at any moment, when a person-self is relocated into another creature form, it will experience whatever sense facilities that form exhibits.

But this begs the question:

What would that self do, if it had no access to any life form?

In other words, can it function sensually without being identified with a physical form?

Moral Regulations

Each society, in fact each home, each business enterprise even, has moral regulations. Some are rigidly enforced. Others are there but are barely observed by the people concerned. A yogi must observe whatever morality he is required to honor according to the society.

However, all the religious or secular morality cannot help a yogi with the relationship between the core-self and its adjuncts? That observation and alteration occurs through meditative practice when the yogi becomes isolated and focuses on the components of the psyche and their relational interactions.

Instead of being concerned about which person lied to him (her). A yogi should be concerned about how the buddhi intellect produced false justifications to support the schemes of the sensuality.

Instead of making sure that he does not steal from someone, or that someone does not steal from him, a yogi should be sure that what is conjured by the mind, does not steal his attention or that his attention does not steal his focus and place it in ideas and images which are randomly conjured.

Instead of worrying about the infidelity of a spouse, the ascetic should be concerned about the disloyally of the kundalini lifeforce's constant pursuit of sensual objects which imperil the psyche and the intellect's constant flirtation with the lifeforce in disobedience to the core-self.

Morality is important in self-tantric practice but only in relation to the core-self and its adjuncts. This may be termed as introspective morality with emphasis on increasing the autonomy of the core-self and reducing the influence of the intellect and the kundalini lifeforce's sensual outlay.

Chapter 3
Self-Tantric Described

Male / Female Difference

Self-tantric can be practiced by either gender but in certain areas the approach to practice is different. This is because the construction of the reproductive glands are different in each case. Due to this difference, the transit of pleasure energy varies between the genders.

Even in the subtle world, female anatomy is different. However the aim remains the same which is the full discovery of the gender capacity.

On the physical planet it is easy to sort the male from female. The essential fact in this is that in the human species, only the female body is capable to developing an embryo while only the male is capable of developing sperm.

The male body is not concerned with nurturing an embryo or with breast-feeding after birth of the fetus. Gender expression in the male in relation to sexual intercourse is targeted to depositing sperm in the uterus of the females. The pleasure involved in this does not in any way change this reproductive purpose. Even though it affords a pleasure experience in the process, nature stays on que with its mission for producing babies.

Regardless of whether pleasure is experienced or not, a viable sperm in a woman's uterus has the potential for becoming an embryo. This proves conclusively that the pleasure aspect, the sensual excitement, is superfluous when we consider this from the angle of reproduction.

In a sexual intercourse, the partners may feel that their pleasure is integral to the occurrence. In fact some partners testify to their pleasure as being part of the child produced in the pleasure act. However when we take a cold look at this, the pleasure aspect is superfluous and has limited function. In terms of reproduction, the pleasure of a sexual act does contribute to the mobilization of the sperm directly because of the force of an ejaculation. Is the pleasure merely a man's interpretation of the bio-electric force which operates the pump which generates ejaculation? If it is, then pleasure is merely a man's interpretation because of his emotional position during the act.

If we single out the pleasure climax, what would be its worth if we were to separate it from its ejaculatory function. Stated otherwise: If there was a climax experience with no emittance of sperm, what would be the function?

Is it a fact that pleasure is a function or a fulfillment all by itself without being tagged to reproduction?

If no fetuses are created in the astral world, why on earth are astral beings indulging in sexual intercourse?

Reproduction Studied

Reproduction or the generation of children must be studied by the self-tantric. He or she must decide on participation in the expansion of the life form of the body, which means to use the body's genetic material to create babies. Reincarnation of ancestors is related to this. That too must be studied. The views of Krishna in Bhagavad Gita should be learned and applied to one's lifestyle.

A question arises as to how much should the ascetic contribute to the generation of progeny. How much time and energy should he dedicate to that? Many ascetics have the opinion that they should not be part of a sexual partnership. They make such declarations on the basis of renunciation. The idea is that if one becomes involved, it will consume time, making it impossible to become liberated from material existence.

On the surface these arguments for renunciation seems perfect but when we apply insight these may be faulty. An ascetic should consider his obligation to the ancestors of his body, in regard to assisting them to relieve themselves of the need for new physical forms.

If the yogi waivers himself, will there be an unpleasant repercussion here or hereafter?

If he complies with the ancestors and acts sexually to reproduce children, how many should he have?

Who will protect him from losing the spiritual disciplines which are worn away by family involvement?

There is a similar query proposed by Arjuna in the Bhagavad Gita:

अर्जुन उवाच

अयतिः श्रद्धयोपेतो

योगाच्चलितमानसः ।

अप्राप्य योगसंसिद्धिं

कां गतिं कृष्ण गच्छति ॥ ६.३७॥

arjuna uvāca
ayatiḥ śraddhayopeto
yogāccalitamānasaḥ
aprāpya yogasaṁsiddhiṁ

kāṁ gatiṁ kṛṣṇa gacchati (6.37)

arjuna — Arjuna; uvāca — said; ayatiḥ — indisciplined person; śraddhayopeto = śraddhayopetaḥ = śraddhayā — by faith + upetaḥ — has got; yogāccalitamānasaḥ = yogāc (yogāt) — from yoga practice + calita — deviated + mānasaḥ — mind; aprāpya — not attain; yogasaṁsiddhiṁ — yoga proficiency; kāṁ — what; gatiṁ — course; kṛṣṇa — Krishna; gacchati — he goes

Arjuna said: What about the indisciplined person who has faith? Having deviated from yoga practice, having not attained yoga proficiency, what course does he take, O Krishna? (Bhagavad Gita 6.37)

कच्चिन्नोभयविभ्रष्टश्

छिन्नाभ्रमिव नश्यति ।

अप्रतिष्ठो महाबाहो

विमूढो ब्रह्मणः पथि ॥ ६.३८॥

kaccinnobhayavibhraṣṭaś
chinnābhramiva naśyati
apratiṣṭho mahābāho
vimūḍho brahmaṇaḥ pathi (6.38)

kaccin = kaccid — is he; nobhayavibhraṣṭaś = na — not + ubhaya — both + vibhraṣṭaḥ — lost out; chinnābhram = chinna — faded + abhram — cloud; iva — like; naśyati — lost; apratiṣṭho = apratiṣṭhaḥ — without foundation; mahābāho — O Almighty Kṛṣṇa; vimūḍho = vimūḍhaḥ — baffled; brahmaṇaḥ — of the spirituality; pathi — on the path

Is he not like a faded cloud, lost from both situations, like being without a foundation? O Almighty Krishna: He is baffled on the path of spirituality. (Bhagavad Gita 6.38)

Personal Introspective Investigation

Self-tantric concerns personal introspective investigation while being engaged in sexuality and while observing the sensual attitudes of others. It is mostly a self-observation process with little viewing of the sensual life of others.

For this practice the ascetic should use what was made available to him by providence. He should not force circumstances just for experience sake. The ascetic should cooperate with fate, while astutely studying the emergence of sensual energy in the psyche. The way that others display their sensual needs should be noted but not to criticize others, only to get insight into sensual operations.

Self-tantric applies to the self and the self only. It does not include others except if providence causes the association, and only in so far as being with others gives one self-insight. The self in this case must review itself, critique itself, make plans to reform, readjust or changed itself as it can. It should understand its potential.

Even when the ascetic is sensually or sexual involved with another person, self-tantric still means self-investigation by introspective meditation. Some of the insight gained by an ascetic may be gained through associative sensual involvement only. But if that can be avoided then there is no reason for an ascetic to be partnered with another person unless providence suggests.

Pleasure Commodity

Pleasure is a commodity in human society. It was always that and will continue to be that for as long as there is sensual perception. Pleasure is a psychological product which is in much demand. It is contrasted by pain which usually is not desired, even though some individuals have psyches which regard what most others feel as pain to be desired pleasure.

Commodity means a product which can be sold or bartered to some other person for this or that value. Prostitution by any gender is a way of using sex pleasure as a commodity. However any sensual product can be used as a commodity. It could be bought, sold or traded for some other emotional, mental or physical thing.

For self-tantric practice, an ascetic should not be involved in the commercial exchange of any sensual product. Our concern with pleasure including the sexual type is for investigation into the gender potential. This is not a social review but an isolated personal one, which may or may not require involvement with a partner.

Involvement causes complication of energies which makes it harder to sort the components which comprise a pleasure experience, hence only when necessary or when fated, should the ascetic be partner-involved.

Pleasure Sharing

Pleasure sharing may be viewed as a type of pleasure access which could not be experienced if one person did not couple with another. In other words, what is the purpose of sex pleasure sharing?

Is it to beget new life forms for the perpetuation of the species?

Is it for yielding a unique pleasure which each partner could not experience through self-expression?

For self-tantric this must be investigated? If for completion, one must have a partner, that should be considered. Otherwise, it should be avoided.

Reproduction does require contribution of sexual fluids from a male and female. But can the pleasure involved in sexual intercourse be stripped out?

Is the pleasure so embedded in the coupling experience, that it is integral to it?

Obviously the pleasure is not required for production of an embryo. Some raped women successfully produced children from a sex experience which was never to their liking and which they detested.

Comprehensive Celibacy

Comprehensive celibacy is an ideal which is hardly realizable except by a few ascetics. Partial celibacy is possible. Hypocritical celibacy is the most likely achievement.

Comprehensive celibacy takes into account three factors, a physical body, a subtle body and a core-self. It does not, like partial or hypocritical celibacy, underwrite what happens to the physical body with no insight into the activities of the subtle one and the gender potential of the core-self.

Self-tantric concerns comprehensive celibacy which could very well mean no celibacy except here or there, in this body or that body, in respect to the time, place and circumstance.

Physical celibacy is terribly flawed because the subtle body is not permanently affected by anything the physical form does. An ascetic has to target the subtle form directly if he or she is serious about making changes in the psyche.

Even if the subtle body is altered successfully, the ascetic is still left with the task of gender uncertainty. Is the core-self male, female, bi-gender or completely neutral?

The task of reining in the subtle body is so fantastic, that any ascetic who achieves it may be regarded as a siddha perfected being. But there are many ascetics who feign it or whose followers falsely advertise their teacher as having attained it. The determination of the gender potential is such an abstract feat that there is no discussion of it by most ascetics.

Hatha Yoga

Hatha yoga is necessary in the self-tantric practice. It is the method of targeting the subtle body, first by changing the feelings-format of the physical one and then by directly manipulating the energy in the subtle form. This includes mastering the kundalini lifeforce and its energy distribution subtle passages.

Physical yoga practice has value only if it allows the ascetic to perceive the abstract subtle form. That subtle body in turn has value only in so far as it would allow the ascetic to begin targeting the core-self which is the most subtle component in the psyche.

It is not what the ascetic wishes to be or where he or she wishes to go. It is rather what the ascetic will discover and how he or she could produce permanent transformations in the psyche. Whatever is there is the reality. The task is discovery.

The ascetic must learn about, infuse energy into, and redirect the kundalini lifeforce psychic mechanism. This psychic operation has its own sense of gender which may or may not be consistent with the gender of the core-self. An ascetic must single-out the kundalini lifeforce for clarity about the core-self and the psychic material nature in emotional form.

Physiological Pleasure

If sensual pleasure of any type is merely physiological, it means that it would end for the person when the physical system dies. Any necessary pleasure which is fully or partially reliant on physical substances is stress-consuming to the self when it is deprived of the physical body.

If there is a pleasure which the enduring self can only access when it has a physical body, we are left to question as to the value of that enjoyment and as to why the subtle body, or psychology, has a component within it which requires a pleasure which can only be accessed through a physical system.

Suppose we positively identify a pleasure which can only be accessed when the self has, or is, a physical body, then how can we determine which part of the subtle body needs that pleasure?

The need for material bodies will continue endlessly if there is no way to remove the subtle body's craving for physical sensuality. In that case, the quest for liberation from physical existence would be futile.

Conversely if the self can exist without a physical form, and if it can have subtle pleasures to its satisfaction and does not have to consume physical sensations, then what are those subtle pleasures?

Pleasure Exhaustion

For self-tantric, pleasure exhaustion must be studied. This happens frequently in sensual intake, where the psyche invests in pursuing a pleasure, then gets a return on its investment by exploiting the pleasure. After the climax, the person experiences a depression which is due to exhaustion of the energy which was used to sponsor the pleasure.

Exhaustion means down-time, where the psyche must rest and recuperate, to make itself fit for living. Then again when it accumulates enough energy to invest in the pleasure, it again pursues the same. When that pursuit is successful, it again exploits the pleasure, which again climaxes after which there is depression due to exhaustion of the pleasure-energy.

This type of pleasure though desired for its enjoying phase, is undesirable in its exhaustion. The ascetic should study this and figure if it is possible to eliminate such pleasure pursuits. If anything, the self should locate a pleasure source which in its expressive state has no exhaustion, where the self remains without negative moods or stupor.

Pleasure Efficiency

Pleasure efficiency is the expending of pleasure energy in reference to the exhaustion, such that if a pleasure reaches a climax and then it converts into a depressed state where its pleasure-energy is exhausted, that is low efficiency. It is unacceptable for self-tantric practice. No one wants to invest energy into an enterprise which will fail soon after it reaches its peak development.

High efficiency is desired, whereby when a pleasure reaches its climax and then it continues or even terminates but without converting into a depressed state. It should leave the participant with insight so that there is no need for rest and recuperation to replenish the pleasure-energy. It should be a depression-less experience all the way.

Pleasure Energy Accumulation, Use and Exhaustion

In the practice of self-tantric, the physical and subtle forms must be meticulous observed and studied. No one needs to understand the self more than the self. At birth one is quite unfamiliar with the psyche. A human being cannot see into its body. Many have no idea where specific organs are located. In fact, by the grace of science, many human beings have some insight about the organs in the physical body. Otherwise if it were not for modern education very few human beings would know where any gland in the physical body is located.

The reason for this ignorance is that nature does not award penetrating vision when it gives the physical body. Even the slight sensual expressions should be investigated but the sensational and grand ones like sex pleasure must be researched. For self-tantric the sensual energies must be contained and transformed. There should be no excess, which means diet must be controlled. It is through diet that the sense organs get power. A reduction in diet means less stored energy. An increase means more reserves, which in turn means more pleasure production, where it is likely that the self will be overpowered by the energy.

More production also means more exhaustion. Less production may result in less sense participation. What is sufficient? How does the yogi determine how much to eat?

Pleasure Energy Stimulation through Exposure

Environmental triggers may cause excessive sensual stimulation. This applies to all forms of sensuality. It is not restricted to sexual intercourse and for the purpose of self-tantric, the ascetic is observant of any stimulation not just the sexual type.

Too much stress on sexual excess will be the undoing of an ascetic, because he or she will be less vigilant when involved in other expressions, which will result in breaches in other activities which will damage the practice nevertheless. Many persons who safeguarded their sexual abstinence and brought these to nil, were fractured by some other sense participation because they failed to recognize that any sense could be the cause of weakening the autonomy of the core-self. Weather deteriorates houses in an obvious and very telling way but so do termites with their silent and invisible gnawing methods.

Self-tantric also means sense vigilance of every type even of the very abstract expressions. The ascetic has it as a task to leave aside the socially-obvious means of sense expression, such as sexual intercourse. But in time he or she must switch the focus to the subtle non-obvious sensations which operate behind the scenes with the power to undermine the authority of the core-self.

Since many moral authorities listed sexual intercourse as number one enemy, and since it is the focus in sexual tantra (not self-tantra), it should be studied by the self-tantric. The fact that it was given so much attention and that a practice developed just for it, means that it is potentially, a huge barrier to progress. However the prominence of sexual tantra does not remove the threat of the non-obvious sense expressions.

Ship captains are alert for large rocks which protrude the oceans. These can surely wreck their craft. But some captains who are unaware of the dangers of submerged reefs became wrecked all the same.

Any exposure in any physical or astral realm carries risks. The reason being that beings in need of anything usually make efforts to procure sense objects which satisfy urges. For instance if a man is hungry, he will eat whatever edible item he finds in the environment, irrespective of if he owns the item or not. Our sense of ownership is flexible. It leans to our favor. It excuses us when it sees fit. Some urges are so forceful as to create a seemingly-righted sense of possession on the spot. A person who is hungry, and who stumbles accidentally on a mango tree, will more than likely appropriate the fruits just as if he planted and tended the tree. He may not consider if someone owns it.

This means that if a person is sexually exposed, and he or she wanders into someone who has an active sex urge, that exposed person runs the risk of being forced into a sexual participation. Even if there is no forced participation, the mere sight by the urged person may create visual appropriation. Even though that is not physical it will have a psychic impact.

The converse is also true. If the ascetic is not exposed, he or she may still be affected if he or she encounters someone who is exposed. The sexually exposed person will not be appropriated by the yogi or yogini necessarily, but there will be a psychic impact nevertheless. In the case of the mango tree, it will not be affected by the desire of the wandering man if that man restrains himself or just does not feel a need to pick the mango. But this exception occurs only because the mango tree did not have a visual means of sense perception. If the exposed ascetic held one of the mangoes and squeezed it the tree would be affected by that action, even if the ascetic did not tug the fruit from the tree. Through its touch sensation the tree would become aware of the ascetic and the threat implied.

Self-tantric requires as much isolation as possible, otherwise the practice cannot be instituted due to constant manifestations of urges and exposures of the ascetic and of any other sense object. To study the sensual energies, the ascetic needs two circumstances to do research:

- no access to much sensual stimuli
- limited access to specific sensual stimuli

For a time an ascetic would require no access to particular stimuli. This gives him (her) the opportunity to study the urges in the psyche when they are not triggered by external association. From this the ascetic can gage what is native to the self.

The ascetic must, from time to time, be isolated with specific sensual stimuli, so that he (she) can study the effects of the triggers given by those external aspects, as to their worth, as to their corruption of the integrity of the self, as to the self's innate need for these expressions.

Physical Body's Sensual Influence

The physical body has sensual influence which the subtle form is conditioned by. In fact there is a danger that whatever tendencies one develops while using a physical body, one will carry those features in the subtle body long after the physical one dies.

Some features of a subtle body are innate to it. But there are other aspects of a subtle form which are exhibited because the subtle either has or had a physical form.

The ascetic is required to sort what is innate to the subtle body and what it adapted under physical influence. For the research of kundalini self-tantric, there should be no extra features in the subtle body. This research inquiries into the subtle body's basic format and its adaptations to physical needs.

The ascetic should practice yoga to sort the influences. Once he or she comprehends what is natural or extraneous to the subtle body, a process can be applied for deleting the excess so that the self can review its segregated condition. A good place to begin is with the reproduction physiology.

How does the physical system generate sexual hormones?

How is the urge for sexual indulgence formatted?

What does food have to do with sex desire?

Insight through Physical Restraint

Self-tantric begins with curbing the physical body from all sensual excess. First one must recognize what is a sensually-excessive experience. All desirable experiences carry with them an energy which discourages insight. If a person likes an experience, it goes to his disadvantage if he tries to analyze it. This is because the mere desirability erodes whatever insight the person may gain from it.

Negatives experiences, those which the person does not like, also carry in them an energy of rejection which discourages unbiased review. This is why some persons commit undesirable acts repeatedly.

The first step is to decrease the frequency of the indulgence. If the ascetic commits an act which cause an increase in indulgence, he or she will find that there is little or no power to curtail the act. I will use sex pleasure as an example to explain how one can reduce the frequency and come to the basic format one's psyche has for indulgence.

There are two initiations into sexual activities. These are:

- nutrition
- sense stimulation

Sexual urge is sponsored primarily through nutrition. It has other supports but unless there is good nutrition, the urge cannot express itself in a grand way. If the body is starved it will cease producing sex hormones. Those hormones are created by food consumption. This is an important hint. It means that the ascetic should regulate diet. If he or she eats more than necessary there may be impulsion for excessive sexual indulgence.

If there is sense stimulation it should be identified and curtailed. During the experience the movement of sensations should be mapped. Conclusions which are drawn from this should be applied when the exposure is encountered again.

Sexual Apparatus Design

The ascetic should study the sexual apparatus design, as to its construction, as to its distribution channels, as to the mix of energies and organ functions which comprise the experience. Those who do not have a partner may study sexual encounters on the astral planes. Those who have no partner and who also do not recall astral life should study the digestive system to gain insight into how what is eaten is converted to digestive energy which powers each cell of the body.

Yoga Postures

Yoga postures are required in the self-tantric process. These exercises make for a more efficient energy distribution in the physical and astral bodies. Some postures support and enhance the celibate aim of ascetics but in self-tantric we expect that the posture would sponsor the entire psyche. On the physical plane the posture should help every part of the body resulting in efficient energy distribution. The focus is the entire body, not just its sexual organs.

However the ascetic may focus on certain parts, like the sexual organs and the reproductive apparatus, and then step by step investigate the whole psyche. The fact that much of yoga was used to sublimate sexual desire, informs us that to have the sexual and reproductive functions as the prime focus for reform could be a basic premise for a beginner. If one gains success in the sexual restraint, that would be a plus for the ascetic. That would cause much self-confidence giving the ascetic the courage to reform even the abstract parts of the psyche.

Yoga / Muscular and Mental Locks

There are many contractions used by yogis for containing, identifying, compressing, scattering, purifying and directing energy in the physical and subtle bodies. Many of these are unknown. Some are mentioned in the ancient yoga texts like the *Hatha Yoga Pradipika*.

The well-known contractions are:
- anus lock
- sex lock
- navel lock
- neck lock

- mind lock

These correspond to the chakra energy gyrating centers.

The **anus lock** is the act of pulling up the anal sphincter muscle. When the ascetic becomes sensitive and develops psychic insight, the physical action of applying this lock causes energy in the subtle body to remain above the anal sphincter muscle, so that this energy does not express itself through the anus region in the subtle body. If energy is effectively prohibited from passing through the anus, it is likely that the energy may go upwards through the center of the spinal column.

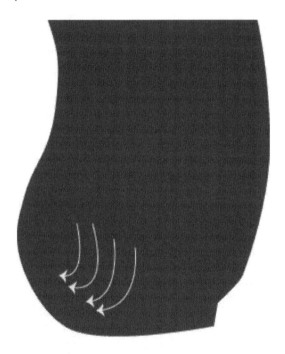

expression of energy downward
and outward because of relaxed
anal sphincter muscle

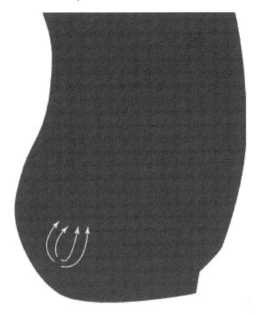

pull-up anal sphincter muscle

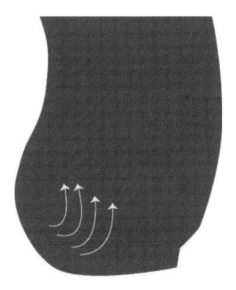

expression of energy upward
and inward due to contraction
upward of anal sphincter muscle

The **sex lock** involves contracting the urinary and sexual organ apparatus at the perineum. This contraction is an upward slanted action. It compresses sexual energy and causes conservation of hormones. It may cause the absorption of hormone energy into the blood stream so that cells in other parts of the body, may gain access to the hormones.

Initially the sex lock involves the urinary and sexual organ apparatus. In the advanced stage the two applications are segregated and the ascetic would apply the contraction to the sexual or urinary aspects, or both simultaneously. The target is the sexual apparatus contraction which must be pulled up and back at a slant. It is focused in the perineum area.

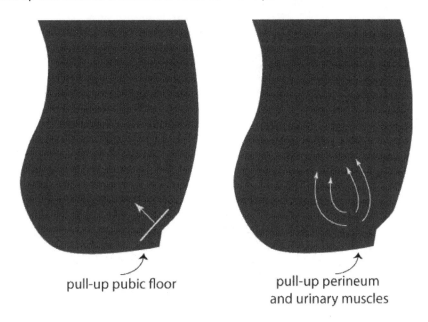

pull-up pubic floor   pull-up perineum
                                         and urinary muscles

The objective is to close the energy orifice which emits physical and subtle sexual energy. This orifice remains open in most adult bodies. The aim is to close it so that the sexual hormonal energy is routed to the base chakra where it is fused into the kundalini psychic lifeforce.

There is also a method which is more advanced. This is the process of pulling the sex hormone energy upwards through the trunk of the subtle body, so that it does not go downwards but is dissipated upwards as soon as any of it is produced.

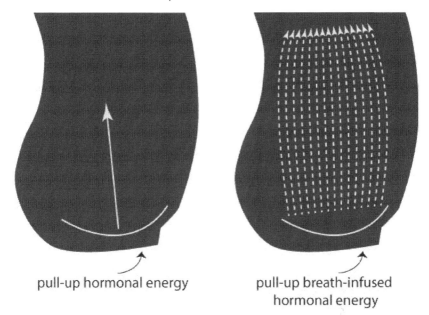

pull-up hormonal energy   pull-up breath-infused
                                    hormonal energy

The **navel lock** is important because it involves control of the digestive process. Even the sexual and reproductive areas which some ascetics are desperate to control is supported by the digestive process. If the ascetic can bring the navel area under control he or she can gain the upper hand and eliminate the need for physical sustenance. This is a feature which affects many ascetics after they depart from the physical body. They find that the subtle form feels hungry. This produces a need to develop another embryo just for the purpose of ingesting physical meals.

For the navel lock, the navel is pulled back towards the spine while on either side below the navel the abdomen is pulled upwards and backwards towards the spine.

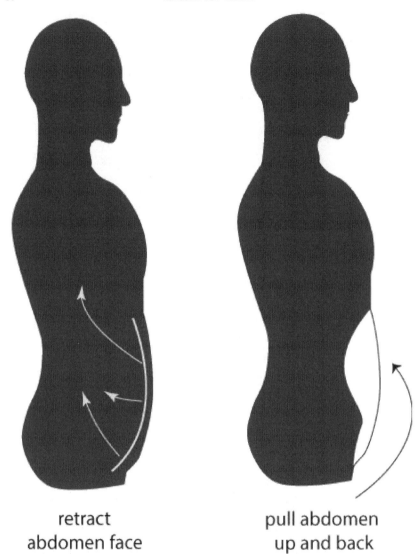

retract
abdomen face

pull abdomen
up and back

The **neck lock** is for keeping any energy which passes through the neck centralized so that if it reaches the brain it does so under mental management. It does not diffuse through the tongue and throat. This is important for controlling the ascent of the kundalini psychic lifeforce into the subtle head. If this force enters the head in a haphazard way, the ascetic will lose control of the physical body and will find himself or herself to be in an altered state of consciousness for the time that kundalini remained in the head. As soon as it subsides down through the spine to the base chakra, the person will resume normal awareness with or without memory of what occurred.

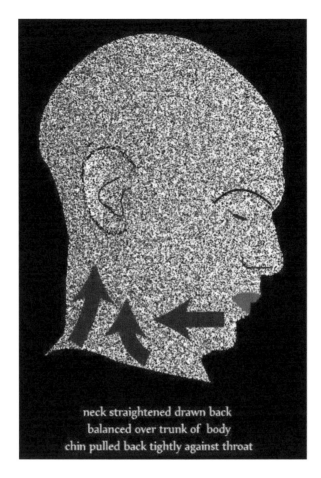

neck straightened drawn back
balanced over trunk of body
chin pulled back tightly against throat

The **mind lock** is the habitual centering of the core of consciousness within the head of the subtle body with applications within the psyche at any other place within it. This is practiced by sitting to meditate and pulling all sensual expressions to the existential center of the subtle head. When a person does breath-infusion practice with asana postures, he or she should remain centered so that the energy which is generated becomes attracted to the intense radiance of the core-self.

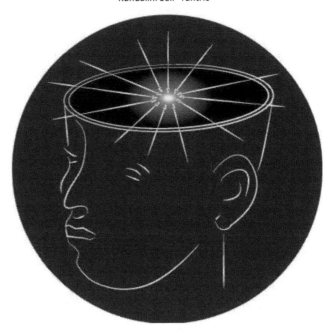

This mind lock is used throughout the breath-infusion practice even when the other locks are relaxed. Its cultivation, however is developed in meditation sessions when the yogi pulls in the sensual energies and commands them to cease their extrovert tendencies.

These locks are used in the subtle body to study its configuration and to implement pressures for required changes. All sensations are features of the sensuality but their transit relates to the type of medium through which they are conducted. The same sensations give different experiences according to the medium used for the sensation transit.

Most students are bewildered by this but in time, if a student practices ardently, he or she will realize that his or her opinion of the pleasure is incorrect. This does not mean that the person will become detached or will have a neutral attitude in the future. However the initial insight gives some clarity, so that the parts of the experience can be regarded and analyzed.

The evidence is, that because of existential limitations, some students may never transcend certain desirable pleasures. Even if such students are shown how to be neutral, they may never abandon certain features. This is due to innate need for those fulfillments.

Chapter 4
Subtle Body

Subtle Body is the Target

The subtle body is the target. It is not the physical form. However some practice begins with emphasis on the physical body. The ascetic should not under-rate the physical form. Actions committed with it do affect the subtle one. For that matter most self-tantric practice begins physically.

Fixing the physical body will not completely adjust the subtle form but still, a student should realize that many of these practices begin with physical actions. At no time, should a student become so obsessed with the physical body, that he or she forgets that the subtle one is the target.

The subtle body's need for a physical system is itself a challenge to an ascetic.

Physical Actions / Subtle Impact

Any physical action which affects the sensuality in the long term should be known to the ascetic. Those physical actions which only have short-term impact should also be known. If something occurs repeatedly on the physical side, it may in the long term develop as an instinctual urge.

Every sensual feature should be checked for its impact on the subtle body. Whatever physical process causes the subtle body to become more addicted to using physical forms, should be noted. Actions should be taken to curtail these influences so that the subtle body becomes freed from the need for physical participation.

Beliefs and doctrines provide false confidence but do not change the subtle body. The ascetic should always check to be sure that his or her physical yoga practice, results in desired subtle effects. Whatever does not assist, should be abandoned.

Food Supports and Informs Sensual Desire

Food is the key factor in any type of sense desire which is fulfilled through a material body. Due to helplessness in controlling food, due to having little or no insight into how food is transformed into full blown desire, a human being does not make the effort to restrain food intake and to make digestion as efficient as possible.

Instead of focusing on the primal support for desire manifestation which is food, the ascetic may instead focus on controlling the result of food intake, which is hormone production in the body. However once the hormones are created, the person can only make an effort to control that energy or to express it in a regulated way.

It would be better if he or she were to control food intake so that the minimum quantity is ingested, resulting in the minimum hormonal production, which would cause the minimum sensual expression, which in its turn would give the yogi the insight into what is essential and into how to safely procure that.

If for instance a human being requires a minimum eight (8) ounces of milk per day, that would produce a certain quantity, say X amount, of hormones. Once this hormonal concentrate is produced, it will then boost certain desire urges. As motivated, the person would indulge in a certain quantity of sense gratification.

But if another human being used, say, ten (10) more ounces of milk per day , then the excess too, would also be converted, so that this person would have say X + Y amount of hormones. This concentrate would then boost desire urges. As motivated the person would indulge in a larger amount of sense gratification, which is not efficient because such energy would result in a depression after the sensual experience climaxed.

All sensual expression of this nature climaxes but some experiences are a more sensational event. This is why sexual indulgence is singled out. However, one type of sensuality, even a non-sensational type, is just as dangerous as the other.

The value of a sensational experience is that it is easy to identify. Its sensation is easier to focus on even though it is not as easy to observe because of the lack of objectivity during the experience.

Sensual Energy Encasement

The sensual energy in the psyche is encased generally and specifically. It is not distributed evenly in a material body or in the corresponding subtle form. In the spiritual body, the sensual energy is distributed evenly in each part, so that there is no advantage to express sensations in any part, like for instance through the genitals.

However the situation of the spiritual body is fantasy because right now our experience is physical for the most part. For a few who shift attention to the subtle level that is the primary means of enjoyment.

The encasement of sensation in the psyche as well as the bunching of the energy in particular areas, must be examined thoroughly. It would not be possible to figure the format of sensations if a yogi did not apply himself to this.

Some people claim to have experiences of evenly distributed pleasure throughout the physical or subtle body but when this happens that pleasure usually originates from a specific part of the body. This is different to the pleasure experience in a spiritual body where the pleasure occurs simultaneously in every part without any original burst of energy.

Yoga is the technique which is used to discover the psyche's sensation-container and the particular parts in which sensations concentrate or disperse. Some study of physical anatomy is helpful because the physique of the physical system is based on the energy distribution channels of the subtle body. The physical system is studied first in hatha yoga which is the skill of kundalini manipulation for subtle body transformation.

Collapse of the Abdomen

Bad eating habits are the primary cause of collapse of supportive musculature having to do with the abdomen. If the supportive muscles stretch or become distended, there will likely be an increased in food quantity with a resulting further collapse. The increased food will cause the manufacture of excessive hormones, which in turn will produce more powerful sense urges for this or that fulfilment of this or that pleasure.

Over-eating and wrong times for eating are the primary causes of a distended abdomen. When the stomach, and intestines are regularly stuffed and when they are subjected to food intake at unfavorable times, they become distended. Their efficiency decreases. This affects the general condition of the physical body, which in turn affects the subtle form.

A yogi must get diet under control. He or she should eat such foods and at such times, to facilitate asana postures and breath-infusion practice. One should do what is necessary to prevent the abdomen from becoming distended. An inefficiency in hormone production is counterproductive for a yogi as this affects the consciousness in the subtle body and ruins the possibility of increased insight.

Mood Swings

Mood swings must be studied by yogis and yoginis. Both males and females are subjected to influences which produce undesirable attitudes. One must recognize the variations and side-step them. As every creature on earth is affected by weather and has preferences according to its lifeform, so every ascetic is subjected to mood variations.

It is not what another person does but rather how I act and react. Each ascetic has a task to come to terms with mood swings, to learn how to recognize and avoid these. No one should feel that he or she will never experience a counterproductive attitude.

There are so many influences which prevail. Many of these are more powerful that the puny willpower. If we gain objectivity and can recognize the onset of a negative influence, we can sidestep it. Once an ascetic is predominately stationed in a high level of consciousness, it is likely that he or she will not succumb to moods but will allow them to come and go as they will. No one should feel that it is his task to abolish the spread of mood energy. Let it be but be distinct from it. Let nature do whatever it so pleases but be objective to it. Allow it to run its course without becoming a stooge of it.

Those who enjoy being critical of others will find that their peace of mind cannot be maintained when they determine that someone is faulty. This is because they make the observation from a lower mode of consciousness. When there is sufficient insight, one also sees the faults of others but with the vision there will be detachment such that one will not become disturbed and will not speak in a caustic way to satisfy one's need to criticize and to prove one's superiority to others.

An ascetic who has a vindictive nature will hardly realize that he or she is on a lower plane. Assuming the self to be lofty and posing as having an interest in others, that person will misuse any situation in which the other person can be logged as faulty. If the faulted one is a senior the critic will be caustic, which is the sure indication of being on a lower plane of consciousness.

When one ascetic criticizes another, it should always be out of a sense of responsibility. This means that a senior should criticize a junior but never should there be a circumstance of a junior criticizing a senior. If one finds that one has a mind to criticize one's teacher or a person who at some stage was one's teacher, one should restrain from it.

The criticism of a teacher should come from the teacher's teacher not from someone who is or was a student. In fact one should not be irritated by the real or imagined faults of a teacher. Such irritation is a sure sign of being on a lower level of consciousness which means that one's perception of the person is faulty even in cases where that senior made an error.

Superfluous Sensual Agitation

The senses are such that even a minor contact, even an accidental expression, even memory of an event, could trigger a new pursuit. It does not have to be logical or reasonable.

Odors of a food preparation might induce someone to eat even though that person might be satisfied with food taken prior. Sight of a sex organ, might create sex desire in a person who had no sexual ideas. Memory of anything might cause the senses to motivate the body to acquire the same or a similar object unreasonably. Once the senses become alert to a real or imagined sense object, it is likely that the psyche will be forced to procure it. Or it may become frustrated if the item is not within reach.

For this practice, the ascetic should reduce all superfluous agitation whenever possible. What sensual expression one must exhibit or be exposed to, is sufficient for existence. It is inefficient to increase it even one iota. Superfluous sensuality means extra exhaustion which is a rip in consciousness, a lack of vigilance and mandatory entry to lower planes of reality. It means more dulling influence, resulting in gaps where there is no insight, with decisions which are detrimental to the self.

Positive Sensuality is reduced in Elderly Years

The full range of sensual grasping is always present but depending on the body being used the person may not exploit certain features of it. In the elderly years the full range of sensuality is present but much of it becomes unavailable because of the deterioration of the body. Instead of getting pleasure from familiar activities, the person might experience pain, which is another form of sensual expression.

Some ascetics are of the opinion that the reduction in sensuality in elderly years is an indication of advancement. This is untrue. Dormant sensuality is reserved potency. As soon as the person develops a new body, the force of the dormant energy will emerge.

In the elderly years, serious ascetics should transfer their interest to the subtle plane. There they can continue the research in self-tantric practice even if the material body is elderly or incapacitated.

Reduction of Sensuality during Elderly Years

Like it or not, there is reduction in sensuality during the elderly years. In fact after sexuality maturity as time encroaches on the material body, its sensual efficiency becomes more and more reduced. Finally there is no sensual response. The body is pronounced dead.

An ascetic should be wise and appreciate that this reduction in sensual expression and response cannot be successfully exploited by anybody. It is nature's reduction plan for nature's convenience only. If the ascetic feels that he or she transcended some sensual expression when in fact nature reduced that to nil, that ascetic will get a rude awakening when nature reverses and again develops the full expression of that sensual feature.

One should not be proud of nature's achievements and should certainly not think that whatever nature does which is desired, will remain in force for all time. People who aim for celibacy should not be proud of achieving it when nature reduces the sex drive in old age. Instead one should study the subtle body because in it, the sexual energy will be dormant and would manifest again if one takes some other mammal body.

Reincarnation Considered

A practicing self-tantric must know about reincarnation. He or she must investigate whether there were previous lives and if there may be more in the future.

What is the subtle body?

How does it function as the core for an embryo in one or the other lifeform?

What are the subtle body's recurring tendencies which are supported by specific lifeforms?

Why does the subtle form use a physical body?

Why is it not satisfied with the subtle dimensions?

Unless the ascetic can investigate such queries, he or she cannot be successful in self-tantric practice.

Reincarnation means that the observing-self will, more than likely, assume another embryo after the death of its physical form. It means that this happened before. The transiting form is the subtle body which takes possession of a birth environment and is unified with the sexual fluids of parents-to-be. The core-self travels in that subtle body from life form to life form. Usually, when it is focused on physical existence, it does not perceive the astral world in which it constantly resides.

Dietary Violence Considered

The ascetic should consider dietary violence which is the degree of harm one must do to life forms for the sake of diet. What is the least harmful way in which one can maintain life in a body?

Is flesh food necessary?

Do we have to eat eggs?

What may happen if one cultivates a tendency for eating foods which can be acquired only by killing animals?

Is it possible that one could be born as another predatory species in a future birth?

For the purpose of self-tantric, one should eat only dairy products, vegetables, nuts and fruits. Dairy products mean food items which are based only on the milk of the cow not its flesh, and only from cows which are tended with care.

Even for a vegetarian, there is violence to plants but this violence is the least we may commit in the struggle for survival. It is much less than the violence committed to acquire flesh, fish and eggs which comes from life forms which are more acutely aware.

Ultimately an ascetic should consider forgoing this type of existence completely. To do this he or she has to transform the subtle body such that it does not require physical sustenance.

Organ/Muscle Malformation

Whatever happens to the physical body is registered in some way in the subtle form. The subtle body may retain whatever it sensed from the physical system or it may not be affected in any way. The ascetic should keep a log of whatever transfers from physical to subtle. In the long term, hereafter or in some other life, a tendency which the subtle body developed will again influence the behavior of the psyche.

Over-eating is one area which the ascetic needs reform. If there is excessive foods, there will be excessive pleasure and exhaustion but there will also be organ and muscle abuse. Over time this will affect the health of the physical system and produce undesirable afflictions.

When the gut becomes distended and when the abdominal muscles become stretched beyond recognition, one can expect that in the subtle body, there will be deformed subtle organs and warped astral energy strands. The subtle pubic floor will be stretched because of the heavy astral energy which compacts on it.

This does not concern anyone but the ascetic himself or herself. This is task enough for the person, such that there will be no interest in the defects of others. An ascetic who continues with the obsession about helping, reforming and criticizing others, has no deep interest in self-tantric practice. Such an evangelist is not suited to these methods.

Expulsion of Pollutants

Prompt expulsion of physical and liquid waste is preferred in this practice. Any effort to hold waste in the body, beyond the call of nature, will result in an increase in the body's unwanted matter. When solid waste is retained in the intestinal track, the body extracts and retains some pollutants from it. This in turn increases the percentage of pollutants in the body. These pollutants support a lower state of consciousness. Hence it is undesirable.

A yogi should always have prompt urination and evacuation. His or her diet should not promote constipation. It should not have a negative impact on meditation. A yogi should be sensitive, so that he can make dietary changes which aid yoga.

Excess Sensual Stimulation is Undesirable

There are many types of sensual stimulation which one may enjoy while using a human body, but any excess carries with it a downside in the form of extra exhaustion with accompanying lowering of consciousness. For this reason excess stimulation is undesirable.

Self-tantric is about discovering one's gender potential. It avoids both excess and denial because both are degrading. Excessive stimulation causes excess sensual energy to accumulate, which in turn causes excessive participation, which results in exhaustion and depressed states. Denial of the potential of the self's gender causes false pride which is uncovered later to the dismay of the ascetic. This arrogance causes grand delusions in the form of artificially-enhanced self-opinions which the self just cannot maintain and which brings downward-spiraling states.

Any excess of any sensual intake will result in a proportionate quantity of exhaustion and depression. For instance, if the ascetic over-eats, he or she will have to deal with increased digestive activity, increased hormone storage, increased pressure on the lower trunk of the body, increases overt or covert sexual participation and increased exhaustion and depression.

This applies to any type of sensual expression. Sex excess is obvious because of its sensational feature. Yet, the other pursuits are just as or may even be more dangerous to the ascetic. In all respects, a yogi should curtail the sensual stimulations.

Illness/Disease a Distraction

Illness or disease is a distraction in the practice of self-tantric. These cause inefficient use of energies, negatively altered states of consciousness and loss of focus on the gender research of the self.

A yogi should be alert so as not to do anything which will result in illness or disease. There will be illness or diseases because that is the fate of a material body. It is also the fate of the subtle form when it is on the lower astral levels. However the person concerned should be intelligent enough not to aggravate what is fated. One should eat in the healthiest way and should learn from bad incidences about undesirable foods. One should also avoid places and people with contagious diseases.

Chapter 5
Sexual Access of Ancestors

Kundalini self-tantric concerns the discovery and application of gender. That includes a study of celibacy. There are two aspects of celibacy which will be examined. These are nature-imposed celibacy and self-imposed celibacy which defies nature's sex indulgence compulsions.

A yogi should investigate his or her gender to be certain that the gender being used as male, female, neuter or bisexual, is in alignment with the core-self and is not a mere imposition on the self, where the core is used as an energizer for a gender development as a particular body.

In deep meditation, the yogi is required to peel back the various subtle layers of sociology to reach the core-self and determine its gender or its lack of definition. If it is discovered that the core is genderless, the yogi is left with the task to determine if it should continue in this creation or if it should be translated to some other dimension in which a genderless being could function without being forced into supporting gender designations.

If the yogi determines that it is a male, female, or bisexual, it should check to see if its social role matches that configuration. If it does not, it should determine the best way to retract and then apply itself somewhere somehow to a matching sociology. It could either relocate to a place where its gender or genderless condition is the social function or to a place where the core-self assumes a subtle format which matches its neutrality or polarity.

Celibacy

A study of celibacy is required. The core-self should determine if it can exist as it is without sexual engagement. This has nothing to do with its social role in a creation like this, where it is circumstantially or otherwise forced to participate in certain gender designations in a celibate or non-celibate way.

Can the particular self exist without being subjected to full-blown sexual engagement?

Is the particular self such that it must be sexually linked because it is existentially designed for that?

Is it existentially celibate such that even when it is designated a sexual role, it is still not sexually engaged but is only providing support for sexual operations?

Is there such a state where the core-self has a male, female or bisexual gender which does not need involvement with any other self, where it can function in every other social role besides sexual coupling?

Coupling

In the gender investigation, persons who discover their cores to be genderless have a simple outlook which is to find an allowing environment in which there are no demands for polarized gender designations. The search for such a place would be on for that yogi. It would be the solution to all of his or her problems. In this case, *his* or *her,* is title for the current gender role which was nature-assigned to the particular body currently used. Realizing that the role is temporary and has no deep impact, the self would meditate deeply. Its only challenge would be to locate and gain access to a compatible dimension.

On the contrary those who discover their core-selves to be gender-polarized either as one gender or the next or as both genders alternating or simultaneously manifesting, have a big task in this spiritual investigation. The essential self should locate an environment which perfectly facilitates his or her or its gender polarity. Whatever is the essential person, the core of the psychology, is the true personality.

Elementary Practice of Celibacy

The elementary practice of celibacy begins with the understanding that sexual intercourse is at the heart of social problems. This concerns moral rules for social conduct which lubricates society. Sexual intercourse is supervised by the feeling of jealousy, which is sponsored by a strong sense of proprietorship.

Who should be blamed for the progeny which results from a sexual relation?

Conversely, who should be praised for the family?

Elementary efforts at celibacy are governed by the needs of society. It is the effort to regulate who will have intercourse with whom for the purpose of assigning responsibilities for the progeny produced.

Initially the yogi is harassed by the enforcement of morality. Thus he or she comes to consider the need for celibacy. Why bother to engage in sexual intercourse if the result will be intimidation about the welfare of progeny?

Why not be celibate and avoid the risk of being condemned for moral misconduct or irresponsible behavior as it is defined by government officials and families?

These perplexities which the beginner considers have little to do with kundalini self-tantric. However one must begin where one is. Thus celibacy as an alternative to complicated social life was always defined as the effort to avoid sexual interactions and to remain free of spousal complication.

When someone considers celibacy for a lifestyle, he or she rarely considers reincarnation. This is a flaw in the calculation. The reason being that ancestors have shares in the lives of their descendants, such that the descendants do not have total autonomy. The body itself will be disobedient to the will of the ascetic if a psychic ancestral influence prevails. Though dead and gone, an ancestor may wield considerable influence over what happens to the body. For this reason, the ascetic will be unable to resist certain overpowering sexual feelings.

Advanced Practice of Celibacy

The advanced practice for celibacy was conducted by persons who felt that so long as they were involved in sexual partnerships the complications would result in near total absorption of the materialistic way of life, with so much focus on social matters concerning the physical body, that there would be no time to investigate if there would be any remnant of the self after death of the physical system.

Ascetics who were that advanced split off from social living, went into isolation, avoided partnership attractions, reduced associations in dreams, practiced the six higher stages of yoga and made a bid to translate over to higher dimensions.

The eight stages of yoga which were delineated by Patanjali are:
- Yama behavioral restraints
- Niyama behavioral approvals
- Asana physical postures
- Pranayama breath-infusion
- Pratyahar sensual energy retraction
- Dharana effortful focus of interest to higher levels of existence
- Dhyana spontaneous focus of interest to higher levels of existence
- Samadhi continuous spontaneous focus of interest to higher levels of existence

An advanced ascetic is not concerned with the first two stages. Those are for suppressing or promoting various behaviors. If there is no physical association with others, there is no need to monitor interactions, except those which arise in the astral world or which reach the yogi by psychic transfer.

There is a higher application of the first two stages, where the ascetic is required to monitor the interaction between the core-self and its adjuncts but that development results as part of the meditation practice and not as a moral behavior. It is not related to social interaction between the ascetic and others. It is a total inside monitorship of the core-self and its assistant functions within the psyche.

For these reasons in defining hatha yoga kundalini manipulation for psyche transformation, Gorakshnath Mahayogin listed only six stages of yoga, neglecting to mention the first two which were itemized by Patanjali. Since a proficient yogi already broke off from social relationships with others, and only completes obligations superficially, Gorakshnath listed the six higher stages,

In the stages listed by Gorakshnath, the first three are preliminary but for beginners, these are the most important achievements. These three are:

- Asana physical postures
- Pranayama breath-infusion
- Pratyahar sensual energy retraction

There is a two part aspect to the **asana physical postures**, which are the physical stretching and tensing and the subtle stretching and tensing. Gorakshnath process has to do with stretching and tensing the subtle body. Even though the physical body may be involved, it is not the focus in Gorakshnath's practice. In fact there are ascetics who do this practice in the astral world after being deprived of a physical body. The astral yogis have no physical system to stretch and tense, hence their doing their practice would include only the subtle form. However for those who are physically functioning, they would stretch and tense both the physical and astral bodies simultaneously but they are required to focus primarily on the astral one.

Pranayama breath-infusion has two parts as well but with each of the two parts split into sub-aspects which become known to the ascetic as he advances. The two aspects are the physical and subtle with stress on the subtle after the ascetic did sufficient physical focus to understand that when the physical system is plumb full of fresh air, this causes a shift in focus to the subtle body with insight into its energy.

Once the ascetic shifts to the subtle aspect of pranayama breath-infusion, he will in time realize that this is the way to achieve the third stage of Gorakshnath process which is **pratyahar sensual energy retraction**. The pranayama breath-infusion serves as an enrichment process for the subtle body, which causes the mind to internalize as it becomes attracted to the enriching energy which is infused into it. The mind then no longer has an interest in pursuing the conventional interests which are outside of the psyche.

With this insight, the yogi begins to perceive the grasping, relaxing and introverting postures of the mind. When he identifies these, he can better monitor the psychic operations. He can terminate those features which are undesirable.

The completion of the pratyahar sensual energy retraction is the end of the preliminary practice of yoga. Then the three highest stages commence. Fortunately Patanjali listed these as samyama or the complete restraint of the mento-emotional energy in terms of its automatic and very conventional operations. These three process are:

- Dharana effortful focus of interest to higher levels of existence
- Dhyana spontaneous focus of interest to higher levels of existence
- Samadhi continuous spontaneous focus of interest to higher levels of existence

There arises a question as to the selected or assigned focus. Unless one has an advanced yoga-guru, one may not have a valid objective. Hence the practice will be haphazard and will in the process of time become discouraged. There is no simple way to determine the focus. It hinges on the particular yogi and on what he needs for advancement at the time. The focus is tailored to suit the particular student. It should be recommended by the yoga-guru.

Books like the *Bhagavad Gita* and the *Hatha Yoga Pradipika*, as well as the *Yoga Sutras* map the course for meditation. Still the student should get directions from a physical or astral yoga-guru.

Advanced Celibacy as Non-Participation in the Enjoying and Begetting Processes

There are two features which are tackled in advanced celibate practice. These are:

- Distancing the self from sexual enjoyment
- Totally avoiding any involvement in the reproductive functions

Sexual expression has two parts which are the enjoying energy generated and the biological formation of new lifeforms (embryos). Nature presents the enjoying energy immediately. It shows the new lifeform(s) at a later date. When there is contraceptive interference new life forms are not generated.

Some ascetics want to distance themselves from sexual enjoyment while they remain contributory to the embryo production. Others want the sexual enjoyment but are suspicious of the reproductive intent. There are yet others who are adverse to both. Some have no aversion to either but retreat from participation because they wish to be spared social complication.

One thing is certain: The process of material nature will endure. It will not be altered essentially by any limited being, nor even by the Supreme Person. It will endure as it is with the detractions or contributions. Hence the celibate achievements which are unnatural, will be reversed by nature.

Details of Sexual Construction

In the study of sexual polarity and participation as it applies to yogic celibate achievement, the yogi should study the construction of the sex organs and the distribution of sexual energy before, during and after an arousal. The problem with this advice is that it goes against the celibacy tradition, which is that the ascetic should restrain from all mental, verbal and emotional sexuality. However for the purpose of self-tantric, the ascetic is required to study his psychology and its relationship to physical behavior.

Traditional celibacy is different in that it concerns moral behavior for the interaction from one person to another in the social environment. That is not self-tantric practice.

One has to leave aside the morality of human society to study this. However it does not mean that one becomes specialize in upsetting moral rules. In fact one should be sure to be moral and only rarely should one breach that.

An ascetic will not be protected from condemnation if he breaks moral stipulations. Hence any action which is contrary to society's standards may bring unfavorable reactions. Thus the ascetic should only rarely breach rules.

There are many moral stipulations which cause immediate approval in human society but which in the long term are detrimental to the person concerned. Everything must be studied carefully to determine what risk one should take and for how long.

The details of sexual construction of each gender should be studied. This is easy because of the advances made by modern science in its use of imaging technology which renders graphics of things in the human body which a human eye cannot see. Formerly mystics penetrated with psychic perception. Now even a beginner can have some idea of the construction of the genitalia by studying medical diagrams.

The ascetic needs to study the system from within the mind both during sexual participation and when there is no sexual access or interest. It must be studied both in the physical and subtle systems, with the subtle being the primary objective. An ascetic who has no partner and who is sincere as a sexual non-participant, should be alert to sexual encounters on the astral planes. It is near impossible for someone to be free of sex desire in the astral body because the nature of that form is raw sensuality which is spearheaded by sexual matching to neutralize polarity.

The theory is that by physical celibacy, the ascetic will eliminate sex desire and remain aloof from its vulgarity. However the practice on the astral plane goes to the contrary. Physical control is not related to subtle life necessarily. Honesty is important but it is only viable if the ascetic is aware of all psychic encounters. Completing approved vows and having high self-esteem for moral objectives, in no way curbs the subtle body. In fact the ascetic may be unaware of his subtle sexual activities.

Sexual Tendency Adjustment

Traditional celibacy is an effort to thwart nature's sexual indulgence tendency, so that the ascetic stops all physical interest in sexuality and makes an effort to curtail sexual thinking and imaging. This is both a physical and mental effort. For some ascetics it is a mental effort mostly because their physical bodies have little or no sexual drive. For others it is primarily a physical effort because they are plagued with sexual urges which cause arousal at the slightest sexual exposure. There are some others who have both the physical and subtle challenge of stamping out sex desire.

Self-tantric has a different objective. For that matter self-tantric is not concerned with the social approval gained by becoming known as a celibate person.

The self-tantric must study the tendency of the physical body and that of the subtle form. He must gain clarity about the relation between that two. There must be clarity as to which part of the sexuality is merely a physical tendency and which is physical on the basis of a subtle urge. He must know which sexual tendencies will persist after the physical body become incapable of being aroused sexually.

Questions will arise:

What cosmetic sexual tendencies can be rooted out of the physical or subtle forms?

Which innate tendencies cannot be removed?

Which tendencies can be suspended for a time?

What is the value of willpower in the quest to remove a sexual tendencies?

Is it necessary to apply physical constraints to eliminate sexual responsiveness?

Can the ascetic cause his sexual polarity to disappear permanently?

Natural Celibacy

Natural celibacy is experienced before puberty and in old age when the body is no longer capable to exhibit the urge. However, when we inspect these situations we admit that natural celibacy only means a hidden sex urge.

Strangely, a few humans lack the sex urge even in the adult stage but that does not mean that their sexual polarity is absent. It may be dormant from infancy through the elderly years.

In so far as the subtle body is the basis of the physical, it follows that on the psychic plane, celibacy is doubtful and would have to be verified closely to be accepted as a permanent condition and not a suspended one.

Does the individual have absolute rights to determine his or her gender or lack of sexual polarity?

How much control does nature have?

Why does nature have the power to put the individual into situations where a gender role is enforced or even where so much identity must be invested into the gender energy, that the individual loses objectivity?

Are those who take credit for celibacy being superficial?

How do we explain why a pre-pubescent person is denied celibacy after the development of sexual maturity?

Are monks who experience sexual arousal, really celibate?

Celibacy as a Personal Objective

Celibacy, for all it is, may be flawed in cases where there is some supernatural objection to it. This objection may come from an ancestor or deity. In the Mahabharata, there is the case of Jarat Karu. This ascetic was an avowed celibate with full intentions not to ever be sexually involved.

In his wanderings, he chanced to see some ascetics hanging upside down in a cave. Being curious and feeling compelled to relate to them, he questioned about their situation. They explained that the cause of it was a person known as Jarat Karu who insisted on being celibate, when the right thing to do was to be sexual engaged for the sake of the ancestors.

After hearing this Jarat Karu agreed to be sexually involved but only for a limited period of time, just enough to beget an embryo in a woman's womb. An ascetic who has an obligation to assist his ancestors in acquiring embryos for their rebirth, and who sticks to celibate vows, is a hypocrite. Sooner than later he will suffer a breach in asceticism.

The ugly question of, *who owns the body*, rears its ugly head again. In fact it is a question of who owns the genitals.

Does the ascetic, the central power source in the body, own it?

Does he own the least shares in it?

If the ancestors own most of the body, it is in order that they should use the genitals to acquire embryos.

However this poses the question of how much of the body the ancestors have rights to?

Is their claim on the body infallible?

Obviously it is not. In modern times, we observe the widespread use of contraceptives. Of course there may be a reaction in future lives for any human beings who thwarts nature but that is to be seen.

Celibacy as Required for Spiritual Translation

According to the Bhagavad Gita, celibacy is required before anyone can be translated spiritually. Here is the statement:

प्रयाणकाले मनसाचलेन

भक्त्या युक्तो योगबलेन चैव ।

भ्रुवोर्मध्ये प्राणमावेश्य सम्यक्

स तं परं पुरुषमुपैति दिव्यम् ॥८.१०॥

prayāṇakāle manasācalena
bhaktyā yukto yogabalena caiva
bhruvormadhye prāṇam āveśya samyak
sa taṁ paraṁ puruṣamupaiti divyam (8.10)

prayāṇakāle — at the time of death; manasācalena = manasā — by the mind + acalena- by unwavering; bhaktyā — with devotion; yukto = yuktaḥ — connected; yogabalena — with psychological power developed through yoga practice; caiva = ca — and + eva — indeed; bhruvor = bhruvoḥ — of the two eyebrows; madhye — in the middle; prāṇam — energizing breath; āveśya- having caused to enter; samyak — precisely; sa = saḥ — he; tam - this; param — supreme; puruṣam- person; upaiti — he goes; divyam — divine

...and that meditator who even at the time of death, with an unwavering mind, being connected devotedly, with psychological power developed through yoga practice, and having caused the energizing breath to enter between the eyebrows with precision, goes to the Divine Supreme Person. (Bhagavad Gita 8.10)

यदक्षरं वेदविदो वदन्ति

विशन्ति यद्यतयो वीतरागाः ।

यदिच्छन्तो ब्रह्मचर्यं चरन्ति

तत्ते पदं संग्रहेण प्रवक्ष्ये ॥८.११॥

yadakṣaraṁ vedavido vadanti
viśanti yadyatayo vītarāgāḥ
yadicchanto brahmacaryaṁ caranti
tatte padaṁ saṁgraheṇa pravakṣye (8.11)

yad — which; akṣaram — imperishable; vedavido = vedavidaḥ — knowers of the Veda; vadanti — they described; viśanti — they enter; yad — which; yatayo = yatayaḥ — ascetics; vītarāgāḥ — free from cravings; yad — which; icchanto = icchantaḥ — desiring; brahmacaryam — life of celibacy; caranti — they follow; tat = tad — this; te — to you; padam — process; saṁgraheṇa — in brief; pravakṣye — I will explain

I will briefly explain the process to you, which the knowers of the Veda describe as imperishable, which the ascetics who are free from cravings enter and who desiring to be transferred there, they follow a life of celibacy. (Bhagavad Gita 8.11)

Everyone will be singled out sooner or later and have to account for sexual expression. Unless one does self-tantric, one cannot know one's true gender. Hence one will not assume full honesty because of wearing the profile awarded to oneself by the psychic material nature.

However this life of celibacy is not the same as social morality and celibacy in terms of physical behavior who is approved by religious and self-righteous people.

The shedding of the cravings is a thorough process regarding all the involvements not just the sexual one. It is a parting off even from the conventional moral aspects in the physical reality and the lower astral levels. Here are the following statements:

सर्वद्वाराणि संयम्य

मनो हृदि निरुध्य च ।

मूर्ध्न्याधायात्मनः प्राणम्

आस्थितो योगधारणाम् ॥ ८.१२ ॥

sarvadvārāṇi saṁyamya
mano hṛdi nirudhya ca
mūrdhnyādhāyātmanaḥ prāṇam
āsthito yogadhāraṇām (8.12)

sarvadvārāṇi = sarva — all + dvārāṇi — entrances; saṁyamya — controlling; mano = manaḥ — mind; hṛdi — in the core of consciousness; nirudhya — confining; ca — and; mūrdhny = mūrdhni — in the brain; ādhāyātmanaḥ = ādhāya — situating + ātmanaḥ — of the soul; prāṇam — energizing breath; āsthito = āsthitaḥ — remain fixed; yogadhāraṇām — yoga concentration

Controlling all openings of the body, and restricting the mind in the core of consciousness, situating the energizing energy of the soul in the brain, remaining fixed in yoga concentration, (Bhagavad Gita 8.12)

ओमित्येकाक्षरं ब्रह्म

व्याहरन्मामनुस्मरन् ।

यः प्रयाति त्यजन्देहं

स याति परमां गतिम् ॥८.१३॥

omityekākṣaraṁ brahma
vyāharanmāmanusmaran
yaḥ prayāti tyajandehaṁ
sa yāti paramāṁ gatim (8.13)

om — the uttered sound om; ity = iti — thus saying; ekākṣaram — one syllable; brahma — spiritual reality; vyāharan — chanting; mām — Me; anusmaran — meditating on; yaḥ — who; prayāti — passes on; tyajan — renouncing; deham — body; sa = saḥ — he; yāti — attains; paramām — supreme; gatim — objective

...uttering Om, the one-syllable sound which represents the spiritual reality, meditating on Me, the yogi who passes on, renouncing the body, attains the highest objective. (Bhagavad Gita 8.13)

This means departing from all social involvements. At some time the ascetic must ceases regarding social norms, irrespective of if they are approved and disapproved, considered to be good or bad. He must turn away from the material existence and the desirable aspects of the lower astral world, otherwise he will not be able to reach the higher astral dimension or the places which are beyond that.

Sticking to anything which is good or bad about human society may in itself become an impediment which will restrict the ascetic's access to higher dimensions. He must at once not be faulty and also not be attached to the privileges awarded to those who do what is considered to be auspicious on the physical or lower astral planes.

Motive for Celibacy Effort

The celibacy effort is as good as the motive. Hence unless the motive is proper, the effort will be corrupted by the psychological energy from which the endeavor was derived. The rash motive for celibacy and perhaps the most popular one among males, is to escape from the travails of family life. Since sexual intercourse is likely to result in pregnancy and since females tend to be emotional, many males resort to the celibate effort to escape from family responsibility. They want to have nothing to do with female emotions or with hassles which result from having children.

Since so many ascetics began the quest for celibacy with the motive to escape family responsibility and emotional management of a relationship with a woman, this motive for celibacy is praiseworthy as a beginning effort. It is however terribly flawed. Unless the ascetic graduates from this initial basis, his endeavor for celibacy will fail in the long term, either in the current life or in some other, or in the world hereafter.

Nature only has to change the sexual profile of his body or put him in some other body which has a sex-prone tendency, and his efforts at celibacy will be demolished.

Someone might be celibate because he has no sexual urge. Such people are successful celibates because for the time being they are supported by nature not to have libido, the feelings of lust for some other human being. These persons will do well as celibates provided nature does not change their gender profile in the current life or in a future life or hereafter.

Someone might become castrated and lose the sex urge but that will only last for as long as the current body is present because as soon as that body is lost, the subtle form will manifest the sexual urge in full. It will again generate another physical body which is patterned to manifest sexual polarity.

Someone, a woman for instance, might also want celibacy because of being raped by a man. However for that person there might be a genetic change in the body, whereby that person will feel no sexual urge for anyone, but sooner or later when the traumatic feelings of the rape are relaxed, that woman will again feel the sex urge. This may happen in the current life or in a future time or hereafter.

An advanced yogi does celibate practice for the reason of gaining a nature which is compatible for residence in higher dimensions, where the life there is one of sensuality without stress on genital contact. This would be a proper motive for becoming celibate. It is not reactionary to physical existence. It is not referenced to any positive or negative feature of this physical history. It is based on attraction to a higher dimension and is referenced toward being pulled to the higher place.

But even though it is instrumental in causing a yogi to advance to higher places, this motive is flawed. The perfect motive for celibacy is derived from the investigation into one's true gender, regarding if it is male, female, bisexual or neuter and how that should be expressed in the highest dimension one could attain as a spiritual being. Such a person if successful would be celibate just for the investigation into true gender and then would make endeavor to manifest that truth and to transit to the world where that truth would naturally manifest.

Full Celibacy is Near Impossible

A few ascetics over the centuries attained full celibacy. Many attempted it and failed. This does not mean that partial celibacy is not praiseworthy or that full celibacy is without flaws. Some who did full celibacy were prone to criminality anyway. Celibacy itself does not remove every unwanted trait.

Unless a person is assisted by an able yoga-guru and by a deity who has extensive supernatural power, the bid for celibacy will fail. This is because the psychic material nature is against it. No limited person's willpower can go up against the psychic material nature successfully. As it is we take so much assistance from nature, that if she withdraws support our plans will crumble. There is not a single thing we can do and this included being celibate, which we can successfully complete without the assistance the psychic material nature.

People who feel that celibacy is merely a matter of willpower, or a decision to be exempt from sexual participation, are unaware of the components of reality. They feel that the volition of the individual is all that is needed for achievement.

A full onslaught against sex expression is admirable but it may not be pragmatic. In fact many who achieve some degree of celibacy find that at a later date, they are again assailed by sex desire and must give in to sexual participation, all because the psychic material nature changed the profile and only provided energies which support indulgence.

We must also take into account that physical celibacy, even if it is complete and it rarely is, does not in any way guarantee that the subtle body is celibate. The subtle form may indulge sexually while the physical body totally restrains. The result of this is that in the future due to subtle pressure, the present physical system or some other physical body will be forced to indulge.

Sexual Energy / a Composite

Sexual Energy is a composite physical and psychic force. Dissecting it to determine the ingredients is important in self-tantric. The ascetic should not waste time trying to control that which belongs to others. Sexual energy concerns both the living and the disembodied. Since we are the living, we should tally the influence of the disembodied and not take their presence for granted.

What is called my sexual energy is not all mine. Much of it is ancestral power which resides in my psyche and which does so with its own motivational force. It is a hidden force which is difficult to segregate. The ascetic has a task to sort himself from the one or many ancestral influences which comprise his sex urge.

Bisecting the sex urge we may find these factors:

- The female partner
- The male partner
- Ancestor(s) who requires an embryo(s)
- Sexually-charged hormones

This implies a minimum of three persons besides the sexually-charged hormones.

If there is a pregnancy we will see two physical persons, with one having a protruding abdomen. Before the pregnancy there were two physical persons involved but there was another person a subtle one, the ancestor(s).

For self-tantric, we need to tally the subtle persons not the physical ones. The tally of physical reality which is the conventional way of viewing circumstances is misleading because it fails to take into consideration the subtle reality which influences the physical outcomes.

Before the pregnancy we had three persons on the subtle side. During the pregnancy we had the same three subtle persons but then we were sure of the location of the ancestor because of the development in the mother's abdomen.

The residence of the ancestor before the pregnancy is a mystery but that puzzle disappears as soon as there is a pregnancy, because then the subtle residence of the ancestor registers as being that which is becoming enlarged in the mother's abdomen.

Before the pregnancy the ancestor was a real something but it was unseen except for those with psychic perception. That unseen real something became the basis for the developing embryo.

The sexually charged hormone energy was used to accomplish the sexual intercourse mostly but some of it was part of the embryonic development.

Can the yogi know before a pregnancy how much sexual pleasure energy is the force of the ancestor? Could the yogi have the detachment and insight necessary to see that only a portion of the enjoying energy is his?

This vision would not change the mixture of energies from the three persons but it would render clarity amidst the joint venture, whereby the yogi would not mistake the total energy as being his own.

Sexual Pleasure as an Ancestral Conveyance

Sexual pleasure has a draw to it, a pulling force. This causes the physical person(s) involved to be compulsively focused into it. His or her attention is drawn to the flow of the energy and experiences its fluctuations. The central force of this energy is a disembodied ancestor who is in the process of becoming an embryo. If there is contraception involved, the effort for the embryo will be frustrated. The disembodied ancestor will experience the denial as an energy depression.

The journey of the departed ancestor from within the body of the father into that of the mother is a convention of nature. Where was the ancestor before he became part of the father's body?

In the male body, during a sexual intercourse, the focus of attention is on the climax experience which is produced by a bio-electrical pump system for discharging semen. The interpretation of this bio-electrical current is that it is a form of intense pleasure. From an energy viewpoint, it is a high current for running a pump discharge system.

During sexual climax, the male experiences a rise in the bio-electrical current. There is a shock-sensation like being electrocuted. When this current increases to its maximum, there is discharge where semen is squirted into the female body. Once there, the sperms in it, move up the cervix. Common sense shows that if the bio-electrical pump did not operate the semen would have no way of getting out of the male body.

The male perceives the movement of the ancestor from the testes through the tubing in the penis and then into the cervix but this perception identifies the ancestor as a central bliss force, as sexual pleasure which increased to a climax at the point of discharge of semen. A yogi must endeavor for clarity, so that the ancestor is regarded as an ancestor with potent sexual energy force, and not merely as intense sexual pleasure.

If we proceed backwards in history, to before the man had the productive sexual intercourse with the woman, who later became the mother of the ancestor's body, then the trace of the ancestor would not be easy unless one had psychic perception and could see the movement of that departed soul.

Taking for granted that the ancestor came from somewhere and that there was a psychic presence of this person in the astral dimensions, the location of the departed person before the sexual act, was the reproductive fluids of the father, residing there as sexual emotions in reproductive fluids.

Prior to residence in the reproductive organs of the father, the ancestor existed in the emotions of the mother or father. Prior to that the ancestor would have existed in the astral world hereafter. Prior to that the ancestor lived as a material body on earth. This completes the missing residences.

Here it is in sequence:

- Ancestor as its last material body
- Ancestor as astral being (ghost)
- Ancestor as part of the emotional feelings of a living human being
- Ancestor as part of the sexual feelings in the reproductive fluids of its potential father

- Ancestor as a sperm particle which was emitted into the uterus of its potential mother
- Ancestor as a developing embryo in its potential mother

That is the journey, the conveyance, from being physical to being astral and then to being physical again.

Chapter 6
Transit Hereafter

Romance as Ancestral Energy

Romantic feelings when sorted are more than the love or affection between two persons whose sexual involvement could produce a child. The child in question even if it does not acquire a body because of a contraceptive interruption, is part of the romantic energy. He or she is a substantial part of the love interplay. How then could the potential parents realize this? They would have to be detached from their feelings, segmented out, so that they would perceive the portion of energy which was theirs individually, as well as that which was the contribution of the ancestor, who is to become the embryo. This segregation of the shares in the romantic energy would clarify the situation and remove the illusion of either parent about owning the pleasure energy.

Thus the romantic energies which are so desired by most human beings is for the least a tripartite investment of the father, mother and ancestor. It begs the question as to who really enjoys the pleasurable emotions.

Appreciations Due

At this paragraph, the author expresses appreciation to the deities who provide the inspiration and literary energy to write this book. After doing chapter one, I was perplexed as to how to continue this work. The reason is that some years prior; I wrote a series of books on the celibate effort of yogis. The information given then was to be presented again in this volume but when I attempted to do this the literary format of the previous books did not fit this presentation. However now the deities reset my energy so that I can complete this text. I am confident now that I can do this work on their behalf.

For all I know, right now I can be dead and gone. I completed most of the information which I was commissioned to publish. This book and anything I write later is extra information. This is advanced information for persons who would be relocated with the siddhas or with an advanced yoga-guru hereafter. This information and any other books which I write later would be of lessons which a student would have if he passed on and achieved the association of advanced yogis in the hereafter.

Kundalini Lifeforce Energy Generator

The hormonal energies and other power sources of the material and subtle body are generated under the supervision of the kundalini lifeforce which is an energy with emotional intelligence. It is a force in the subtle body. From there it creates the physical system. When given the opportunity, it designs for itself a parallel system of energy distribution which is based on chakras and nadis. Chakras are subtle energy gyrations centers. Nadis are routes of energy distribution from the chakras.

Of the chakras, the residence of the kundalini lifeforce is the base vortex. From that habitat, the lifeforce sends out instructions to every part of the physical and subtle bodies for the functions and maintenance of everything.

In the hatha yoga system expounded by Gorakshnath Mahayogin, the yogi takes control of these functions. He maintains the bodies instead of relying on the kundalini to make most of the decisions in this regard.

Most human beings pay little attention to the maintenance of the body. This is due to being absorbed enjoying the various sensual facilities, of which there are five varieties, namely smelling, tasting, seeing, touching and hearing. These five senses come in a variety and in combination with each other as well, in an array of sensuality which is bewildering.

The senses themselves are outshoots of the kundalini lifeforce but their information is processed by the intellect which is a psychic organ in the subtle head. The senses are emotionally sensitive. That is their expression of intelligence. This is subsided by the rational sensitivity of the intellect which uses references in memory to identify and catalog the information provided by the senses. The kundalini for its turn patiently waits for the intellect to provide knowledge about what is detected by the senses.

As soon as the kundalini gets information about any sensual instance from the senses, it checks to see if the intellect made related deliberations. If there are any the kundalini will take that in account before making a decision. This is done in a flash, so fast, that it may not be perceived by the core-self who is supposed to be the master of the psyche. What the self usually sees is the instruction for an action to procure or ignore the particular sense object under investigation. Hence the core-self is usually at a disadvantage in relationship to the kundalini and intellect because these two psychic adjuncts form a conspiracy which is more than the core-self can handle unless it meditates and comes to terms to control the functions and maintenance procedures of the psyche.

Sexual Termination

Sexual acts have four common endings:
- Frustration without progeny

- Frustration with progeny
- Fulfilment without progeny
- Fulfilment with progeny

Sexual arousal carries with it a need for intense pleasure fulfillment. If the relationship does not produce that, it is interpreted by the mind as frustration.

There may be frustration with or without progeny. The appearance of a child complicates matters but it also provides emotional fulfillment which in some cases, serves to counterbalance the frustration.

Because it implies obligation, the presence of a child may spook either parent. The child is itself a factor of cohesion which needs the parents to stay together even if they are not agreeable to each other. Based on pure selfish need, the child claims the parents:

- You are my father!
- You are my mother!

This is to make a claim for liability so that the parents feel obligated to raise the infant through its minority years. Either parent may be spooked by this claim. One or the other parent might ignore it completely.

One sexual action which is fulfilled or frustrated and which produces a child makes it obvious that sexual acts may be costly in terms of the liability for a child produced. A sexual act which might last for say thirty (30) minutes could carry with a sixteen (16) years liability for the child. This means that a reproductively-successful sexual intercourse is costly. Even if the child rearing years bring joy to the parents, the liability for the child is still time-expensive.

Father and Mother are Conveyed

In a productive sexual intercourse, one from which an embryo develops, the father and mother are conveyed by the pleasure feelings in their respective bodies. Even if the incidence was planned by either or both parents, still the rhythm of the feelings during the experiences, is conducted by lifeforce operations and not by the design of either parent. The parents might be compared to a rudderless canoe in a rapid stream or a dry twig in a fast moving river. The plan of either parent, if there is any, is more a plan to be conveyed as soon as the sexual urge is aroused. Even a deliberate sexual liaison is inspired by the sexual energy itself. It operates on subconscious levels.

The conscious operation of the sex urge is merely a cosmetic attempt to trigger a nature process which cannot be managed fully by either parent. No parent can truthfully say that he or she created the sexual apparatus and developed it through puberty into the adult stage. From another perspective no human being can say that in youth he or she shut down the puberty development by willpower.

Either parent is a utility of nature, even in cases where they planned the pregnancy. In the background of their planning is the subconscious level of their consciousness, which operates to project ideas for fulfilment into their minds.

There is urge. There is fulfilment. First from the subconscious comes an urge. From the same subconscious comes the means for executing the urge. This process produces the fulfilment.

The active role of either person is superficial for the most. It is not meaningful in terms of the creation and execution of the urge, but nature allows the parent some token self-esteem as a contribution for supporting natural pride.

Format of Sexual Activity

During sexual behavior both the male and female who would contribute to the formations of an embryo are emotionally active. The stirring of emotions does not rely on willpower participation. Nature's emotional conveyance operates with or without the application of willpower. In fact nature may use enjoyment as a force which attracts, controls and directs willpower.

The male is conveyed as a dart-force which runs through the genital tubing and is throttled there for squirting into the female passage. The female is conveyed as an absorbent force which spread through the genital reception area for collection of the squirted male fluids.

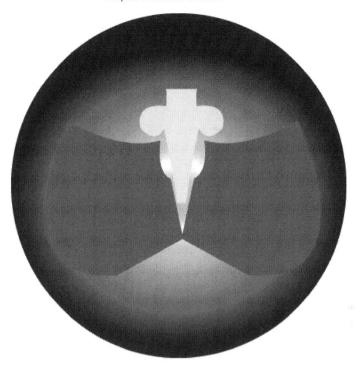

As nature would have it, the male and female are distracted in regards to the objective of the sexual unity. The male is influenced to keep track of the increasing electric current which runs through the pump mechanism which squirts sexual fluids. He mistakes that electrical flow for pleasure.

The female is misled into thinking that wave-like bursts of electric energy are pleasure climaxes. In both cases, the objective is to facilitate an embryo development. For the male, the race of the sperms, particular that of the most viable one is the focus. For the female the sensitivity of the receptor cells as well as the anticipation of safe docking of the most viable sperm is the headline experience. In both cases, nature misleads the partners. It direct them away from its plan, which is not pleasure for the potential parents but rather reproduction of a body for an ancestor(s).

Deeper more insightful inspection of the sexual process should be made by the self-tantric ascetic. Nature rendered a farcical opinion to the self. That is misleading but it serves nature's purpose of not being interfered with by the dot-like core-self. Without disrespecting nature, without feeling that nature can be conquered by the self, one should inspect the process to understand its layout and authority. Please begin this investigation.

Route Taken by the Ancestor

From nature's perspective fulfillment occurs only if there is a successful birth. Any other outcome is a frustration for the ancestor. This causes a levy of unfulfilled desire on the psychic plane. The parents do become aware of this but their mental interpretation of the energy becomes warped because of focus on genital pleasure as the objective. Regardless of getting enough genital pleasure or of not getting sufficiency in it, the parents are oblivious to the plight of the ancestor who was or was not successful in the embryo bid. Those parents who desired a pregnancy will express dissatisfaction after noting that there was none, but these same persons are usually unaware of the plight of the ancestor involved in the bid for that embryo.

Parents usually consider an embryo to be their baby, their infant, their biological and social property. Even in societies where the belief in reincarnation prevails, most people adhere to the feeling that the embryo is their child. They do not presuppose that it is an ancestor with adult content.

Once the bid for an embryo fails, the ancestor is rerouted through the same potential parents or through some others. The effort made by nature to create the embryo is repeated because the ancestor possesses that routine energy.

There may be many unsuccessful attempts for an embryo by one particular ancestor. Such a person exist as a sexual urge and has tireless energy to try again and again to become someone's child.

As nature would have it, the potential parent has no memory of its pre-life stage as a sexual urge. All the same the ancestor who was converted into being sexual energy has no idea of its prior state as an adult human. The identity core of anyone is shorn of its various profiles by acts of psychic nature, which make it impossible to be objective through many states.

Nature's Many Expressions

Nature has many avenues of expression with each carrying certain short and long term advantages and disadvantages. How is one to know, which facility will yield a certain immediate and remote response? What should one do if one does not have the insight to view the consequences of a behavior which nature endorsed or objected to?

Is Nature Always Correct?

What happens when nature gives a dual indication and it is left to the individual to use an alternative?

Self-tantric is for determining the essential gender of the yogi (yogini) and how best to service that gender configuration in whatever body the yogi currently has? How should the yogi live so as to attain an environment in which the true gender is perfectly expressed?

A yogi should not get into the mindset of judging opportunities on the basis of social morality or religious stipulation. He or she should be aware of those moral recommendations but should not be guided essentially by them because they do not wholeheartedly support yoga practice and are designed for social status not gender clarification.

Social alignment is not self-tantric practice. Even though the yogi should be aware of social approvals and should comply with them for the most part, he should know that it does not yield deep insight into what nature affords as the consequence of actions. Nature has its operations which are different from the way human society is administered. The conclusions of these two environments do coincide on occasion but still they are segregated. In the final analysis nature's view will have the impact not human design.

Transit: Physical to Subtle

The transformation of a person from being physical to being subtle and then to being physical again is simply an operation of a series of forced or voluntary shifted focuses. Even the voluntary ones are forced for the most part. We usually interpret pleasurable shifts as being voluntary ones even though much of it is forced with a pleasure lubricant which removes our resistance before we could decide to reject anything.

Beginning on this side of existence, we have the physical person whose social identity is tagged as being the son or daughter of certain parents. That physical person has a subtle body which is ignored for the time being. That subtle apparatus is not recognized by either the person or by most other human beings. Thus for all practical purposes and in terms or relation and focus, that person is a physical being.

However for this self-tantric practice, we must recognized both the physical person and the psychological aspects of the person. The psychic energies form the subtle body. Just as in the physical existence, the body of the person is identified as the person, so in the subtle existence, the psychological aspects are regarded as one subtle person, one subtle body.

There is constant interaction between the physical aspect and the psychological ones, such that physical changes may cause similar adjustment in the subtle body and subtle changes may alter the physical one.

At death of the physical system, the psychological aspects which are not reliant on the physical system continue existing. Some of the psychology fades away because of lacking physical support. For instance Tommy's sister brought food for him each day. He developed a reliance on her for this. Then Tommy's physical body died. Seeing this his sister ceased the food delivery.

Even though his physical body died, Tommy, for his part still expected the food delivery. However his sister, who was physically focused, showed no psychic interest in delivering food. Hence Tommy's subtle expectation of her meals gradually faded away for want of being reinforced by deliveries on the subtle plane. This affected Tommy's psychology such that his subtle body was reduced in the part of it which was nourished by the subtle energy which was consumed through the physical food.

Tommy's sister had no idea that her physical food delivery had a subtle counterpart. Hence she did not feel the need to make food from subtle energy. She was unaware of the fading away of a part of Tommy's subtle body because of the absence of her meals.

Much of the subtle body continues as is after physical death. Some of it fades away because of a lack of physical support or because of a lack of subtle support which was physically based.

Tommy being dead to physical reality, continued existing in the subtle world but only in part. Most of his psychology continued to exist as something ethereal. A small part of it faded away. Tommy had to get used to being the surviving part of his subtle self. He had no choice, because he could not access physical reality.

Most people do not value their psychology as an existence in its own right. Instead people feel that the psychology is part of the physical existence. This results in a sharper focus into physical reality with a corresponding neglect and lack of recognition of the subtle body. It does not however terminate the subtle form which will for the most part survive the physical system.

Transit: Subtle to Physical

Once the physical body is dead, the person or the collection of psychological energies which used that form, can no longer make a direct physical register. It can however impact history by influencing the actions of someone who has a physical form. This influence may be obvious or unknown to the physical person who is possessed.

Immediately after death of the physical system, the surviving psychological content of the deceased person may be hazy. It may be indefinite. It may be a confusion of energy. Just as upon arising from a state of intoxication or from a coma, a physical person may be at a lost as to whom he is and as to what he should do, so in the astral domains, a recently deceased person may be in a vague state of consciousness with uncertainty about whom the person should be.

However eventually there will be clarity, even though it may be less than what the person experienced when that person had a physical body. To some extent, once a person becomes a physical body, that person's psychological content is altered and reinforced by that physicality. Hence when that physical system is no longer available, that person may become a reduced self in terms of the content of the psychology.

During the physical life, the person commits actions to develop and express the personality. This is based on social interaction, from which the person gets hint as to what psychological traits have value and can cause favorable recognition in the world of the living. This effort at status has all the value in physical history but when the physical body is dead, the subtle body finds some of the status energy to be inconvenient. This is because physically-reinforced astral energy dissipates as soon as the physical support for it is no longer present.

To be clear the total psychology energy of the person when he used a physical body will be reduced once he loses that form. The reason being that on the loss of the physical system, certain portions of the psychology would no longer be supported and thus would fade away either immediately or gradually.

The remnant psychology which survives the death of the physical system organizes itself to be a functional person in the astral world. Some persons experience this organization instantly at the time of death. Others experience it over a time of days, weeks, months or years.

When this remnant psychology feels as if it is the whole person, when the person no longer feels undone by death of the physical system, then the coast is clear so that the person can turn in the direction of getting an embryo. The settling down and reformation of the confused psychological energies which remain as the person in the astral world, after death of the physical system, is the event which is pivotal in that person's acquirement of another embryo.

As soon as the fragmented energy is formatted into an astral person, that one becomes attentive again to being physical, to being part of earth history. This causes a feeling of wanting to be someone's dependent, of wanting to rely on some person. The patron could be a descendant, or a friend who still has a material body, or even a deceased person who has authority to influence living persons to beget children.

At this stage the astral person who feels drawn to the patron person, feels relief in that person's presence. The astral body of the deceased person becomes interspaced in the astral body of the patron person. While people who are emotionally close must remain close but do not become interspaced into each other's physical bodies, this astral entity actually becomes interspaced in the subtle body of the patron person. Due to this the astral person feels a kinship with the patron person and feels satisfied to be existentially related in that confidential way.

Eventually through this closeness, the feelings of the patron person become stitched with that of the astral person, so that the astral person loses track of self and feels as if he or she is the patron person. This is due to confusion of astral emotions, where one cannot discern which feelings are objective and which are subjective.

Due to the fact that the astral person's energy carries in it the need for an embryo for being alive physically to be part of earth history, the patron person begins to think of sexual acts. This happens spontaneously. The patron person then seeks out opportunities for having sexual intercourse or for influencing someone to have sexual intercourse. The presumption for this is the need for an embryo which is in the intersected form of the astral person who needs to be physical again.

As soon as the patron person locates a sexual opportunity, the astral person who needs a body will detect it and will move into the body of one of the persons who might be the parent. This movement is totally emotional. It is that the astral person's psychology converts into a colossal emotional force which is saturated with affection and lusty impetus. The potential parent who becomes possessed of this saturation affection energy which is itself a person requiring an embryo, experiences himself or herself only as a romantic feeling or sexual urge.

The possess person, the parent-to-be will feel that urge and identify it as local energy, as a need to complete copulation. If this happens, and if both parents are fertile, there will be an embryo for the astral person who will come out into the physical world as a baby. That is the end of the journey from one life, into the astral existence and then to another physical life.

Subtle Body as Emotions and Mental Energy

If we accept that the subtle body is composed of emotions and mental energy, and that it is the basis of any material body, our focus would switch to the subtle as the primary entity and the physical as the incidental factor. If during the physical life, the primary components of the personality are the emotions and mental energy, and not the physical system, then it follows that if we trace the subtle aspects during the life of the physical body, we could easily keep in touch with that subtle person after he or she is deprived of a physical form.

The collection of emotional and mental energies constitutes a body, the subtle form, just as the collections of liquids and solids in the form of flesh and bone constitute the material body.

The variations in the subtle body does not eliminate that body. It continues existing around the core-self despite the energy alterations. This is similar to the changes in the physical body which itself continues through the life of that form.

As soon as we understand the reality of the subtle body, as being the composition of emotional and mental energy with a limited agency, the core-self or decision maker, we can focus attention on the subtle form and understand the possibility of its transmigration from a dead physical form to being just itself on the psychological plane where feeling and thinking are enacted with or without physical correspondence.

Components of Psychological Consciousness

In considering the components of psychological consciousness, the basic listing is

- Emotions
- Mental energy
- Agency

Initially there is little clarity about this. For a start this is a confusion of energy in which parting out the emotions from the thinking force and the agency, can hardly be sorted. It is one psychology which we can isolate and that is all we know.

When one sorts the mental energy, one finds thoughts in a mental environment with an uncertain observer which appears to be nothing but a pin-point object in the mindscape.

When one sorts the emotions one finds attractive feelings which either deny an observer or pin-points it further.

When one sorts the agency, one finds that an objective self appears and dissolves out miraculously according to the emotional or mental condition. In most instances, the agency appears to be token with very little self-definition.

Regardless of what it is, our concern is about the agency's functionality. It is perplexing because the psyche may function as an agent without participation of an objective self as the decision maker. Moods, feelings or emotions may result in decisions being made which the objective self has no say in. Thoughts may progress into decisions or conclusions which the self is overpowered by, with the objective self not even surfacing. Is this self an alternate existing and nonexistent psychic operator?

Chapter 7
Identification of an Ancestor

Search for the Living Ancestor

The search for the living ancestor results in failure because we are oriented to physical existence. We remember the ancestor as a physical being, as a physical senior of the family. In that view, the ancestor is dead and gone. It cannot be found astrally because our reference for it is a physical body with flesh and bones.

In searching for a psychic substance or subtle person, one has to use psychic reality itself as the reference. That would require a new way of inquiry.

During the life of someone, the yogi should shift focus from regarding the person as a physical entity to the person being a psychic entity which has the components of emotions, mental energy and agency. Even though physical death results in some reduction of the person's psychology, still the reduction will be so small, that the person is still recognizable. If a physical being's finger is amputated, we can still recognize that personality. Thus a small change or omission in the psychological content of a person at death of the physical body cannot prevent recognition of that personality.

The transit of the ancestor after the death of its body can be tracked if one knew the person's psychic profile. We would look in psychological places for the person and be able to follow the person's movement through the astral domain and even if the person became an inhabitant in the subtle body of a living physical person, as for instance an embryo.

Movement of an Ancestor

To track a departed soul, one would have to be on the lookout for the transit of a psychology. One would have to track the movement of emotions, signature mental activity and psychic agency. Emotions from one physical being for instance, can shift to another human being without any corresponding physical behavior of either person. Thinking energy can be transferred without any indication of it on the physical plane. However it is a fact that in the physical world we are habituated to identifying an emotional or mental movement by its physical conclusion. Usually, we expect a physical conclusion. We accept that as confirmation or denial of what we sensed on the emotional or mental plane.

To be successful at psychic tracking, we must first rid ourselves of the need to get physical conclusion, whereby an emotional or mental perception becomes the singular proof of an activity, where that is itself a conclusion. This natural habit of confirming an emotional or mental activity with a physical action which mimics the emotional or mental intention, should be discarded. One should develop trust in the emotional or mental perception. Even though this will include some erroneous and misinterpreted moods and thoughts, still it should be done. In either case if the yogi's intuition is faulty or perfect, he or she should use the psychic detection as reference. One should cease dependence on physical confirmation.

A psychic act is qualified by itself. It does not need a physical action which repeats or mimics it. While using the physical body, the yogi should regard his psychic actions and that of others as complete, as not needing physical reproduction or completion. This will cause the development of psychic insight.

The recognition of the subtle body of a living person is the same for that of a departed soul, except that the physical person's psychic actions may have physical confirmation. Hence if a yogi cultivates this reliance on the subtle without physical reference, he or she will experience psychic perception which will result in perceiving the movements of people who have no physical bodies but who are relating to physical beings through the transit of emotional and mental interplay.

What is the transit of a departed soul from being a subtle being in the astral world into being an embryo in a physical female?

It is the transit of emotions, mental energy and willpower agency into the would-be mother's psyche. The departed soul's subtle energies are interspaced in the subtle energy of the would-be mother. To find that departed soul one should search for its psychic energy.

Sex Focus as Ancestral Pressure

In so far as an ancestor becomes a subtle format of emotions, thinking and willpower energy, we as those with sexually-mature physical bodies, are under constant psychic pressure to engage in sexual activity. Our physical presence has with it, the psychic parallel of being in a world which has sexual energy for its atmosphere.

Everywhere we go, in any direction, we are assailed but we can hardly perceive the origin of sexual lust. This lack of insight results in a bloated self-impression where we identify ourselves as sexual agents. We try to get sexual fulfillment as a solution to the pressure.

As soon as someone dies to the physical existence, that person, you or me, is likely to become a sex urge, a romantic force, which will merge with the sexual energy in the body of any physical person who is sensed as being sexually attractive. This could convert into a full blown pregnancy whereby an embryo is produced. Or it may pan out in an abortion, miscarriage or sexual expression which produces no embryo.

Sexual Supernatural Influences

Apart from ancestral influences of limited entities, persons who have little or no power over the country or planet, we have supernatural force from people who can influence us even against our desire.

A levee can frustrate normal tides but it has no such effect on a tidal wave. One might resist the sexual inspiration which develops from ancestral influence, but one surely cannot resist if one becomes the focal of sexual energy which is inspired by supernatural beings who have national, global or universal power.

There is no reason to disbelief the existence of supernatural entities. Just as we have cosmic forces which are beyond human control, we also have personalities who have vast power. The only thing lacking is our perception of such people. Science assisted us to have some grasp on cosmic energy and manifestation. We are left to consider cosmic people and influences.

Even the limited entities on earth, do on occasion as they are facilitated by time and circumstance, exercise national or global influence. An attractive celebrity who acts in movies or who is a musician, may induce millions of people to indulge in sexual intercourse. For some fans this may result in fruitful pregnancies. That is evidence that we can be influenced supernaturally, at least by physical people whom we are not related to in the present life. One celebrity may be a supernatural being with extensive natural powers. Another one may be an ordinary person who is facilitated by time and circumstance.

Content of the Psychological Body

Krishna precisely described what transmigrates as the psychological body of a deceased individual:

शरीरं यदवाप्नोति

यच्चाप्युत्क्रामतीश्वरः ।

गृहीत्वैतानि संयाति

वायुर्गन्धानिवाशयात् ॥ १५.८ ॥

śarīraṁ yadavāpnoti
yaccāpyutkrāmatīśvaraḥ
gṛhītvaitāni saṁyāti

vāyurgandhānivāśayāt (15.8)

śarīram — by body; yad — which; avāpnoti — he acquires; yat — which; cāpi — and also; utkrāmatīśvaraḥ = utkrāmati — departs from + īśvaraḥ — master; gṛhītvaitāni = gṛhītvā — taking + etāni — these; saṁyāti — he goes; vāyuḥ — wind; gandhān — perfumes; ivāśayāt = ivā — just as + āśayāt — from source

Regardless of whichever body that master acquires, or whichever one he departs from, he goes taking these senses along, just as the wind goes with the perfumes from their source. (Bhagavad Gita 15.8)

As the core-person with its psychic adjuncts in the form of the subtle sensing moods and mechanisms, the individual survives the death of its physical system. The core-self is licensed as the master of the psyche but practically speaking its autonomy is circumstantially franchised to the intellect and the sensual energies. These mechanisms inefficiently uses the self's psychological powers.

Krishna explained this:

श्रोत्रं चक्षुः स्पर्शनं च

रसनं घ्राणमेव च ।

अधिष्ठाय मनश्चायं

विषयानुपसेवते ॥ १५.९ ॥

śrotraṁ cakṣuḥ sparśanaṁ ca
rasanaṁ ghrāṇameva ca
adhiṣṭhāya manaścāyaṁ
viṣayānupasevate (15.9)

śrotram — hearing; cakṣuḥ — vision; sparśanaṁ — sense of touch; ca — and; rasanaṁ — taste; ghrāṇam — smell; eva — indeed; ca — and; adhiṣṭhāya — governing ; manaścāyaṁ = manaḥ — mind;-- ca — and + ayaṁ — this; viṣayān — attractive objects; upasevate — becomes addicted

While governing the sense of hearing, the vision, the sense of touch, the sense of taste, the sense of smell and the mind, My partner becomes addicted to the attractive objects. (Bhagavad Gita 15.9)

Irrespective of the core-self's control or indulgence, it has to remain with the sensual energies even when it does not have a physical form. Though it appears to be dependent on a physical system, this core-self is not a physical reality.

The core-self's reliance on the senses for environmental information, results in dependence or a loss of autonomy. Thus the attractive objects are an indirect cause of the self's costly indulgences.

Basic Condition for Rebirth

The basic condition for rebirth is the urge to be a physical body. The psychology of the individual must have a rebirth need in it for this to take place. However such a need is natural to the psyche. It does not come about by a willpower generated desire, even though such a desire may reinforce the urge.

There are two types of subtle bodies. One, the superior type, has no physical needs. The inferior type has the rebirth need built into it. Even if there is no desire for birth, even if the individual vehemently does not want to take another body, he or she will have to accept the self as such a body as soon as nature facilitates and produces one. This is because the willpower of the individual is a cosmetic agency.

There is no fair balance between the willpower of the individual and the mento-emotional energy in the psyche. The willpower is the weaker force. It will be forced to comply even when it detests something. In circumstances when the willpower commands the psyche, we can assume that it is being allowed to take charge for a time. This allowance will be suspended as soon as the moods and mentality shift.

Conflict between Desire and Facility

In this existence, there is constant conflict between a person's desire and the facility which forms as opportunity. It happens as well that sometime a desire seems to perfectly fit the opportunity. Or it may fit it partially. A perfect fit happens for a time only, then there is reversal which frustrates everyone concerned. People are left with cherished memories only.

Desires are a composite energy, a mixture of urges from many sources, memories and anticipation for a bland, stimulating or intense pleasure. The psychic material nature produces these desires and imposes them on the core-self, which for its part feels compelled to ardently pursue the fulfilment or to reluctant tag along as the psyche endeavors for the outcome.

The emergence of a desire does not guarantee that nature will service it. Part of the range of experiences offered by nature is frustration. That is also the manifestation of a desire which is within nature. Thus for many desires which nature produced, it has no intention of servicing or it may service the desire partially and then undermine the effort for it.

The opportunities are preset in that their raw materials must be created before the emergence of a desire. If only part of the materials are in existence, the desire cannot be fully manifested. If none of the materials are present, the desire will be fully frustrated. This is the system of urges and fulfillments in material nature.

If someone understands urges and their fulfillment or the lack thereof, he or she will appreciate both the fulfillments and frustrations. Otherwise the person will crave the fulfilments and be baffled by remorse when frustrations occur.

Core-self ~ a Superficial Agent

If we study what Krishna told Arjuna in the Bhagavad Gita, we may come to the conclusion that as the core-self we are superficial agents. Consider these verses:

न कर्तृत्वं न कर्माणि

लोकस्य सृजति प्रभुः ।

न कर्मफलसंयोगं

स्वभावस्तु प्रवर्तते ॥५.१४॥

na kartṛtvaṁ na karmāṇi
lokasya sṛjati prabhuḥ
na karmaphalasaṁyogaṁ
svabhāvastu pravartate (5.14)

na — not; kartṛtvaṁ — means of action; na — nor; karmāṇi — actions; lokasya — of the creatures; sṛjati — he creates; prabhuḥ — the Lord; na — nor; karmaphalasaṁyogaṁ = karma — action + phala — consequence + saṁyogaṁ — cyclic connection; svabhāvaḥ — inherent nature; tu — but; pravartate — it causes

The Lord does not create the means of action, nor the actions of the creatures, nor the action-consequence cycle. But the inherent nature causes this. (Bhagavad Gita 5.14)

नादत्ते कस्यचित्पापं

न चैव सुकृतं विभुः ।

अज्ञानेनावृतं ज्ञानं

तेन मुह्यन्ति जन्तवः ॥५.१५॥

nādatte kasyacitpāpaṁ
na caiva sukṛtaṁ vibhuḥ
ajñānenāvṛtaṁ jñānaṁ
tena muhyanti jantavaḥ (5.15)

nādatte = na — not + ādatte — perceives; kasyacit — of anyone; pāpaṁ — evil consequence; na — not; caiva = ca — and + eva — indeed; sukṛtaṁ — good reaction; vibhuḥ — the Almighty God; ajñānenāvṛtam = ajñānena — by ignorance + avṛtam — shrouded; jñānaṁ — knowledge; tena — through which; muhyanti — they are deluded; jantavaḥ — the people

The Almighty God does not receive from anyone, an evil consequence nor a good reaction. The knowledge of this is shrouded by ignorance through which the people are deluded. (Bhagavad Gita 5.15)

This is a disclaimer by the Almighty God about not creating or absorbing the favorable or unfavorable results of an action of the limited entities who abound in the creation. And yet, many religions thrive on just that, on stating that the deity will render favors to the follower if donations are given in the name of God.

Krishna even distances himself from the means of action, the actions of the creatures and the action-consequence cycle. He leaves all of it to be settled by the individuals involved and the inexorable psychic material nature which is exacting within its time frame.

This clarification about the involvement and commitment of the Supreme Lord rids us of any false assessments about God's liability of our actions. It leaves us to fend for ourselves in the physical and psychic material nature. The result of this is a change of attitude of the yogi. Krishna explained it like this:

ज्ञानेन तु तदज्ञानं

येषां नाशितमात्मनः ।

तेषामादित्यवज्ज्ञानं

प्रकाशयति तत्परम् ॥ ५.१६ ॥

jñānena tu tadajñānaṁ
yeṣāṁ nāśitamātmanaḥ
teṣāmādityavajjñānaṁ
prakāśayati tatparam (5.16)

jñānena — by experience; tu — however; tad — this; ajñānam — ignorance; yeṣāṁ — of whom; nāśitam — removed; ātmanaḥ — of the self; teṣām — of them; ādityavaj = ādityavat — like the sun; jñānam — revelation; prakāśayati — causes to appear; tat — that; param — Supreme Truth (explained in two previous verses)

However, for those, in whose souls the ignorance is removed by experience, that revelation of theirs, will cause the Supreme Truth to appear distinctly like the sun. (Bhagavad Gita 5.16)

तद्बुद्धयस्तदात्मानस्

तन्निष्ठास्तत्परायणाः ।

गच्छन्त्यपुनरावृत्तिं

ज्ञाननिर्धूतकल्मषाः ॥५.१७॥

tadbuddhayastadātmānas
tanniṣṭhāstatparāyaṇāḥ
gacchantyapunarāvṛttiṁ
jñānanirdhūtakalmaṣāḥ (5.17)

tadbuddhayaḥ — those whose intellects are situated in that supreme truth; tadātmānaḥ — those whose spirits are focused on that supreme truth; tanniṣṭhāḥ — those whose reference is that supreme truth; tatparāyaṇāḥ — those who aspire to that supreme truth as the highest reality; gacchantyapunarāvṛttim = gacchanty (gacchanti) — go + apunar — never again + āvṛttim — rebirth; jñānanirdhūtakalmaṣāḥ = jnana — experience + nirdhūta — removed + kalmaṣāḥ — faults

Those whose intellects are situated in that Supreme Truth, whose souls are focused on it, whose basic reference is that, whose faults are removed by the experience, who aspire to that as the highest reality, never go again to rebirth. (Bhagavad Gita 5.17)

Once a yogi realizes that he is on his own in the material nature, both on the physical and subtle planes, he can sober up because he knows that the liabilities for actions rest squarely on his shoulders. These will be enforced by material nature in its own way at its convenience. The yogi knows that he does not have to willingly commit an act to become responsible for it. Even if he is induced to act by another agency, even if he is force to do so, still the returns for the act will find him sooner or later so long as he is in the environment where the causative energies of the act operate for a resolution.

Understanding this, the yogi will strive to make the subtle body lose its urge for manifesting physical embryos because that is the first step away from haphazard rebirth.

Unnecessary Exposure

A yogi should reduce his exposure so that the reactive material nature has the least possible opportunity to target him. No matter where one goes there will be a reactive energy operating to pressure one to do this or that. There is no escape because every bit of the physical and psychic material nature is highly reactive. To decrease the incidences a yogi should be as isolated as fate would permit.

The yogi must be sensitive to know how much exposure he should display because total concealment may cause bigger mandatory exposures at another time. One must study the circumstantial energies and play the agent when it is the easiest way out of a situation, otherwise if one denies nature one's participation it may create an unpalatable future in which one will be forced to be the victim or actor.

Within the mind however, one should maintain a space between the core-self and its adjuncts. There should be a gap between the core-self and the enjoyment energies which abound in the psyche as well as between the self and the depressive moods.

Sexual Intercourse ~ an Ongoing Need

Sexual intercourse, any which way, is an ongoing requirement on this physical level and on the related astral planes. In every species which reproduces through this type of intercourse, it is a necessity. Its need harasses everyone who is capable of it.

How much of a person's existence is under that person's autonomous control? In gender research, one has to figure in the impositions of the physical and psychic material nature. One must subtract these from the sexuality of the psyche, to determine what will be left as one's gender expression. The difficulty will be to sort this. Once it is sorted a new enigma arises which is how to segregate the self from nature's portion of the energy.

As a man walking into a TB ward could readily contact the disease, so in this creation one may become infected by ancestral people, even ones who are not related to one's physical body. Each departed soul who needs an embryo is a sexual energy unto itself. That departed person exist on the psychological plane as emotions, mentality and volition. This produces a sexual-inducement format which a human being will interpret as romantic energy once he is possessed by it.

One must understand that one floats in a sea of sex indulgence, with nature intending to reproduce through it. One can be victimized at any given moment. One may be in the victimization energy as a departed soul becoming an embryo or be a victim of it as a sexually-mature physical being as a parent. In the world of sex indulgence one may take turns being the victimizer (embryo) or the victim (parent), all depending on if one has a material body or if one requires one.

Sensuous Energy Power Supply and Directive

The highest directive passages in the body is the nervous system which includes brain cells. This is a bio-electrical operation. In the yoga system, this is termed as the kundalini-lifeforce/chakra/nadi energy distribution layout. For self-tantric, the yogi is required to study this system.

Sensuosity in the physical body is the flow of energy through the nerves. From an objective viewpoint, this concerns the movement of electricity. The kundalini lifeforce is rooted at the base of the spinal column and operates the bio-electricity distribution. By practicing pranayama breath-infusion, the yogi can gain insight into how this energy operates. He can modify it. He may even transform it so that its basic instinct changes to facilitate an aim of yoga which is to be relieved of the need for physical life.

The senses are a development from the sensual energies. The control of the senses by external means is a temporary effort which fails in the long term. When the yogi realizes this he researches to find the root cause of the senses which is the kundalini lifeforce. If the yogi tackles this kundalini, his effort to rein in the senses would be successful because he can cut or restrict their power supply.

The senses also take help from the intellect but the intellect is not the producer of the senses. However the yogi has to restrict the communicative flow between the senses and the lifeforce as well as between sensuousness or feelings and the intellect. This segregation, once achieved, gives the yogi more autonomy, such that the senses and the intellect are restricted in how they operate self-destructively.

The most important exchange medium for a physical body is fresh air. This is because the kundalini lifeforce uses that for its main energy consumption. In the subtle body the subtle counterpart of fresh air, subtle air, is used in the same way. This is why a yogi should become proficient in pranayama breath-infusion. By extracting most of the used air in the body, the yogi causes the energy status of the system to be upgraded, to shift to a higher plane. This gives increased insight. It renders deeper meditative states.

Kundalini Lifeforce as Gender Creator

Until a person becomes totally freed from the psychic material nature, he or she is manhandled by the lifeforce and must adhere to the gender which is developed by it. This means that for the most part the effort at self-tantric will be a failure because the person will be unable to discover his or her true gender, as to if it is male, female, bisexual or neuter.

The initially effort for gender discovery will result in discovering the preferred gender designation of the kundalini life force but that is not the gender of the core-self even though it may be a mirror image or a complete distortion of the self.

Despite this setback, a yogi should not be discouraged. For the time being, whatever will be will be, at least until the yogi can negotiate freedom from every aspect of the psychic material nature?

In material nature, the self is really a neutral sexual factor but it is shrouded by the composition of the kundalini lifeforce, as that energy shifts through constant waves of cosmic energy. A living entity is stuck with one lifeforce and must use that assigned psychic mechanism for the duration of the creation. Hence there is no alternative but to reform and redesign that energy. If it is changed into a neutral emotions generator, there is a chance that the core-self can assess its true gender.

Aside from the kundalini's actual gender, there are impositions from the numerous environments which it is transited through. The environments react to render sexual polarities which run contrary even to what the kundalini would naturally be. This means that we have three gender configurations to trudge through, the environmental impositions, the kundalini complex sexuality and the core-self's undiscovered gender.

This makes a tall order for the research in self-tantric practice. The sooner we hone in on this process, the better we will be, because of the clarity which we could derive from it.

Study of Celibacy

The study of celibacy and its partial or full attainment is for the most part the study of the life force's sexual profile and exploits. Without understanding the lifeforce's sexual needs and without upsetting its process, one cannot have any meaningful success as a celibate ascetic. Volition or willpower, religious or philosophical beliefs are useless for this objective. One must have the grace of providence, so that it does not force into one's life ancestral obligations.

Sex expression in the form of acute pleasure is sponsored and produced by the life force. The expression itself is not the issue but the design of the experience is such that it veers one's focus into the expression, thus shrouding the cause which is the manipulations of the lifeforce.

Once hormonal sexual energy is produced by the life force it is polarized by the reproductive organs. Once polarized it causes the core-self to feel an urge for sexual expression. This drives the person for sexual release. The core-self is directed by the intellect towards the pleasure expression. This directive force is misleading as it causes the core-self to ignore the kundalini lifeforce which is the creative energy which operates sex expression. Even though celibacy means termination of sexual interaction, still unless one understands the part played by the life force, one cannot successfully be celibate. In fact celibacy which happens without this achievement, occurs superficially. It will be reversed in the near future, resulting in a breach of sex restraint.

An ascetic must have a thorough study of the kundalini lifeforce mechanism if he is to conquer sex desire in any long-term meaningful way. The study of sexuality should be done with the idea that sexuality is part of sensuality. Sensuality is the problem not sexuality which is merely one expression of sensual interest. The kundalini lifeforce is the generator of sensuality and thus it must be brought to fore.

Celibacy Effort in Two Approaches

The celibacy effort has two valid approaches and many hop-scotch methods which are used by people who have no inkling of the kundalini operation. The valid methods are:

- Arrest and diffusion of sexual hormonal energy
- Arrest and diffusion of digestive energy

Even though other haphazard and superficial methods have value in social negotiations and reputation building, I will not discuss them. For self-tantric only the two methods listed have application.

- **Arrest and diffusion of sexual hormonal energy**

Once the sexual hormonal energy is produced, the ascetic is faced with the task of using it sexually, neglecting sexual expression or diffusing out the energy by some physio-psychic technique. If he uses it sexually he may benefit if he has insight into the components of the energy and mixing regulations which nature observes during a sexual intercourse.

Production of sexual hormonal energy is itself a sign of a lack of celibacy. This is because the production is itself the manufacture of the sex urge. How can one be celibate if one's psyche is already possessed of the urge?

The system is that the digested hormonal energy is transported to the genitals where it is treated for fertility concentration and gender polarization. The ascetic must then do something to use this energy in some other way besides sexual expression.

Yogis have methods for the upward travel of the sexual hormones. These pass under the general term of urdhvareta, meaning upward movement of semen. The hatha yoga practice by Gorakshnath Mahayogin includes practices to cause the already produced sexual energy to be sublimated and diverted to the muladhar base chakra where it strikes the kundalini life force. This causes kundalini's arousal at the base chakra as contrasted to sex energy arousal in the genitals. Kundalini's explosion of psychic energy is then piloted through the spine into the brain. This method became the standard for dynamic celibacy but it is flawed because it includes the production of sexual hormones.

Why are the hormones produced in the first place? Why not stop the production completely?

This method is admittance that the yogi cannot cease the production of sexual hormones. It is the best attempt for this process of celibacy with the continued production of sex energy. Many ascetics who mastered this process were successful in becoming siddhas after leaving their material bodies and journeying through higher dimensions to the places called siddhaloka.

- **Arrest and diffusion of digestive energy**

The arrest and diffusion of the digestive energy before it converts into hormonal energy which is sexually polarized, is the best celibate method. This means that the ascetic does not have to deal with environmental or internal sexual polarity. The environmental energy comes from other persons, dead or alive. The internal energy is that which would be created by the genitals as supervised by the kundalini lifeforce.

Before it is converted into a sex hormone power, the digestive energy is neutral. Its arrest by the ascetic means that it would retain that neutral aspect but be a bliss force. With this bliss experience, the ascetic can research the core-self's gender without being influenced by prejudices from the environment or from the kundalini lifeforce.

Sexual Expression Limits

Unless the digestive energy is diffused and does not form into a sexually polarized force, the ascetic like everyone else must deal with the possibility of arousal.

How will it be dissipated?

Will he masturbate?

Will he ignore the urge?

Will his physical body efficiently absorbed the hormonal energy?

Will he express himself in astral sexual intercourses?

The answer to any of these questions raises many others queries, which harry the uncertainty about absolute sexual energy control.

Assuming that the aspiring yogi is isolated, we may assume that he will face no physical sexual arousal because of exposure of himself or anyone else. But that pertains to physical application only. Physical isolation does not certify astral exclusion. In fact physical isolation is likely to promote astral exposure.

Gender Definition Uncertainty

The gender of the physical body is determined by its genitals. The gender of the subtle body is understood by the inner feelings of the person. Both genders may be consistent or one may be contrary to the other. Can we use the gender of either body to determine the gender of the core-self?

Can it be that someone who has a female subtle gender also has a male physical body? Or that a male subtle body may have a female physical form.

Is the core-self a neuter person which adapts to whatever gender the subtle or physical body displays?

Chapter 8
Understanding Celibacy

Celibacy: Is It Impossible?

Since sexual indulgence is part of the reproductive action for extension of creature forms, the effort to rid the self of having to participate in sexual affairs is more or less a lost cause. Yes, there are phases of the body when celibacy occurs naturally, as for instance before puberty and also in the elderly years when libido is lost. Yes, there were successful celibate monks who somehow experienced bodies which have no sexual urge. However these instances do not prove that ongoing celibacy over the span of many bodies is possible. What happens when the monk passes on, does not reach a celibacy-catering dimension, and takes another embryo from parents who are genetically coded for sexual compulsion?

Celibacy in any life as a true achievement is to be honored but it does not guarantee celibacy in any other subsequent life. The ascetic does not have that control over nature, over every form which will be produced as himself or herself in some other life. The ascetic cannot command that this will happen or that will happen unless he or she has absolute control over nature.

Social Celibacy

Social celibacy, when that is defined as no sexual interaction on the physical level, where human beings can monitor the behavior of the ascetic, has nothing to do with real celibacy. Celibacy, for it to be real, must be a lack of sexual impetus on the subtle plane, on the psychological level. That cannot be verified by human society because most humans lack the insight to determine the activities of a subtle body.

Not participating in physical sex in no way shows that there is no subtle interaction. In fact the lack of physical intercourse may have the effect of increased sexual participation on the astral planes. Who could observe that sexual behavior?

Some ascetics who master physical celibacy are unaware of their subtle activities. They do not know and cannot verify even to themselves, if they are engaged in sexual acts in dreams. This is because many incidences on the astral level go unnoticed to the objective mind. Thus the only honest statement these ascetics can make is that they have no idea if their subtle forms are sexually involved. This means that their celibacy is partial. It is superficial because the main body, which is the subtle one, transcends observation.

Celibacy is Impractical for Rebirth

If an ascetic does not become transferred from this earth life influence, from its physical and astral ranges, then his attempt at celibacy will be a failure as soon as he has to become an embryo.

Think of it!

You are a physical celibate monk. You are a partial subtle celibate ascetic as well because you do some mystic practice where you can curtail and reform some of the subtle body's sexual adventures. You pass from your physical body at its death. You find yourself to be a subtle body only, to be only psychological energy. Then what?

How will you progress further without become involved in a sexual intercourse? How will you get the next material body without merging into the sexual intercourse energy of your potential parents?

Does it make you a celibate because your parents are duly married and are upright religious people?

Does that sanitize their sexual act?

Does that prevent your subtle body from becoming a sexual urge?

As soon as a successful physical celibate person passes from the material body, he or she if the person requires a physical form, will be attracted to the sexual energy of potential parents. This means the reversal of celibacy at least on the mento-emotional level. The very same ascetic who was averse or who disregarded the genitals of any and every one, will now live in the genitals of the potential parents. He or she would have to do this without complaint.

Will this previous physical ascetic resume the celibate effort? How can we guarantee that he will do so? How will he be affected when the sex urge is manifest in his new body? Will he or she have control over that or terminate that before it becomes a full blown sexual expression?

Limits of Understanding Sex Energy Transfer

The two aspects of understanding sex energy transfer, are the theoretically view of it and the insight of it. Neither of these may give control over the urge. The theoretical view is the least effective but even the insight if the ascetic has it, may render him little control of the urge.

Control, and then the elimination of the sexual urge, is sponsored first by having direct insight into how the energies interact and operate, but the insight itself is not sufficient to stop the ascetic from sexual participation.

Those who have no direct insight but who rely on theoretical views about sex indulgence, are hypocritical when they try to push sex restraint in the lives of others while in their own psyche, they have no control. This writer is himself a victim of people who take his information and use the theory of it to ridicule and shun others. This is a negative action which I do not support. If anything one should use this information for self-reform, not for insulting others, or morally corralling others, because they do not live up to one's expectations.

Insight into sex indulgence may be inspired into the mind of an ascetic by some other person or it may be discovered by the ascetic when he develops the related mystic perception. However this award may not include having the power over the urge. People may be surprised that a person with insight into indulgence, does not resist the urge. This is because those critics have a misconception which is that the insight is accompanied by effective resistance. Usually it is not. Usually the insight is there, the ascetic sees the sexual dalliance for what it is, but he cannot restrain his body. When he attempts to do so, the sexual urge ignores his willpower.

Lone Ascetic

The ascetic who wishes to be successful in the quest of true gender discovery, is a lone ascetic. He or she has little to get in the form of support from others. Even those who identify themselves as being interested in celibacy, as being supporters of morality, are inimical to the true ascetic. Here is why:

They do not understand a thing about the composition of sex energy. Their idea is that the ascetic needs only willpower and sense desire control to attain full celibacy. They are naïve, having no insight into the reproduction force.

First of all the ascetic does not control the sexual energies of his ancestors. If he is deceased, he may not have control over the sexual energy of his potential parents. Without control he cannot operate autonomously. He is limited. The award of full control either by willpower or by sex restraint desire is a fantasy of inept minds, even his own.

Before we rate the ascetic, we must determine what percentage of the sexual energies are his, and which are his ancestors. What control does he have over the portions of energy which are not his to govern? Can he really say no to a sexual influence which his ancestors sponsor but which he has no interest in?

The power of the ascetic over his body is not a complete assumption of every activity of the body. It is partial only. If anything, it is there to monitor what the body does rather than to dictate everything it performs. If an ancestor wants to use the body to derive an embryo, what say does the ascetic have? Suppose the ascetic can say no, suppose he does have that leverage, might there be a negative reaction because he blocked the desire of a departed soul who had rights to use his body.

Destruction of Sex Desire

Destruction of the sum-total sex desire is never going to happen until the entire manifestation is mothballed by time. No limited entity can bring on the destruction of lust which is an integral part of what this is. The hold that lust has on this creation is such that it cannot be wished away by any limited entities, certainly not by earthlings who are wishing for a sex-free or lust-free human society.

One ascetic may side step this energy effectively but most of the aspiring celibates have the odds against their success just because of the prevalence of the sex energy which is saturated in every physical and in many of the astral domains.

To be realistic, an ascetic would begin with this understanding, so that he or she does not waste energy fighting a losing battle against a universal power which cannot be wished away.

Passage through the Would-Be Parents

To track the passage of a departed soul, into the parents and then forming as an embryo and out of the mother's body, we need to consider the departed souls as being an invisible body with emotional feelings and mental energy. That departed person, or psyche, could blend into the psyche of either parent. He or she could live in the psyche of the father or mother. The problem in developing the required insight, is that we usually consider a person as a physical body and not as psychological energy in the form of a human being. If we cease the physical body reference and develop the psychological body perspective, the tracking of an ancestor would become easy.

Feelings intermix with feelings, emotions with emotions and mental energy with mental energy, one to the other. Thus when the departed soul as an emotional and mental form, relates to its future father or mother, it does so as an energy which blends with similar energy. This results in mergence of these energies which is difficult to sort. The would-be parent will not know which energy is his or hers but will identify the composite as his or hers only.

Nature could care less about this misidentification especially if it would serve the purpose of causing the person not to interfere with sexual transmission of a sperm to the potential mother.

The emotions and mental energy body of a departed soul becomes merged with the energy of one parent, either the mother or father to be. This mergence is so bewildering that either parent identifies with it as his or her own, but as a desire for experiencing sexual pleasure.

The sperm particle is essential in reproduction. Hence if the ancestor was attracted first to the would-be mother, it would have to transfer to the feelings of the father to develop the sperm body. Then it would transit to the mother's body during ejaculation, whereby it would target an egg and become hedged into the uterus.

The embryo which forms in a pregnancy does so on the basis of its emotional body and the genetic tendency of the sperm and ovum which were contributed from the father and mother.

An ancestor can live for years in the body of its descendant or in that of a friend of its descendant. The ancestor might become the child of that person. Its first unification in the parent's body occurs on the psychological plane as feelings, emotions and willpower

Passage through the Parents

The parental perception of what happens in the formation of an embryo lacks psychic insight. The operational shifts of the ancestor who is to be the child go unnoticed by the parents because nature attracts their attention to the sexual flow of energies which cause them to interpret the experience as pleasure.

Generally, the departed soul enters into the feelings of the would-be mother or father, according to which parent is more submissive to the ancestral emotions. From there the ancestor enters the blood stream. If it enters the mother's feelings, it is transferred into the father's feelings through an emotional exchange where the father becomes charmed or induced into accepting the particular life-energy vibration of the departed soul.

Once the ancestor is in the father's feelings, the father only perceives that ancestor as a feeling, as an emotion, or as a thought energy of affection. This is where the parent misinterprets. To a human being, all emotions and thoughts of his heart and mind are his own. As such he cannot identify outside influences. Through misplaced identity, he becomes impelled in numerous sexual acts without sorting the proprietors of the energies.

From the subtle body of the would-be father, the ancestor is transferred into the bloodstream because the blood stream of the gross body is surcharged by the energy of the subtle form. This is a spontaneous psychic process which transcends the willpower and observational capacity of the parent.

After entering the bloodstream of the father, the ancestor travels to the genitals. From that position the ancestor takes possession of semen and becomes familiar with the father's lifeforce which is in the base of the spinal column.

After passing through the testes of the father, where semen is manufactured, the ancestor becomes eager to leave the father's body. He travels into the seminal vesicle which is in the father's pubic area. From there he urges the father to acquire sexual access. He pesters the parent until he is ejaculated from the father's form.

The father for his part does not interpret this urging correctly. He erroneously considers it to be a personal sexual urge requiring fulfillment through sexual intercourse.

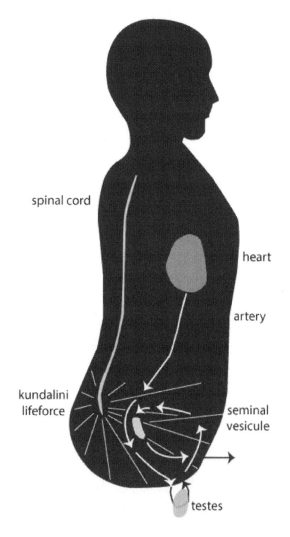

spinal cord

heart

artery

kundalini
lifeforce

seminal
vesicule

testes

Misinterpretation of the Ancestor

In this case, though the victimizer, the ancestor is not conscious of the natural process which facilities his need for an embryo. Its interpretation is skewed. That disembodied entity is conscious of the transit through the father's subtle and gross bodies but it has an interpretation which is incorrect. It is circumstantially perceptive of this because of the way nature's restricts its access to deep insight.

The ancestor regards its travel though the parents' bodies as an eagerness for life. It feels itself as being eagerness for life, as being a mere urge which is required to move here or there in the parents' bodies. It does not understand that it is moving into someone else's emotions or that it was transferred from a potential mother to a potential father. It does not understand that it is transited through tubes in the father's sexual apparatus. Instead it considers itself to be an affection of the father for the mother or of the mother for the father, or an overwhelming affection which is irresistible, or as intense sexual pleasure.

When the ancestor's liquid sperm body is squirted into the mother passage, the ancestor experiences that as an eagerness to be embedded in the mother's psyche. For the father that is experienced as intense sexual pleasure or as an unbearable electric sensation but the ancestor experiences that as a flash movement in the form of an irresistible urge to get into the mother's body.

Sex Desire as All-Penetrating

This present condition of human beings in the creation of which we are a part, is sponsored by sex desire. Every human being arrived here as an embryo through sex desire. We may thank this desire for sponsoring physical life. It is all-penetrating. It saturates social interactions. When the accounting is done, this manifestation of human beings can continue only by subscribing to sex desire.

No one can settle any score in a future life without using sex desire to manifest some other physical body. The pleasure goes with it. So does the responsibility. The good people depend on it. The questionable humans do as well.

Ancestors as Romantic Feelings

The ancestors do exist, certainly. They are present as feelings of affection. From that perspective a part of sexual love is the content of the emotional body of a departed spirit. One physical being may be sexually attracted to another but in that transfer of affection, there are ancestors. Thus in sorting the energy, the yogi must isolate parts which are the energy body of others and parts which are the attraction-force between the would-be parents.

The union of the ancestor with the father or mother is temporary. As soon as the embryo is delivered, it will make efforts to segregate itself. For nurture, it will unify itself with the mother. Eventually in the young adult years the ancestor will desire to step away from the mother, with whom it was so closely attached.

Power Base of an Ancestor

I will list the main base of power of an ancestor, a power through which it can enter out the emotional energy of a physical body without the person's consent. The victim may be totally oblivious to this possession.

- Piety in former physical bodies
- Non-obstruction by fate

The main permit for taking a body is the pious activity done by the ancestor in a previous life. As a speeding comet which is destined to hit the earth cannot be intercepted by human agency, so the force for rebirth which is a past act done by an ancestor in a past body, cannot be thwarted by a descendant who is to be that ancestor's parent.

It is a fact however that some ancestors are thwarted again and again in the bid for getting an embryo. This is done by contraceptive means. On close inspection we find that the act for birth of the ancestor in the past life, carried in it a self-destructive energy. Thus the frustration of someone who desires an embryo, comes because of a self-destructive component in a past pious activity.

For instance:

A school teacher taught a student well. Subsequently that student acquired a high paying job because of the education invested by the teacher. During the teaching sessions, the educator stressed that career was more important than family cultivation. Thus the student dedicated herself to a job and took steps not to have children.

In the meantime, the school teacher passed on. He wanted to be born as that student's child or grandchild but he could not develop an embryo because the student avoided pregnancies. His good social act of giving an education allowed him to fuse into the student's subtle body and be part of her reproductive energy, but his stress about career caused frustration because the student used contraceptive methods which frustrated pregnancy.

An ancestor may be obstructed by fate. It does not have to be the action of the person which causes misfortune. This is a grand universe in which the limited persons may be subjected to enforced expansion or contraction, imposed by supernatural agency. Even if the parents are agreeable and the ancestor has the positive energy to support a pregnancy, there may be obstructions which effectively block the formation.

Supernatural Agency Rarely Interferes with Rebirth Efforts

Even though as human beings, we are ever obsessed with individual specialness, nature gives no more preference to us, than it does to any other life form. On this planet, the human being is the pinnacle of nature's productions. Yet the archeological evidence does not show any preference of time and place for humans. The crudest life forms were facilitated all the same; some for longer periods than the humans.

Human agency is there but the individual and collective volition adds up to very little when we consider cosmic time and space. We are however impressed with ourselves. The truth is that nature's sexual outlay is its investment in reproduction. In some life forms it appears to be efficient. In others like the human type, it appears to be inefficient with many sperms which do not come to fruition as embryos.

Supernatural agency is more an ongoing permit for the sexual activity with success or frustration. Rarely is it a specific allowance which guarantees a successful embryo. The psychic material nature is such that it does not require supernatural supervision for each pregnancy attempt. The supernatural permission is continuous.

Sex Indulgence Distracts from Spirituality

For the most part, sex indulgence is a distraction from spirituality. It is an attraction to sensuality. It represents sensual addiction. A yogi should study sexual feelings to rate their sensuality. He should measure his resistance to sexual feelings. If the ascetic focuses on sexual pleasure as a distinct pleasure energy, he will make the mistake of not seeing where it fits in as part of sensuality.

For those who pursue spiritual life, all sensuality is in question. Sensuality is misleading because it pivots the interest of the core-self into sensual experiences while depriving the self of insight.

Even though the sexual energy is a major sensation, superficial success in curbing sexuality does not free the self from other sensual addictions, especially some which are not as sensational but which all the same could prevent the development of spiritual insight.

It is detachment or existential distance, which allows the yogi to be involved sexually and to be objective to the energy so that what is normally regarded as sexual pleasure is seen for what it is which is bio-electric energy.

Those yogis who are not sexually involved, may perceive the bio-electric interplay of sexual partners and will not consider them to be pleasure engaged.

Even though a homeowner enjoys the cooling effects of an air-conditioner, a technician considers the machine as an electrical device which manufactures frozen air. The cooling experience is real for the homeowner but to the technician it is of little consequence when considering how the machine operates.

Abandoning Reactionary Moods about Sexual Pleasure

For self-tantric, the yogi or yogini must clear up the misinterpretations about sex. This is achieve through clarity about the composition of the sex drive, regarding where it originated and which parts of it came from which sources. He must also trash the idea that sexual pleasure is a problem because the condemned feature is sensuality, of which sexual pleasure is merely one sensational part.

Sexual pleasure is a distraction but it is not the main culprit in the obsessions we have with sensuality. It is the kundalini lifeforce psychic mechanism which is the cause. Unless the ascetic integrates into this information and switches focus to the kundalini lifeforce, he cannot be successful in discovering the core-self's gender.

If the ascetic is to gain clarity, reactionary moods and opinions about sexual pleasure must be abandoned. When we dissect sexual pleasure, we find that it has little to do with pleasure because it is powered by the bio-electric energy which is generated in a physical body and by the psycho-electric power which is produced in the subtle form.

First of all one cannot remove the energy because it is an essential part of the sensual force in the body. What we can do is to change the interpretation of what this energy is and how it affects us.

Chapter 9
Reincarnation

Freedom from Responsibility

Modern people have ways of avoiding sexual responsibility. The modern civilizations offers contraceptives cheaply. Most modern people see that if a contraception is used, the person could have the sexual pleasure with no embryo liability. This mean that sexual pleasure no longer carries the risk that there might be a child whom the parents must support for eighteen years.

The interplay of a sexual relationship also carries with it risks. One partner might become attached to the other, whereby if the relationship ends, the attached lover experiences psychological trauma. This might surface as resentment, jealousy and other sordid feelings which affect all concerned.

Sexual life does not free someone from responsibility. In fact it pins the person down with liabilities which can only be resolved by executing responsible acts on the physical, emotional and mental levels.

This causes some persons to become ascetic with a plan to avoid partnership so as to not be involved in a way where any type of trauma could be produced. However, this does not settle the issue of what the ascetic owes his ancestors, as to if he is duty bound to beget bodies for them.

Responsibility for family life, though counterproductive as an investment for spiritual progress, is still something that most ascetics cannot safely avoid. Hence it is best that the ascetic services the family obligation.

Reincarnation ~ Impossible to Prove

How does anyone prove reincarnation to the self?

Collective proof for reincarnation cannot be provided but a person can investigate the self in meditation to get personal evidence about his or her past lives and future possibility. It begins with understanding if anything will be left of the person after the physical self dies. Will a psychological content survive beyond the physical body? How does it again become a physical person as someone's child?

In this life, we could research on the psychological plane to locate what will survive and what will disintegrate. With the insight derived, we could surmise what survived from the last body, to become the core around which this present physical form was created.

What should be done now with sexual life which will facilitate my need for another embryo? If I will not need one why should I participate in the anxious-ridden begetting process?

To the contrary, how should I invest in family life, so that in the future when I derive an embryo it develops into an adult form with preferred privileges?

Is there is a preference of what I could have as my childhood upbringing and as to my financial status in the adult years?

When all is said and done, when the material body reached its end, whatever is left of the psychology will continue existing on the astral planes. This collective of energy will be the surviving self which will again become unified with physical parents. It will eventually be the core around which a physical embryo will form. It will be established again as an infant, which will grow to be an adult, which will progress into being someone who is elderly. This will in turn die physically leaving its trace as whatever psychological content remains on the astral planes as the transmigrating self. This in turn will again develop an embryo unless this loses the urge to be physical.

Selfish Calculations about Reincarnation

It makes sense that one should be selfish about reincarnation. There are two factors:

- Assisting those who need bodies
- Acting in a way which would facilitate oneself if one needs a body in the future

Apart from compassion for the deceased, it makes sense to assist those who need bodies because if those persons rendered one services in a past life, it is in order that one should reciprocate. This does not mean unlimited allowance to the ancestors. It means limited contribution which is efficient and which does not ruin the yogi's spirituality efforts.

One should act in a way which will cause fate to facilitate oneself if one needs a body in the future. First, how does one know if one will not need a body? How can one say for sure that one's subtle body will not require a physical form, that it will not have the need to take energy through a physical system?

If one cannot be certain that one will not need a physical form, it makes sense that one should act in a responsible way so that the outcome of those actions will be favorable to oneself if and when one takes the next body. This will be helpful to one and all if one does not need to take the body, because then the positive energy which is in one's activities will benefit others.

Results of Activities are Parceled Out

The results of activities are parceled out, except that some of the returns come in the future lives. Even if one is not in existence here in the material world, those returns will surface and will be divulged to someone somehow. If a yogi becomes liberated so that he no longer has to take physical bodies, the results which accrued to his previous good and bad social acts, will surface somewhere in the physical creation. They will latch on to someone at some time.

Liberation is assumed to be complete freedom from material existence. However such a meaning is vague. The truth is that liberation happens in stages beginning with the elimination of the need of the subtle body to have physical forms. This means that the subtle body will continue existing but with no attraction to physical existence. It feels complete as an astral reality only. If a yogi attains this, he is considered to attain the first level of liberation. His good and bad returns will remain in the physical energy, so that at some time in the future, it will manifest certain favorable or unfavorable conditions which will cling to some other person(s) or which that other person will appropriate as his very own.

Cultural acts, regardless of if they cause pleasant or unpleasant returns, have potency to affect what is in the surroundings. They are generated for manifestation by the rollout of time. If an ancestor did a favor in a family and if the yogi derived a body in that family, he may have to return the favor. It all depends on the design of time.

If a yogi refuses to assist an ancestor when time suggests that he should, he will get an unfavorable reaction such that his spiritual aspirations become frustrated in one way or the other. It is for this reason that a yogi should not be a celibate fanatic. He should be open-minded to fate, so that he can adjust himself by its decrees.

If possible if a yogi can safely defer what he owes an ancestor, as for instance by referring that person for rebirth to one of his children who is willing to beget, he may do so but he must be certain that providence will not inconvenience him at some future time for avoiding the responsibility.

Sex as an Encouraging Energy

Sexual feelings are an encouraging energy. As with all such emotion, there is risk for over-indulgence. For self-tantric, there is a need to reduce the sexual incidences. One cannot figure one's gender unless one exercises detachment during a pleasure excursion and has insight into the psychic energy of an experience.

The encouragement energy is dangerous. All yogis should dissect it to understand its composition and origin. This energy is there in all sensual expressions. The sexual one is just one such manifestation, albeit a prominent and intense one that cannot be ignored and should not be taken for granted.

If sexual pleasure is such a highlight of physical life, why should it have the most encouraging energy in the whole range of sensuality of a material body?

Encouragement for what?

Encouragement for whom?

Again we are brought back to the answer that it is to facilitate ancestors whose subtle forms which left old or damaged physical bodies, need to create new physical formations.

Moral Principles have Limited Application

A yogi should not become a moral fanatic, where he cannot free himself from moral rules which were set into human society from scriptures or legislative assembles. All the same the yogi should not act in a way which causes religious and judicial authorities to hunt him down for being a moral offender. Unless he calculated the repercussions, he should certainly not influence others in breaking moral precepts.

Yoga practice is for isolated ascetics. People who are socially involved cannot do advanced yoga. They have to bend this way and that way according to what is acceptable to human society, irrespective of whether that undermines the spiritual progress.

Moral principles have social value according to the ethnicity involved but its purpose does not necessarily help a yogi to advance. For instance in the story of Jarat Karu from the Mahabharata, this ascetic was morally approved in his behavior as a single celibate monk. He took a vow of lifelong celibacy which had for it the moral conduct of absolutely no physical sexual involvement.

Later he broke that vow for a short period of time, for the time it took to have one sexual intercourse. That was a moral breach on his part. In addition he offended morality more by not remaining in the vicinity to support his child.

And yet what he did was praiseworthy from the yogic view point. Hence a yogi cannot be concerned with morality as being something absolute but all the same unless one is prepared to absorb the consequences, one should not influence others to breach moral rules.

Passion as a Research Mechanism

The most common means of feeling-research is the passionate energy. This force is sometimes hidden but it resides in the psyche at all times, side by side with the inertia force and the clarifying means of perception.

Even though passion is the easiest means of researching feelings, it is bewildering because it does not clarify the relative position of the feelings in reference to anything else. When it exhausts itself it converts into the inertia energy that causes a lack of clarity, leaving the person with the memory of the passionate experience but with no idea of how that fits into the overall scheme of sensing objects.

In contrast there is the clarifying energy which gives insight but that lacks the stirring impetus of passion, meaning that it does not encourage the person to do further research.

The toss-up for the yogi is either to rely on the passion energy for its vast research capability but its little insight or to switch to the clarifying energy with its insight but its poverty of enthusiasm.

There is pleasure in the neutral energy of the clarifying mode but the self would have to be oriented to that enjoyable neutrality before it could give up its addictive habit of being indulged by passion.

Subtle Perception Development

For self-tantric there must be subtle perception, very keen psychic awareness which accurately shows details of occurrences, both in meditation and during involvements. If the ascetic does not have this perception, he or she should develop it over time. In the meantime he should associate with someone who has it and/or be sure to read books which discuss the cultivation of it. Books like the *Bhagavad Gita* discourse of Krishna to Arjuna, the *Yoga Sutras of Patanjali* and the *Hatha Yoga Pradipika* of Swatmarama will give information on how to cultivate mystic perception.

This mystic practice as it is applied to self-tantric concerns spying into the activities of the psyche itself. It is not for previewing the activities of others. What is hidden within the psyche will be revealed if the yogi can insert his interest into his psychic existence and get clarity about how the mind and sensations operate. It is for self-investigation and self adjustment.

Appreciating Discipline

The ascetic should appreciate discipline and regard it as a precious faculty which should be treasured and applied consistently to develop sensual resistance. Discipline does not mean to discipline others. It is for self-application to rein in habits which are counterproductive and which reduce mystic insight.

There are many such unwanted habits which an ascetic must over time, bring under control by the steady application of restraint with realization of how these ingrained tendencies can be rooted out over time.

Mere restraint cannot permanently get rid of unwanted habits. As soon as the restraint is not applied, the tendencies will surface again and demand their expressions. Restraint is a temporary check of an activity which the psyche naturally wants to express. Thus restraint is ineffective in the long term. The ascetic must study his nature to understand what energies produce the unwanted habit, as to their source-force and as to whether it is possible to rid the self of it or to transform it into what is desirable.

Avoidance of Pregnancies

No matter the reason avoidance of pregnancies results in baring ancestors from taking material bodies. The basis for the avoidance has nothing to do with the outcome which is that an ancestor will not derive a body, even if that person is rightfully due to have one. There are good and bad ways of avoiding a pregnancy but in either situation, the result is the same which is that the ancestor is barred from having an embryo.

Ascetics should not be proud because of having a good reason for preventing pregnancies. Instead one should honestly assess the outcome for the ancestor who would otherwise get an embryo and be able to live again as a physical being fulfilling desires.

This does not mean that an ascetic should forsake his or her good method of avoiding pregnancies but he or she should always keep in mind that the ancestors are being disenfranchised by any activity which prevents pregnancies. This is only fair to oneself, because in the future if one must take another embryo, one may be in the same predicament whereby one may be barred an embryo by an ascetic who is one's descendant. This would mean that one will be frustrated in the attempt to acquire physical life.

Ancestors have merits on the basis of service to families in the past lives. This entitles them to getting embryos from descendants to whom they rendered services directly or indirectly. This service energy produces a tension in the psychic existence which is relieved by the assumption of an embryo. When the ancestor is deprived of the opportunity to take an infant form, the psychic pressure from the service energy creates a tension in the life of the descendants who should or could have assisted.

Process of Return

Once someone passes from a physical body, that person seeks relatives and friends, just as before. This is done on the psychic side only and has no physical activity. A person becomes a purely psychic being once he or she loses the physical body at its death.

The desire for physical life is so compulsive, that a deceased person makes repeated efforts to be physically present with descendants. This continues even after dying physically and realizing that the physical access is no longer available. We experience these ancestors as their thoughts which become evidence in our minds but which we frequently identify incorrectly as our mental constructions.

Sometimes the presence of these deceased people is felt as feelings of love, affection and even feelings of disaffection and indifference. Because we did not cultivate psychic clarity, we misidentify or ignore these feelings. We are confused about their origin.

Crisis of an Ancestor

When anyone requires to be physical and cannot be the focus of a pregnancy, that person experiences a sense of desperation. If the ascetic meditates on this subtle condition, he or she can relive such feelings because every limited entity was frustrated in the hereafter before. This is why it is important to understand the process of rebirth and to have compassion on anyone who needs a body. Harshness towards the ancestors in this regard happens because of not regarding oneself as being in the same position in the past and not seeing its possibility for oneself in the future.

Ascetics who feel that this is the last physical body to be had, should be compassionate to help anyone to get a body but this does not mean that the ascetic should be involved in a sexual intercourse to be the parent of the said ancestor. If one can be the parent, one may be involved for the purpose but the main application is to know that this desperation about getting a physical body applies to one and all, especially to oneself. It does not make sense to feel that one is exempt from the reproduction process.

The good social acts a person performed in the past life and in the present existence become the bargaining chip for that person in the hereafter, so that a new embryo is produced through which the person can again participate in history.

If the person is neglected, barred from getting a body, there arises feeling of rejection, of being cheated by the descendants. This produces a tension in the flow of psychic energies between the world of the living and that of the dead.

Outsmarting the Ancestors

There is only one satisfactory way to satisfy the need of an ancestor for a physical body. That is to engage sexually or to cause someone else to participate. Anything less results in dissatisfaction, disappointment and resentment by the ancestor.

Usually an ancestor tries to get the most desired body based on attraction to a particular couple who could serve as doting parents. These parents would seem to have the potential for being loving, caring and kind, for not ever applying harsh disciplines and not ever rejecting the demands of their infant.

What are the valid excuses for not cooperating with the request of an ancestor?

Such request may not be verbal or even psychically visual. It may be present as the sexual urge only, and as that urge in the body of one or both would-be parents.

Does a monk or nun who took celibate vows have a valid excuse?

Does an ascetic who thinks that raising a family would deter liberation, have a valid reason?

Does someone who has the sexual urge but who cannot find a compatible partner have a valid reason?

How would it be if the desired parent-to-be were to successfully divert the ancestral energy to someone else who indulges sexually?

Reactions will come

If one does not satisfy the need of an ancestor for a body, and if one owes that person the favor, reactions are sure to come, either in this life or hereafter or in the next.

Why?

Because the energy of being deprived of the opportunity is sure to attach itself to the person who owes the favor.

A swami who is now deceased, did in his former life take a vow of lifelong celibacy. He was an advanced yogin. Later when he established an institution for teaching yoga, he got involved with a woman. From that relationship a son was produced.

The Swami arranged to keep the affair under wraps. No one knew of it except for the woman and a few others. Some years after it was revealed that he begat the child. This caused many problems for him.

Once in the astral existence we discussed what happened, he explained that it is best to begat a few children and while doing so do yoga practice, as compared to taking monk status when one has ancestral obligations which should rightfully be serviced.

He also explained that the idea that the obligations go away because one is a monk are false because he said that the subtle energy of the obligation stands for all time until it is absolved. One cannot conveniently absolve the need for a body by an ancestor just by taking celibate vows. The example from the beginning of the Mahabharata about the dedicated celibate Jarat Karu is ideal for understanding that one's vow status does not have the power to absolve the ancestral debts.

Family Responsibility is Time-Consuming

The main reasons for avoiding pregnancies are that progeny supervision and maintenance is time-consuming. Partnership between a father and mother, even under the most ideal conditions, is problematic, with emotional misunderstandings which rupture the encouraging energies of romance. Ideally a person who aspires for celibacy and for self-tantric discovery should go it alone and have no partner. However this is hardly practical because of the pressing ancestral obligations.

Even if the ascetic decides for pregnancies, he or she will still be plagued with the time-consumption of caring for the infant as well as the disruptions caused by emotional misunderstandings with the spouse. Even though one can learn to reduce disagreements, still partners will have flare-ups which disrupt peace of mind.

The allowance of one pregnancy serves as a gateway to a second and a third, on and on until the body of either partner can no longer produce progeny. Even then, the pressure from the ancestors might switch to where another partner is presented for the production of even more infants. How does the ascetic know when to cease participation?

There are ancestors of the father and mother. Which should be accommodated?

Recommending other Parents

If the ascetic refuses to help an ancestor to whom he is obligated, he may induce someone else to beget the infant body. If this is successful the obligation would be absolved for the most part, if the recommended person(s) has the cultural means to produce an environment that meets the expectations of the deceased person who is to be reborn.

For the most part, once an ancestor becomes involved in the development of an embryo, his or her resentments subside for the time being. They become suppressed as subconscious energies which surface later in the new life.

The suppression of resentment energies means that their content is compressed in consciousness and will be used at a later date when providence provides a circumstantial situation to vent them. If an ancestor really wants to be the child of particular parents, if one or both of those parents successfully divert that ancestor to someone else, there will be resentments but these will become suppressed.

There is always this tension in the hereafter, having to do with rejection of ancestors by the persons whom they desire to be their next parents. This energy disrupts the meditation practice even of great yogins.

Yogi Supporting the Plea for Infant Forms

A yogi should support the plea of the ancestors for infant forms but that does not mean that the yogi should himself beget progeny in great numbers. If anyone has an excuse for not begetting progeny because of its time consumption, that person is the yogi. And yet, he or she should beget as many ancestors as one can be responsible for. One should not beget infants and leave their maintenance and upkeep to others.

Children are born with the energy which is required for their upkeep but it is not in every child's case that there will be a silver spoon in the mouth. Some infants will have a copper spoon, others have one which is created out of mud. A yogi should have the insight so that he can divine the cultural returns which will come to his infant children from their social and antisocial activities in past lives. The parent can do only so much to protect the infant from these consequences.

Regardless of how many infants a yogi can reasonably support, he or she should encourage others to contribute to the relieve effort by taking responsibility for progeny. It is a reckless idea to tell people to be celibate. Only one or two people in thousands can be truly celibate. Thus one should advise people to be responsible family managers but with an interest in spiritual cultivation so that some time is dedicated to practice the tenets which are described in the *Bhagavad Gita* and similar texts.

Fallacy of Family Life

No matter what anyone says, family life, though necessary for the continuation of the human species, is full of flaws when considered from the ideal of trying to attain freedom from being subjected to traumatic insecure phases of existence. With family life the ascetic becomes involved with others who have little or no interest in spiritual objectives, who are materialistic to the core.

It is for this reason that many ascetics either rejected the idea of family life or curtailed participation in it, reducing it to the absolute minimum. How many ancestors can one ascetic support as his or her infants? How much influence can an ascetic have in the lives of his dependents where they willingly comply with his views about reincarnation?

This is all uncertain. There is no way the ascetic can enforce his opinions in every case. Some of his influence will be nullified if not rejected outright. And yet, family life remains the only means for departed spirits to get new bodies. Even the ascetics are subjected to this rule of nature. Thus despite the possibility of failure of influencing descendants, the need for the involvement stands.

Other Ancestral Services

Some ascetics get the idea that by some means other than providing an embryo, an ancestor may be repaid for his or her previous services. However the only way these methods can be actual is if the ancestor does acquire a body from some other person and then becomes a conduit for such services from the ascetic.

For instance an ascetic who serves as a school teacher or medical professional may get the opportunity to pay back to the ancestor who becomes the infant of other persons. Instead of providing a body for that ancestor, the ascetic may give that infant an education or some vital medical treatment. This would send resolution energies into the ancestor's psyche. That would nullify resentments towards the ascetic. All of this can be done without the ancestor even realizing that it took place.

Sexual Access is both Necessary and Risky

This world of human beings cannot continue without sexual access. Human effort to regulate this falls under schemes of morality which vary from society to society according to the religious and/or secular definitions of behavior.

In the animal kingdom, there are no written laws or legislative assembles but there are moral stipulations which are enforced by the environment and also by members of the species according to the urges experienced for allowing sexual access.

Use of sexual access carries with it responsibility, which if neglected brings on immediate and remote unfavorable reactions. All the same, sexual access, even when the parties involved are responsible, is risky. It has uncertainty because so much has to be supported by the environment and society.

Witnessing Passion

Sexual access means the expression of a level of passionate energy. The ascetic must be in an existential niche where he or she may witness the passion and not be totally consumed by it. That is the only way to resist control of the passionate energy which abounds inside and outside the psyche.

Even though in most cases this passionate energy is all consuming and possesses the full attention of the person involved, it does not have to overcome the yogi. In meditation, the yogi should practice shifting to a higher perspective, to an insight level, where he or she can perceive the passionate energy from a location besides being in the energy.

The operation of passion is that it surrounds the core-self with an enthusiasm energy which is experienced as pleasure. This compels the self to render full attention to the expression in the form of intense feelings. However the yogi should allow this to take place and should also retreat or relocate the observing capacity of the self into an insight level which renders clarity about the flow of the passionate energy. This is called witnessing passion as it takes place.

When this is done the yogi will develop more insight and will perceive the flow of passion in slow motion. He will see its composites which are a mix of various potencies. This will cause a change in the sensual interpretation, so that it is no longer regarded as only a pleasure force. It will be seen as mixed reserve potency.

The level in which this sexual passion is interpreted as pleasure will remain as it is but the yogi will not be existentially stationed there. He or she will be on an insight level of awareness.

Chapter 10
Lust as a Composite

Removal of the Pleasure Sensations

There is no possibility of permanently removing anything which is already embedded in this existence, or anything which was here before and which is no longer present, or anything which will appear in the future. Everything that is here, that will be here and that was here, cannot be removed permanently by anyone.

What we can do is to shift from one dimension to the next but we cannot remove the various levels. We should also not think that the format of existence which we experience ourselves as, is really just us. In fact, this is a mix which is unavoidable. Even if the ascetic can sort the mix still that does not mean that he can fully segregate himself from whatever mental or emotional energies he is combined with.

Since the pleasure sensations cannot be removed and since their potential is ever present, the ascetic has only one alternative, which is to detach himself from one level and be shifted to some other plane which is preferred. Whatever we discovered in this creation, in the environments or in the inner environments of mental energy and emotions, will be here for all time. The ascetic should cease the effort for removing these. He should instead aspire to transit to other existential locales where preferred energies abound, where what is unwanted does not prevail.

Sensual Restraint

Sensual restraint is the reduction, attenuation and temporary termination of sensual pleasure or pain by the application of non-supportive physical or psychological acts. The idea that someone can cease a particular type of sensual expression forever is ludicrous because no limited being can say for sure if he or she will be placed in a disadvantageous positon in which the restraint applied would not be available for application. Hence for the ascetic to have a realistic ideal, he must understand that if he can terminate a sensual event, his doing so is for the moment, for the circumstance, with no guarantee that it would continue for all time.

The application of sensual restraint without considering the results of such suppression in the long term is not suitable for this self-tantric practice. Here the ascetic is required to apply the restraint towards questionable pleasure and pains but with insight into what will happen to the energy which is squelched, as to if its compression will cause it to manifest with greater force in the future. What is the use of restraining if the pend-up energy will burst out and overpower the psyche in the near future, causing it to indulge with more impetus later.

There are methods of attenuating sensual expressions just as there are methods of reducing fertility in mammals as for instance by reducing their protein intake. However the ascetic should know that such methods are stop-gap procedures which will not result in permanent change.

Despite this, the ascetic should not be licentious, permissive or immoral. All social involvement is risky. Unless it is absolutely necessary the ascetic should avoid social interaction. When he or she must be involved, it should be done in the most efficient way which takes into account the short and long term consequences.

There is nothing that a limited being can do which is for or against another person, which will not bring pleasant or unpleasant consequences. When the ascetic has to act in a way which is disapproved by the social norms, he should do so discretely. One should adhere to one's fate but if doing so brings on the disapproval of society, one should minimize one's behavior so that the least possible repercussions reach one from society.

Continuum of Actions

There is physical continuum of actions. There is also the psychic consequences. Both are interrelated with the psychic overriding the physical. What happens if someone does a criminal act and does not face the reaction within his life time? Unless he is accountable for it in the future, it makes little sense that he should worry about the reactions.

If he will not understand which reaction is from which past-life action, why should the individual be concerned to act in the present for a preferred future outcome? If there is no coherence between the act in one's past life in terms of its reaction which surfaces in the present, why should anyone be perplexed concerning if one act today will cause a reaction in the distant future?

With limited insight, with no perception of past lives, there is no coherence except for acts and their immediate reactions. Actions which will produce remote reactions, surfacing in future lives when the individual will have no memory of the original agency, may give subconscious fulfillment but no integration into the consequential functions of nature.

However an ascetic should act in a constructive way so that his action produces positive returns in the long range. He should do so for the pleasure of one and all, for the satisfaction of the Supreme Being and the yoga gurus.

Sensuality Attenuated

The attenuation of sensuality is done by those yogis who use postures, breath-infusion, muscular contraction, moral compliance, dietary restriction, emotional crushing and mental sorting.

In so far as **postures** can spread compaction of sensual energies, it may be effective in dissipating a certain sensuality which otherwise would have to be expressed.

For as much as **breath-infusion** can do, an ascetic may direct accumulated breath to bombard hormonal energy. This causes loosening up and shattering of hormonal energy which otherwise would convert into reproduction potential with strong sexual expression.

Muscular contractions are part of the hatha yoga. It was developed by Gorakshnath Mahayogin. If one becomes proficient at this, one may redirect all generated sexual energy which forms in the psyche. This allows for the state of urdhva reta, the ascent of sexual fluids.

Moral compliance has importance because it frees the yogi from the curse of public condemnation. This includes responsible intercourse. It depends on the mores of the particular culture where the yogi resides. To avoid getting bad feedback, a yogi may comply morally. Or he may move away from clusters of humanity, so that he can proceed without censorship.

To facilitate the postures and breath-infusion methods, **dietary restriction** is necessary. This allows the yogi to conserve time which would otherwise be spend digesting food matter, and tending to various ailments which arise because of malnutrition.

Emotional crushing is done within the subtle body. Using breath-infusion to locate the pockets of compressed energy, the yogi will infuse those areas with compressed breath. This causes mixing and expanding of emotion-energy. The yogi presses inward on these bunches causing removal of bad emotions.

Mental sorting is done in meditation by careful study of activity within the subtle head, within the mind. There the observing self is segregated from its adjuncts which are examined to learn their secret operations.

Compassion as a Solvent for Restraint

Compassion is a great human trait but it is also a solvent for restraint. Ascetics who endeavor to curb sensual expressions will find that the effort to do so is thwarted by the compassion tendency. Affection is a sensual habit which is innate in all creatures. Since it bridges to other aspects of social relationship, it should be budgeted.

Sensuality is a radiance which is powered by mixes of various energies. These are involved in expression of affection. When the energies begin to move outward, they seek to embrace someone or some object in the environment. Or they cradle something which is in the mind or emotions of the psyche. The radiating power is such that it is difficult to regulate or terminate if there is any compassion energy in the mix. A yogi should study the compassion force to determine how it is expressed. He should be aware of its liabilities.

Liability for Impulsive Activity

The ascetic needs to understand that even though an activity may be natural, even though it may be induced, even though it may be impulsive, still it carries a liability which is enforced in time. Every individual involved in an activity may not be present when the liability is manifested. This means that during the manifestation someone else will be victimized with the energy. Or the energy will remain in the environment until it can attached itself to someone.

So long as one remains in the physical or astral proximity of the earth, one can be certain that the majority of the liability for past good or bad activities will reach one, either here, hereafter, there or thereafter. Nature is not concerned with the absence of recall in our case. It did not equip us with long term memory in terms of past lives but still it will target us on the basis of how we acted before. Hence to ease our troubled minds, it makes sense that we should act in ways which will induce nature to award positive returns.

To escape from the returns of good or bad consequences, one should transit out of the physical or astral proximity of the earth. Then the energy of one's activities will continue to play out in the physical and psychic earth realms but with others being victimized by those energies, where some persons will benefit from the good returns and others will be afflicted with the negative ones.

There are heavenly worlds which allow for manifestation of good returns only. There are also hellish dimension in which only the bad consequences happen. If one is not present during the manifestation of a certain consequential energy, some other person who is present will be the target of the consequence.

There is an identity crisis where a limited being cannot determine if he or she was the source of the original activity which caused a specific good or bad return. In addition the return energy mixes with energy from fresh actions of those in the environment where the return is manifested. This serves to increase the confusion. The natural tendency is to identify with every circumstance but once the yogi becomes advanced in meditation, he can pinpoint the cause of each.

Core-Self is not the Agency

The core-self though deeply involved as a power source for the psychic material nature, is still not the agency. The entire display is enacted by material nature but with it using some power from the observing self. Even though the self is not the agency, it is victimized with liabilities. This is the way it is. This is why it is incumbent for the core-self to seek a divorce from the supernatural mundane energy. Even though from a legal angle it may be proven that the core-self is not liable for what happens, still it is forced to shoulder the responsibilities. This is all the more reason why one should escape.

Influence

Influences must be there. It is a selection of which influence one will be under. As soon as one shifts from one influence, one falls under another. There is no question of being completely freed from influence. A limited being is such that he or she must be in social proximity. The choice to be made is one of, which influence is the most productive for the individual.

Some influences come from other dimensions. An ascetic should use meditation to breach this physical and psychic level of existence, to reach higher planes. This allows investigation about alternative locales. Once the preferred place is discovered the ascetic should practice to transit there. This means falling under a higher influence.

Influences come and go as the universe mutates. A limited being cannot guarantee for himself or herself that he or she will be perpetually under a certain influence. It is unreasonable to feel that one can permanently put oneself under a particular trend. However one should still try to be in a selected environment nevertheless.

Emotional Infection

I am infected by the emotions of others. In turn, my emotions infect others. Psychic vibrations are dart-like, where they leave the psyche of one person and invade someone else.

This pertains to any type of desire which uses emotions for transit and transport. Disembodied souls infect those who are on the physical side. They do this in the same way that one living human can psychically infect some other person. This takes place on the same plane because both the living and the dead use the same psychic conduit to process desires.

Sex desire is only one form of sensuality. Any desire force for anything can begin in one person and then infect someone else. The person who is the source may be living or dead.

Suppose a deceased person needs to be physical. That desire may be transferred into someone who has a physical body. If it infects the person, the victim will experience the infection as sex desire. If this desire for sexual intercourse is fulfilled, the deceased one will become an embryo.

Suppose otherwise, a deceased person needs to have a physical building erected but that person does not feel that he should be physical. Then again this desire may be transferred into someone who has a physical body. This infection would cause that possessed person to feel the necessity of constructing a building. If the urge is strong and if the person have the means to do it, a building would be constructed in the physical world. To all appearances on the physical side, it will seem that the possessed person was the origin of the desire, even though in fact this person was infected by the deceased person's wish. Hence sex desire is not the only type of infection.

Lust as a Composite Energy

Misunderstanding lust, not having the insight to segregate its composite parts, leads to failure after failure for ascetics who wish to eliminate its influence. Lust forces the hand of all limited beings but it does so mainly because it is not understood, because it deprives one of clarity in dealing with it.

The ascetic should sort its components before he uses methods to eliminate it. He must be open-minded when doing the investigation because it may be that for him it cannot be banished for all time.

In so far as lust is a component energy, the ascetic needs to understand what portion of it is his and what parts belongs to nature or to other limited entities. He must also figure supernatural influence which he does not have the power to alter.

In any enterprise, and the psyche of the individual is an enterprise, there are shareholders. The leading person is a shareholder just as any other investor. The yogi should catalog his shares. He should respect the investment of others and not think he owns it all.

The convention is that the physical body and the subtle form belong to the predominant entity who uses it. This is common knowledge but it is not true. Only part of the contents of the psyche belongs to the predominant individual. A yogi should know his part and apply himself to regulating that in his interest. The rest of the psyche belongs to others. Even though the yogi may aid these others in better managing their parts, still those parts are not his.

Sexual Intercourse as an Incidental Factor

Sexual intercourse is an incidental factor but it passes in social circles as a big event. Much of human focus is misplaced on sexual involvements. Sexual pleasure is one of nature's electrifying events but that itself is a distraction because the small exhibitions of sensuality which appear to be so harmless, are actually the real causes of the lack of investigation into self-gender.

In sexual intercourse we have such a mix of energies, that the confusion bewilders one where one cannot understand that it has deceased individuals in its composite of energies. It is more than a pleasure experience. It is the transit method used by nature for departed souls to become physical beings. The pleasure of it is insignificant in that regard. The enjoyment or distaste of it has little to do with the imperceptible individuals who are part of the experience and whose relationship with each other must be settled through social services.

Sexual pleasure is an environment for the conduction of psychological entities into being physio-psychological beings who can participate in physical history whereby there will be manifestation and frustration of desires.

We become obsessed with what we interpret as sexual pleasure but nature is not concerned with this. What we term as pleasure is electric sensation which is the means of converting a psyche into becoming a physio-psychic mechanism, a living physical body.

To be successful in self-tantric the ascetic must depart from convention. He must develop the insight which causes the perception of the individuals who are part of the sexual energy feeling. When someone can see those individuals, that person will have clarity.

Psychic Content of Physical Beings

Understanding the theory of reincarnation, accepting the logic of it, believing it is a fact because a god, God or religious authority stated it, does not give the student the vision to see how it happens.

The key to reincarnation is to first identify which part of a person does the reincarnating. We know for certain that it is not the physical body. It has to be something about the person which is psychological. Travelers who pass through a strict border are subjected to property searches where certain items are confiscated by customs.

When one passes through the death experience, certain aspects of the conventional self disappears. One such item is the physical body. While it is alive, the person repossesses the physical form on a daily basis. This is done by waking up as the physical system. The psychological part which functions as a physical body during the waking hours, is somehow disengaged during sleep. It re-engages when the sleep period is ended.

By identifying the psychological part, one can during the life of any physical system become acquainted with the part which will survive the death of the physical system.

The psychological part is present during the life of the physical system but each ascetic has to develop the ability to recognize it. Then it would be possible to trace a self after the death. The yogi begins this recognition by sorting his conventional self and segmenting out of it the psychological part.

Mix of Psychologies

A romantic affiliation is a mix of various psychologies. There are a minimum of three persons involved. This means three psychologies which are capable of transmigration, or reincarnating as material bodies. There is the potential father's psychology; the potential mother's psyche and the infant-to-be. From a purely psychic viewpoint, each participant is capable of moving on to become an embryo.

It is important to sort that even parents have a psychological remnant of energy which has reincarnation potential. On the plane of the subtle body, the living and the dead are both in registry as living systems which are on par in terms of potential for assuming infant forms. Those who have physical bodies have direct access to physical history but on the psychic level they are no different to dead people.

Remnant Self-Focus

The real self which transmigrates as material bodies cannot be the conventional self. The real self has to be less than the conventional self.

During the life of the physical system, the yogi should discover the real self. He should know what parts of the conventional self will be deducted when the physical body dies.

Those who recognize that remnant self and who focus on that, are likely to make the transition to the hereafter easily and with much objectivity. Otherwise one will become disoriented when the physical system dies.

Most persons who pass on become schizophrenic in the astral dimensions hereafter. This is because of psychic shock due to not being able to repossess themselves as a physical body and due to losing the psychological aspects which were dependent on having a living physical form.

A yogi who anticipates that he will be a remnant of himself in the hereafter, and who focuses on being and developing that portion, will avoid existential uncertainty after death. Some people repeatedly try to awaken as the material body after it dies. Eventually this effort is abandoned because of realizing that it is no longer possible. This causes depression which further lowers the person through the astral planes.

Such persons seek relatives, friends and religious teachers to find solutions to the problem of being disenfranchised from their physical property and social status. Eventually this results in their possessing some living person to whom they are experienced as affectionate energy and/or as the sex urge. This terminates at some stage in a pregnancy.

Diseased People as Memories

Those who are deceased may be present in the bodies of the living as sexual urges. Their most common presence is felt as fond or disruptive memories. As a psychological being hereafter, the self is manifested in the psyche of others, as a sexual urge, a fond memory, an unwanted thought, an affectionate feeling even for some other person or as a desire to achieve something physical.

Once someone is deprived of the physical body and is transited into the hereafter, that deceased person can switch from one energy form to another and can be one emotion or the other, which is not recognized as such by living persons who are so possessed. The deceased one may have no objective understanding of these switches in format of the existential energies.

Deceased People Causing Thought Sequences

Deceased persons can easily cause the mind of a living person to have a series of thoughts which induce physical activity. This may occur so rapidly and so automatically, that the living person cannot discern the ideas as being that of someone else.

Run-on thinking patterns may be those of a deceased person but it would be experienced by the victim as being that of his or her own. As radio signals enter and are emitted by a transponder, so thoughts of a deceased person can enter or be emitted from the mind of a living person. This might occur without the victim realizing that he or she was influenced.

A deceased person can enter into and live in the psyche of someone who has a physical body. That physical person may in turn, identify with that presence as an affectionate feeling, a sexual urge or a desire to achieve something physical.

Based on being possessed by the thinking energy of a deceased person who either lives in the mind or is outside of it, a victim may identify with a string of thoughts about having sexual intercourse. This victim who misidentifies such thinking as his or her own, would then act to facilitate the indulgence.

Deceased People may Enjoy Physical Life

A deceased person may enjoy physical actions through the body of a living person. This happens when the deceased one enters into the emotions and mindal energy of a living person. From that entry, the deceased person can enjoy any of the sensual opportunities which are open to the victim. The deceased one can use any part of the physical body of the victim.

A deceased person can smell, taste, see, touch or hear through the body of a living person. That deceased one can use the body of the victim to experience sexual intercourse or any other pleasure which the physical body may afford.

Non-Direct Relationship with the Deceased

It is possible and likely that one will become influenced by a deceased person to whom one is not related. This happens because of the intertwining emotions. If someone is related to a deceased person, it is easy for that departed soul to enter into and operate the body of the victim. It is also easy for someone who is not directly related but who has some connection to someone who is related.

Wherever emotions flow, an ancestor would take access of anyone in the communication. Ancestors can jump from the body of a descendant to that of the descendant's friend, even to that of a casual acquaintance through a transit of emotional energy.

Ancestral Transit

An ancestor has many routes of transit which are established on the spot. These are natural means to psychic movement in and out of the bodies and minds of living people. One person does not have to be in love with another person for an ancestor in the first person's psyche to be transferred into the other. In the end however, when the ancestor is lodged in the psyche of its potential father, it is transferred into the mother's body for development of the embryo. This terminal movement is always the same in each case.

Before the terminal situation is exploited, the ancestor could be anywhere in anyone's emotions or feelings in route to that terminal mother. The routes are random just as we may say that roads of a city are random. All roads will eventually take a visitor to the City Hall even though some are a confused way of getting there.

The faster route for an ancestor is to enter the feelings of one of its descendants. If the descendant is male, the ancestor only has to be transferred into the body of its potential mother. If the descendant is female, the ancestor must be routed into the body of its potential father and then be re-situated in the body of the potential mother.

Chapter 11
Affection as Currency

Affection as the Only Means

Affection is the common currency used when one is in the hereafter and is desperate for physical presence. Affection is the only means but it has diverse channels for its access to the terminal which is the body of the potential mother. To be given embryo access, an ancestor does not have to be related to either of its potential parents. There only needs to be some routing of affectionate energy from one person to the next until the energy infects one of the parents.

For their part, most potential parents have no insight into this process of ancestral habitation of their bodies. Thus there is little likelihood of blocking access. If one does not see the ancestor's psychological format, its subtle body, there is no event for one in terms of knowing that one is possessed.

Affection is not an Independent Energy

Often, affection appears to be an independent energy as if it is only shared from one person to another, like from a lover to a beloved. However affection is not independent of the social services exchanged. In each case where affection passes, there are implied services to be rendered where the affection is merely the introduction to the service enterprise.

Nature may pay the person before he is made to do the work or service for which he was paid. Nature is all about inducement by offering reward before the service is extracted. Hence we find that many persons come to disagreement over service to be paid because such work is enforced after the person was paid when there is no incentive for the person to commit to the obligation.

For instance it takes only one sexual act to produce a pregnancy, which amounts to many years of child care. Is the pleasure of the act a reasonable reward for the care services? Actually the question is misplaced because the interpretation of sexual acts as being pleasure events, is a misinterpretation. Sexual acts are electrical events in which sensations move through the nervous system. Thus from nature's view point there is no reward. It is all part of the service of producing an embryo. It is an ongoing obligation. However humans are prone to considering it as a pleasure reward followed by a burdensome service enterprise.

Mix of Emotions

The mix of emotions of the ancestor and the potential parents has within it a conflict. Each person has desires which crave fulfillments. One person wants his or her desire to be fulfilled as a priority. Thus the desires conflict with each other on occasion, but desires may also reinforce or support each other.

Usually parents are stuck with the idea that their infants are just that, infants. However infants are adults who were deprived of adult bodies in a previous life. These infants have compressed adult desires in their psyches. This energy may conflict with that of the parents. In the form of the parents there might be a conflict between the father and the infant or between the mother and the infant. There might be contrast even between the mother and father. Or the infant may become allied with the father against the mother or with the mother against the father. As the infant grows, it becomes obvious that it has conflicting desires but when it is a baby, the average parent cannot sort that.

Love at First Sight

Perhaps the most striking moment in a love affair is the one known as *love-at-first-sight*. Is this only between two people, each being the primary observing self in their individual psyches. Could it be that it is actually one ancestor in the psyche of one of the partners making the selection of the other partner as its co-parent?

Assuming that only one partner has an ancestor resident in the psyche, that ancestor may commandeer the eyes of the psyche to see the other partner who does not have an ancestor in his or her psyche. In that case, the selection of the non-possessed partner as an object of love, would be made by the ancestor in the other partner's psyche. This would be a love affair between an ancestor of one person towards another person who does not have an ancestor who is resident in the psyche.

Love-at-first-sight is, therefore, a questionable incident but it is usually mistaken because the possessed person subjectively identifies with the selection energy of his or her ancestor. For clarity in love affairs, each partner must have psychic insight to know if he or she was possessed. This would require a shift in focus so that the ascetic views all interactions in terms of the actions of the remnant psychology of the individual involved.

Instead of seeing the conventional self as the self, the ascetic would recognize and not deny that self but would continuously perceive that as sorted into one or more selves in a composite with each self's participation being clearly seen. Mathematically, psyche is equal to one or more selves operating one psychological person-container. The primary self is not the ancestor but the primary one may be overwhelmed by the ancestor, whereby the primary identifies the actions of the ancestor as being those of the primary. This confusion serves the purpose of the ancestor because then the primary would offer no resistance and would support acts for fulfilling the desires of the ancestor.

Morality Limits

When morality means the physical actions of an individual, that measure will not apply to kundalini self-tantric. The only morality which is useful in self tantric is the inspection and reformation of the subtle body. The preliminary part of this observation is about the behavior of the astral form in the astral dimensions; in other words astral instead of physical sociology. The advanced part is about the behavior of the core-self in reference to its adjuncts.

Do the adjuncts compromised the autonomy of the core-self?

How is the core-self related to its intellect or to its kundalini lifeforce or to its sensual energies or to its memories or to the moods which alternately saturate the psyche?

Physical morality in terms of social approvals have little to do with kundalini self-tantric. Still, the ascetic would do well and would save himself much aggravation if he complies with social mores but he must understand that these agreements for social conduct do not in any way cause progression within the psyche. These do not increase the grip that the core-self has on the internal organs of the psyche.

An external moral conduct which is approved by society, may betray the core-self and gave more power to the kundalini psychic lifeforce mechanism, while a socially immoral behavior might undermine the kundalini and give more power to the core-self. Each incidence must be checked closely to determine how it supports the authority of the core and belittles the adjuncts.

Physical Morality as Subtle Immorality

An external morality which satisfies the moral codes of society and brings status to person may or may not represent subtle morality. It could be supportive of subtle morality. Alternately it could be used by subtle immorality to gain support from the physical social standards.

An example is the case of a married man who was never seen to be with any other woman besides his wife. Once this man met a woman whom he was fond of in his youth. Seeing this lady during his marriage years, he remembered the attraction to her. This caused affectionate feelings to be transferred from his body into the woman's form.

He had no intentions of acting that out physically but later in privacy with his wife, he engaged in sexual intercourse during which he remembered the other woman and felt as if he had an affair with her.

This is an example of how the compliance with monogamy served to protect an immoral subtle behavior. In this case the man was physically compliant while in fact on the subtle plane we know that he was noncompliant.

Suppose this intercourse produced a child. What ancestor became the embryo? Would it be the man's? Would it be his wife's? Or would it be the woman whom he remembered?

Physical Existence as the Reference

In so far as we use physical existence as the primary reference, we surely mislead ourselves. The physical is the least of our problems because the subtle life continues side by side and is of more consequence. Meticulous tracking of the behavior of the subtle body is necessary in kundalini self-tantric. With that information, the ascetic can develop a method to reform that form's involvements.

Apart from the activity of the subtle body there is the tracking of the interplay between the core-self and its adjuncts. These are resident within the subtle body. This is the last feature to be research. It is the final zone for investigation by a yogi.

Ancestral Possession or Transfer

Ancestral possession or transfer is based on the movement of affection. The ancestors use affection as the main transit. It could be affection expressed in the immediate past life of the ancestor or that expressed in a remote antiquity. A human being can suddenly feel an affection for someone whom he or she never met in the present life. This would happen because of subconscious energies which were acquired in a past life but which are unrecognized at present.

One does not have to be related to the ancestor in this life but there has to be a direct or indirect relationship when the affection for the person was serviced in some other life. Affection is not an isolated energy. It develops on the basis of services rendered or services to be rendered.

Affection is like the holding pen for to-be-slaughtered animals. The design is such that the animal cannot back out of the pen. It must go forward to face the knife. Even though the animal is intelligent, it cannot figure how to release itself from the sequences of movements which it is forced to make.

Its death is inevitable. Once affection cordons the person, he or she must comply to render certain services either immediately or in a future life.

The unrestricted, unchecked and uncatalogued movement of affection within the psyche or from one person's psyche to that of others, shows that the individual does not control the flow of emotions. It might suggests as well that even if he or she gained some autonomy it is not possible to gain absolute control. In so far as the psyche participates in events which are a joint enterprise, the primary observing self cannot have full proprietorship and must yield accordingly.

Social Relationships are Obligatory

All social relationships are obligatory, even the hostile and unwanted ones. An ascetic would do well to realize this. He should scale back on creating new ones. Indeed there is pleasure in relationships but there is displeasure as well. There is great happiness to be derived from relationships but there is great anguish to endure as well.

Whatever is forced by fate has to be honored either voluntarily or involuntarily. Yet, a yogi should bow out when he can do so and should efficiently engaged when he must. There is no reason for a yogin to create new relationships if he is not urged on forcibly by fate. Relationships translates to obligation only. Whatever pleasure a relationship awards will convert to service for resolution. Hence by all means the formation of new relationships should be avoided.

Old relationships which are played out presently serve as manure for new phases to be created for future expression. Nature converts old relationships into energy which it uses to sprout as new emotional formations. Hence relationship-energy cannot be terminated. Nature perpetuates the energies in a recycle operation which will pit the actors for or against each other. An ascetic should service current relationship so that they are made dormant or are reduced.

Rebirth under Careless Circumstances

The rebirth tendency is such that even the most principled person can lodge into a birth situation in which either or both parents lack a high sense of responsibility. That would mean that one's upbringing will be less than desired. An ascetic should review the possibilities in meditation. There are two situations to consider:
- Carelessly helping an ancestor to get an embryo
- Carelessly taking an embryo from insecure parents

Regardless of whether one is a departed soul trying to get an embryo or if one is a physical adult having careless sexual relationship which produces an embryo, the same attraction is involved which is attraction to sex pleasure. The mother, the father and the ancestor who is to be their child, are attracted to sex pleasure. That is the emotional circumstances which brings their energies together, and which is experienced by the parents as love.

As a departed soul in the hereafter, one would be attracted to the affection of either parent and to their mutual sexual attraction. This is how one would become an embryo.

As a would-be parent on this side of existence, one would be attracted to sex pleasure with the other parent. One may or may not be aware of the part played by the ancestor as affection and love.

Ghost

Ghost is the remnant subtle body of a deceased person which is seen partially or fully by the subtle eyes of a living person while awake or asleep. If the subtle body was not involved in ghost perception, no one would see ghosts during sleep of the physical form.

Physical eyes cannot see a ghost but it is possible to see a ghost when one also sees physical objects. This happens because when the physical system is awake, the subtle body is interspaced in it and allows for dual vision; that of physical and subtle.

In one sense every person using a physical body is a ghost. Everyone who lives as a physical body does so with a subtle form, the remnant of which will survive the physical system and become an astral being. Any astral being which registers to anyone using a physical body or to anyone who is dreaming, is termed a ghost.

There are trillions of astral beings in the atmosphere. We are constantly passing through the forms of such beings. Yet we do not perceive them as ghosts. This is because we do not have psychic perception or we are not focused into the vision of the subtle body. The convention is to focus only for physical perception.

Instead of dreading ghosts, a yogin should realize that he or she is a ghost. If after death, one tries to communicate with someone who has a physical body, one would be acting as a ghost. One would haunt physical people. One may do so while such persons are awake or asleep. If such persons develop even the slightest mystic perception either during the waking hours or during sleep, one would be successful at contacting the person.

It is likely however that such persons would be spooked if one was successful at making the person aware of oneself. Usually people do not like to be contacted by deceased persons.

Physical Body is designed for Pleasure Indulgence

The physical body is designed for pleasure indulgence. By convention the most intense feature is the sexual one. As compared to females, males experience that in a different way. The females are however the ultimate terminal of sex pleasure. In the human species only the female can develop and then suckle an embryo. That single instance causes the females to be indispensable terminals. As nature would have it the human female is the final objective in the development of a new human being. This means that the human form is designed to consider the female as the final importance.

Wherever one may roam among human beings, one is confronted with the reality that to survive one would have to enter a female uterus to become an embryo. Every viable female one meets is one's potential mother or stated precisely one is threatened by the presence of every adult female to be that person's child, to have to enter that person's uterus. This applies to both males and female because for either the female is the terminal access for becoming an embryo. So long as one is in a world which relies on survival of the species, one must regard the female as the objective.

The ascetic may have preferences but that in no way induces nature to change the way it evolved the human species or any other life form. Our bodies will continue to act in the way nature intended with us making only superficial adjustments.

At death, the physical system and its methods will be finished. Its evolutionary needs and urges will be no more. We will be left with a remnant of the subtle body which consist of feelings and mentality. The question is: Does this remnant have qualities which are mirror needs of the dead physical system?

Genetic Construction of the Body

The physical body comes with a genetic profile. It may have a hereditary disease. There is little that an ascetic can do to change this. The desire of the ascetic for the body to behave in a certain way is realistic only if the body has that capability. A body might act in a preferred way for a while. Then it may revert to an unwanted behavior. Human willpower is not absolute. Nature regularly rejects the volition of the ascetic.

If the ascetic was unfortunate to derive a sex prone body from the parents, what could he do to change that?

Is the ascetic powerful enough to tamper with the genetic behavior of the glands and organs of his body?

Of course he can be restrained but would that change the body?

It is no small wonder when an ascetic gets a body which is sex-resistant and which has reproduction urges which are not compelling.

Mystic Perception is Necessary

If one does not develop mystic perception, one has only information about what survives after death at one's disposal. This is better than having no knowledge whatsoever but it is not sufficient for integration into the reality which is behind psychic transfers.

Everything sensual leads to fulfilment or frustration of desire. Some desires are obvious and known to the conscious mind. Others are covert and are hidden in the subconscious. The more insight one has the more one may curb the behavior of the psyche. In the final analysis it is the relationship between the core-self and its adjuncts which should be reformed. However initially the ascetic cannot achieve that because he does not have the required sensitivity.

Introspection is the only way to come to terms with movements within the psyche. The ascetic must meditate consistently, observe the operations within the psyche, plan its reform and put into place mystic techniques which change the relationship between the core-self and its adjuncts.

The layout of the psyche is described in detail in texts like the *Bhagavad Gita*, the *Yoga Sutras* and the *Hatha Yoga Pradipika* but that information is not sufficient for self-conquest. One must get mystic insight which verifies the statements. That and that alone can give one the final conquest. Here is a verse which supports this:

ज्ञानेन तु तदज्ञानं

येषां नाशितमात्मनः ।

तेषामादित्यवज्ज्ञानं

प्रकाशयति तत्परम् ॥ ५.१६ ॥

jñānena tu tadajñānaṁ
yeṣāṁ nāśitamātmanaḥ
teṣāmādityavajjñānaṁ
prakāśayati tatparam (5.16)

jñānena — by experience; tu — however; tad — this; ajñānaṁ — ignorance; yeṣāṁ — of whom; nāśitam — removed; ātmanaḥ — of the self; teṣām — of them; ādityavaj = ādityavat — like the sun; jñānam — revelation;

prakāśayati — causes to appear; tat — that; param — Supreme Truth (explained in two previous verses)

However, for those, in whose souls the ignorance is removed by experience, that revelation of theirs, will cause the Supreme Truth to appear distinctly like the sun. (Bhagavad-Gita 5.16)

Chapter 12
Kundalini Lifeforce Investigation

Religious and Secular Rules

Religious and secular rules for social conduct should be observed by the ascetic but these do not cause spiritual advancement. The mere idea that a rule is designed to streamline human conduct in reference to others, means that it is useless for spiritual purposes. However this does not mean that the ascetic should breach the recommended behaviors. After all if one becomes antisocial, one runs the risk of being inconvenienced which will be an impediment to mystic practice.

All the same, one should not get into the mindset that strict adherence to social rules will cause one to become advanced. One should not think that it will make one into a spiritually acclaimed human being. Yes, religious people and law-abiding persons might appreciate one if one suits the definition of a morally-upright and law-abiding citizen but this has nothing to do with the relationship between the core-self and its adjuncts.

An ascetic should simultaneously observe social rules and pursue *inSelf Yoga*™ so that progress is made in real terms and there is the least interference into his lifestyle by religious and secular authorities. He should avoid conflict with relatives, friends and neighbors. If required he should move away from people with whom there are chronic problems. An ascetic should back away from hassles and not be a daredevil who relishes confrontations.

Lack of Mystic Insight

Mystic insight is so important that if one lacks it, one cannot be a successful yogi. It is not possible to be a materialistic person and be an advanced yogi. Until one shifts the interest to the astral reality, one should not claim to be a yogi. Yoga means that one shifted one's concerns to the dimensions which will be evident after one loses the physical body.

Information about this other world, the hereafter, is presented in this book as an incentive for doing yoga practice. If someone is interested, he or she should begin elementary yoga practice and then do meditation on a regular basis to develop psychic sensitivity.

Each student has to scan the mind to discover why it is extroverted. The mind must be trained to be introverted. The attention of the self must be redirected so that its interest is the movements within the mind. It should abandon its craving for physical activity. However it cannot do so unless it is trained to turn way from external concerns and invest itself in what is internal.

Ignoring Sex Desire

Since sex desire is all-pervasive because it is involved with survival of physical bodies, some ascetics feel that it should be ignored and that one should eventually become tolerant of it by developing an immunity to it. The advice is that one should develop an insensitivity to it. This may work in the short range but it is very bad advice. That advice causes the sex energy to become dormant at best. In that condition, it increases in potency and eventually it takes over the psyche, whereby the ascetic will crave sex desire more and more and even commit criminal acts to satisfy it later on.

All the same to advise someone to observe instead of ignore sex desire may also cause mishaps. The only persons who could successful observe sex desire and come to a favorable conclusion with it, are those who have the required mystic insight, who can see the movements of the ancestors as explained above. Both ideas, the one about ignoring or tolerating it, as well as the one about observing it, are risky.

Kundalini Lifeforce Investigated

The kundalini lifeforce must be investigated by the ascetic so that he understands its operations. Much of what is conducted as life in the body is done by the kundalini lifeforce with hardly any input from the core-self. This situation should be changed with the core-self doing more tasks and gradually retiring the lifeforce from many body maintenance decisions.

Kundalini yoga practice has pranayama breath-infusion as its mainstay. This is because the most frequent intake of the kundalini is breath energy. By feeding the kundalini a large quantity of breath energy, the yogi will perceive the kundalini more and more. He will in time understand how it distributes energy in the physical and subtle bodies.

Hormonal energy is produced and stored in the body. This is used by the kundalini for various operations, the chief of which is reproduction. The yogi should study how the kundalini uses the hormonal energy for its actions in the psyche. Of particular interest is the sexual hormone energy. In kundalini yoga this energy is mixed with infused breath energy. It is then hurled at the kundalini which is at the base of the spinal column. This results in the movement of kundalini up through the spine into the brain.

The normal nature-given operation of the sex hormone energy is different. The natural passage of it is that it is generated in the genitals and then used there for providing embryos. Such production is possible because of the high electric current which is generated at the genitals by the kundalini. It uses the sex hormone as fuel for generating the high electric charge which humans interpret as sex pleasure.

In terms of bio-electricity, sex pleasure is a highest charge of electric energy but from the emotional view, sex pleasure is an enjoyment experience. The ascetic should leave aside the part of the mind which considers pleasure to be an enjoyment. Instead he should focus through the part of the mind which affords the vision of it being an electric sensation. This will allow him to see the psychic outlay of the energy and the arcing of the kundalini from the base muladhar chakra to the sex chakra and then the expression of it through the genitals

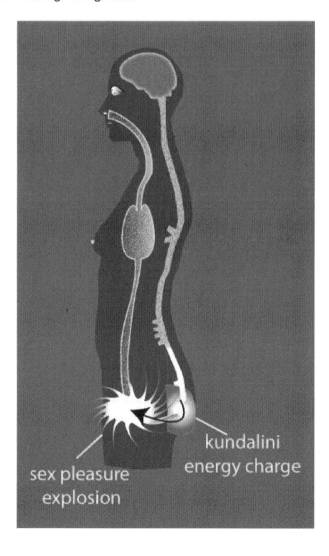

Celibacy as Mind Control or Willpower Action

Celibacy is neither mind control nor an action by the willpower. Celibacy concerns the lifeforce. Willpower actions take place in the head of the subtle body. Sex pleasure occurs mainly in the lower part of the trunk of the subtle body. The lifeforce is located in the lower spine, in the sacral area of the body.

For willpower to cause a termination of the sexual urge, it has to be created in the head of the subtle body and then be transmitted through the intellect to the kundalini lifeforce. That lifeforce must then make efforts to shut down the urge. This is a long-winded process which usually is a partial or total failure.

Controlling the sex urge by trying mind control, means that the ascetic will control the energy in the subtle head so that it does not support the sex urges in the lower part of the body. This may mean to cease all sex-related imagination. However even this is inefficient because what happens in the head of the subtle body must be relayed to the kundalini which in turn must make the effort to shut down the sex urge which was already aroused in the genitals. It is hardly likely that these actions will be completed.

The plan to control sex desire through mind or willpower action is terribly flawed. It is not a scientific method. It is a guessing game due to not understanding how the urge operates. Based on false assumptions a human being thinks that his mind control or willpower would be respected by the rest of the psyche, by the kundalini, but unfortunately the kundalini does not regard the individual's volition in that way.

Assistance from Senior Ascetics and Books

A yogi must take assistance from senior ascetics and from books written by senior yogis who did the research into the practicality of celibacy. The seniors may be astrally present. Wherever they may be, the ascetic should consult with them to get methods which are effective. He must also hear of the failures by ancient yogis who tackled celibacy. Books are helpful to the yogi even if the techniques which worked before cannot yield success currently. Just knowing that the ancients made the effort and were or were not successful is a source of confidence for the yogi.

Puranjan is Every Human Being

In the *Srimad Bhagavatam*, there is narration between Yogi Narad and King Prachinabarhi. Narad explained the life of a king named Puranjan. However the entire story was an allegory. There was no Puranjan, except that after telling the interesting story, Narad explained that Puranjan was representative of King Prachinabarhi.

The story begins with Puranjan wandering on planet earth, trying to find a habitation. He searched for a time but could not find a suitable place. Eventually he found a city on the southern side of the Himalayan Mountains. It had a nice lay-out, in his opinion. The city had nine gates. It was suitable for his needs. It was called Bhogavati, the place for fun and excitement.

Puranjan was relieved to find this place. At the time he was tired of searching. The place had spacious accommodations. It was air-cooled with parks and fit residences. The only strange thing about it was that at first he did not see anyone but himself in the well-arranged city. He was hopeful that he would meet others in that lonesome place.

Puranjan Finds a Mate

As he strolled here and there, Puranjan found a botanical garden. There he saw an intelligent and sexually-attractive young lady. His joy knew no bounds. He noticed that she was followed by ten male servants. Each servant had hundreds of wives. The woman was protected on all sides by a five-headed serpent.

Puranjan assessed the situation. He realized that even though the servants had wives, the woman herself lacked a husband. She was young and beautiful. It seemed to him that she required a mate. Looking at her, he sensed that she was sexually mature. He inquired of her identity. He asked about the servants and the serpent.

The young woman explained that she had no knowledge of how she got to that place. She had no idea as to who produced her, nor could she tell the names or backgrounds of the servants. For that matter all she knew was that the servants were her friends and the snake remained awake always to protect the city and herself.

The Young Woman Proposes to Puranjan

The woman offered services to Puranjan. She invited him to remain for one hundred years. She said,

"O darling, I will arrange this city of nine gates for your satisfaction. While fulfilling your desires in this secluded place, live here with me for one hundred years.

"How fortunate I am to have met you who are capable and intelligent! You glance at me in a romantic way. I can tell that you are sexually expert and experienced. Since you know about sex pleasure and indicate that we would explore the pleasures of this city together, let us join in matrimony and love one another.

"I feel that nothing is better than the union of a man and his lover, especially the sexual connection which gives intense pleasure. I heard that sexual partnership is not only pleasing to the partners but to the forefathers, the supernatural rulers, the great sages, saintly people and just about everyone else. We appreciate a man who dedicates himself to social life."

Narad said that Puranjan was pleased when he heard this proposal. It gratified his heart. All anxieties about finding a suitable habitat vanished from his mind. He settled with the woman. They enjoyed life in each other's company for one hundred years.

Bhogavati ~ Excitement City

This story continues but I will explain the symbolism thus far. The city itself, Bhogavati, represents the human body which is a tool used by Puranjan who represents the individual soul. The woman said that it was a special city because in the human body one is afforded more enjoyment than in any other lifeform. One can exploit the sexual urge in the human form.

In the woman's view, inexperienced persons do not understand that in the human form there is the advantage of excessive sexual indulgence. One can deliberately enjoy sex in the human species while in other forms, one is limited to seasonal sexual contact which is regulated by hormonal secretions. Other lifeforms have sexual contact but they cannot indulge outside of estrus. She explained that the living relatives and the ancestors appreciate when a man focuses on improving the social standing and when he becomes attached to sexual enjoyment.

Narad explained that the woman represents the intellect in every lifeform. The five-hooded serpent represents the lifeforce. The ten servants are the five senses and the five sense objects pursued by those senses. Puranjan is the core-self in the individual psyche. Using a subtle body, this self wanders about on the psychic planes. It assumes various species of life, but it prefers a human body.

At one time Puranjan, a core-self, got lucky to find the beautiful spacious city of Bhogavati, which reflects finding human parents who beget an embryo. When Puranjan first entered Bhogavati, he liked its surroundings, which means that when a departed spirit first contacts the emotions of its would-be parents, those feelings of the parents' love for each other, are experienced as being enjoyable. The feeling appear to be accommodating and spacious.

Sex Enjoyment as the Special Feature

Puranjan considered the human species to be especially affordable of sexual enjoyment, but he needed the cooperation of a queen and servants. Unless we have the intellect and a lifeforce, we cannot get a human body or any type of creature form.

However the problem is that the lifeforce is sexually inclined and the intellect is focused on perpetuation of the particular species one assumes. If either of these adjuncts are not controlled, one is likely to have no spiritual insight. One will contribute to creating more bodies in the species of life one assumed. This is great for the ancestors but it does not provide psychic clarity.

Sexual Exhaustion

Narad related that with the cooperation of the queen Puranjan lived in that city. On occasion he went hunting in the forest and country side. At that time, the queen would become lonely. When he returned, she chided him and deprived him of sexual enjoyment. The idea is that if one misuses the human body by too much activity, the body becomes tired and one cannot enjoy it fully. If one has too much sexual indulgence the lifeforce depresses the emotions for one and two days to allow the sexual hormone energy to accumulate again. In the meantime one's intellect feels uneasy.

Puranjan Died

Eventually, Puranjan was forced out of the city of Bhogavati. In other words, his body died. The lifeforce and the intelligence which was depicted as the five-hooded snake and the queen, reluctantly departed from that place. The physical body is pronounced death when the lifeforce leaves it.

This narration of Narad describes that the human being is a combination of various energies, including a core-self, an intellect and a lifeforce. Narad narrated that when one hundred years transpired, Puranjan, the queen and the five-hooded serpent were forced to leave the city. They were arrested and dragged out by an enemy which burnt the city. They regretted the incidence because the good times came to an end.

For trashing Bhogavati, the enemy closed off the higher gates. Thus Puranjan and his family with their servants had to leave through a lower gate which was the only one left open by the enemy. Every citizen was dragged out in chains by the enemy. Even the city's serpent protector was humiliated in this way. That serpent was fatigued because he alone fought the enemy for many years. While Puranjan and the queen enjoyed a variety of pleasures, the serpent protected the city for one hundred years.

Final Moments in a Body

The explanation is that excessive enjoyment causes ill health which in turn causes the higher faculties to become constricted resulting in brain disease, eye disease, ear infection, heart disease, kidney failure and lung malfunction. Eventually one is left with one working part of the body, which is the rectum. It is such that at the time of death the lifeforce in association with the core self and its other adjuncts, leave the body through the anus.

Since he was addicted to sexual pleasure and abused the related organs, Puranjan's lifeforce always remained in the lower trunk of the body, near the genitals and anus. This caused his intellect which was resident in his head, to focus into the groin area. That preoccupation did not allow him to take higher aspects into consideration.

So long as the lifeforce remains focused on the digestive, sexual and excretory organs of the body, one can never become free from sexual craving. This means there is no possibility of neutrality which is necessary for self-realization.

Willpower Alone is Ineffective

Willpower and pride as an ascetic are insufficient for curbing the sexual impulse of the body. People who accept ascetic status from a religious institution may think that their determination and affiliation will eliminate sex desire but that cannot true. To take something apart one should dismantle the components of the object. What does willpower have to do with sex desire? Since when is the status of a religious institution part of the format of the sex urge?

Which human being can instruct himself or herself to have sexual organs and urges?

Which religious institution constructed the reproductive method of the human species?

The idea that on the basis of volition and religious affiliation one can control the sex urge is preposterous. All teachers of the past, those from the present and those coming in the future, who believe and teach this are either naïve or just plain stupid. None of them should be taken seriously.

In the male and female bodies, the sexual hormone energies and secretions are created in the lower trunk of the body. In a male, it is produce in the testes which are between the thighs. The fluids are stored in the seminal vesicle which is in the pubic area.

In the female body the fluids are created in the ovaries which are in the lower abdomen. These fluids travel into the uterus and vagina, which are also in the lower abdomen. The lifeforce is attracted to these energies which are in its proximity. Unless an effort is made to raise this energy into the brain, one has no chance to complete celibacy.

Can anyone mentally or verbally command the body to create semen? If that is not possible, then why do we think that by mental desire, someone can cause the body to cease sexual fluids production?

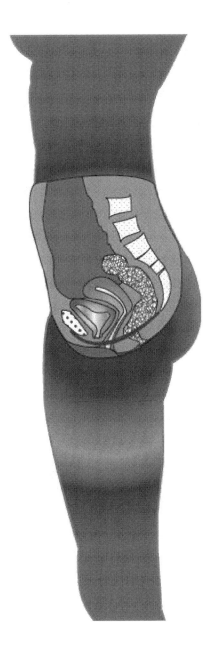

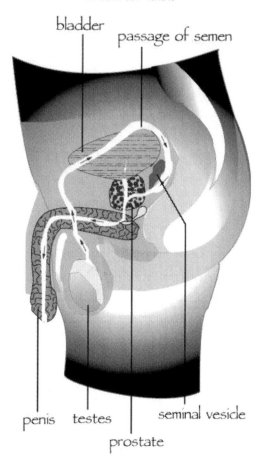

bladder

passage of semen

penis   testes

seminal vesicle

prostate

Take Help from Teachers who dismantle the Components

One must find teachers who dismantled the components of the sex urge. If such teachers are not available in the physical world, one should search the astral dimensions. Some techniques one may discover. Some may be inspired into one's mind by advanced teacher or deities. One cannot discover everything by one self. The practical method is to work industriously to segregate the components which comprise sex desire.

Sannyasis and other types of sex restraint militants are for the most part hypocrites because the psychic material nature refuses to recognize their physical representation as the fact. Physically these people show resistance to the sex urge but on the psychic plane, their situation is murky whereby many are unaware of their astral activities. Those who are somewhat aware, cannot cease sex expression. These religious officials abuse public trust because they represent physical celibacy as total sex restraint while in fact it is more of a misrepresentation.

Many monks masturbate to relieve themselves of the urge. Should we define celibacy as physical sex restraint with masturbation in private? Some monks meet persons of the opposite or same sex on the astral levels and relieve lust. Should we define celibacy as physical restraint with astral indulgence not being considered as a breach?

Some monks have no sex urge because of the age of their bodies. There are others whose sex drive become dormant because of the biological process where the body drastically reduces production of fluids. Should we make definitions for celibacy which take any of this into account?

Attraction of the Lifeforce to Semen

The lifeforce is attracted to semen. Once semen is produce it serves as an attractor of the lifeforce. When the lifeforce consumes semen, that incidence attracts the intellect. Once the intellect is attracted the core-self is helplessly drawn into the experience.

A yogi might apply his willpower to prevent the core-self from being drawn into the experience but that all depends on the intensity and magnitude of the energy. If it is too potent, the willpower will be unable to stop the attraction.

The sequences of events is that semen is produced by the testes. The semen is then stored in the seminal vesicles. The lifeforce is forcibly attracted to it. In proximity to stored semen, the lifeforce will charge the sexual energy with a potency which will result in the person experiencing the urge for sexual linkage.

On another plane of existence, the semen is generated because of the presence of departed spirits, each of whom possesses a sperm. Due to the presence of these entities, the semen has an affection-charge which is irresistible to the intellect. Once the intellect becomes absorbed, the core-self must give its approval to the expressions which would facilitate sexual intercourse.

Lifting the Lifeforce

Hatha yoga is a process of arousing the kundalini lifeforce into the head of the subtle body. The kundalini is resident at the muladhar base chakra which is at the bottom of the spine. For causing it to move through the spine upwards and into the brain, the yogi should strike it with subtle sexual energy which is infused with breath. This is done using the pranayama breath-infusion process. One should learn this from a kundalini yoga teacher who is proficient at raising kundalini.

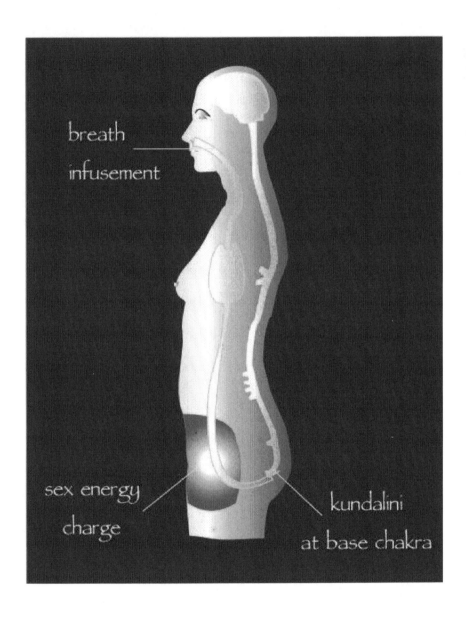

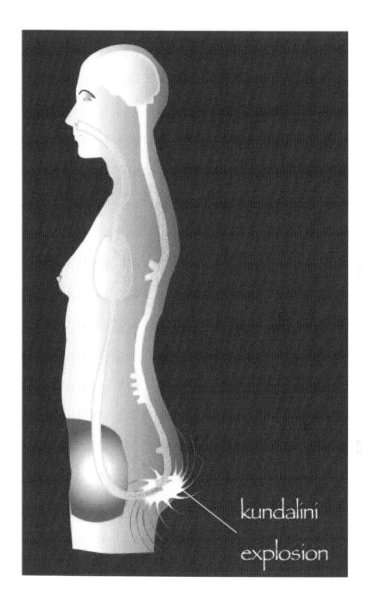

kundalini
explosion

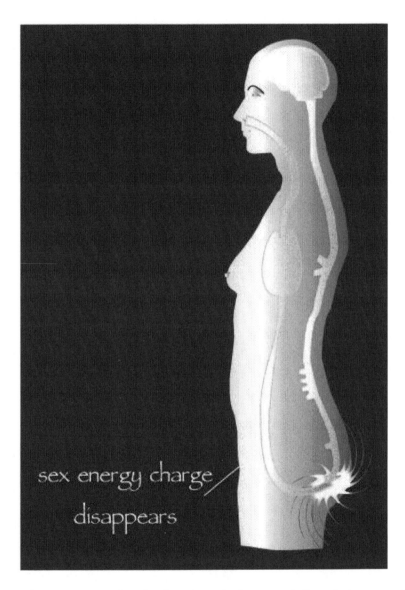

sex energy charge / disappears

First the yogi must infuse fresh air into the lungs and direct it downwards to the reproductive glands. When this is done sufficiently, he should direct that mixed energy to the base chakra, where it can strike the kundalini. This is in contrast to the natural system which is that the kundalini comes to the sexual energy for sex pleasure experience. In sex pleasure experience there is no need for breath-infusion. For kundalini experience through the spine, breath-infusion mixed with sex energy is the definite method of arousing kundalini.

When the kundalini is first struck by the mix of breath and sex energy, it tries to move downward. Thus a yogi must apply the ashwini mudra anus lock. Even though it is applied physically, it is also applied in the subtle body just as well because the physical and subtle are interspaced in a wakeful physical form. The application of the anus lock stops the aroused kundalini from moving out of the spine through the base. Again the yogi should compress the pubic area upwards. This is the sex lock which blocks the outlet from the spine through the genitals.

Again the yogi must apply the navel lock to stop the kundalini from expressing its aroused condition through the abdomen. Then again he should apply the chest lock and the neck lock with the same intentions of not allowing kundalini to discharge itself at these energy gyrating locations. For the neck lock the yogi should direct the energy through the center of the spine into the head of the subtle body. The energy should not be allowed to diffuse itself through the fleshy part of the neck outwards. It should remain in the middle of the spine with impetus to move into the subtle head.

Celibacy as Alternate Utilization of Sexual Energy

For self-tantric practice, celibacy is the alternate utilization of sexual energy by mixing it with infused breath energy and the kundalini psychic lifeforce. The body is designed to use small quantities of sexual energy for purposes other than fulfilling sexual urge. However, this means that the greater portion is left to haunt the yogi. This remnant causes masturbation, physical sexual intercourse, subtle body sexual intercourse or stagnation of the semen in the seminal tubing.

Instead of keeping the stored sexual energy, the yogin should use it efficiently by mixing breath-infusion so that the kundalini is aroused and courses upward through the spine into the brain. This is the celibate expression of it. The yogi must work industriously to consume the produced sexual energy so that it does not accumulate and is not stored as before. If there is no storage, it is likely that there will be no urge for indulgence.

Since nature's system is to store it and use it for reproduction, it is a difficult task for the yogi to interfere with the natural format. We should assume that it will take years of practice, if not lifetimes, for the yogi to completely reform the subtle body from this storage method. Kundalini is designed to go the genitals and then to flash itself during the pleasure climax of sexual arousal. The yogi has to change this method, so that the kundalini stays at the muladhar base chakra. The new method should be that infused breath energy which is mixed with the sex energy should go the kundalini at the base chakra. Then kundalini should move through the spine upwards and not move through the genitals downwards.

No one should think that within weeks or even years, he or she will master the system of moving semen up the spine as described. The plan should be to achieve this over many lifetimes of practice. Eventually when the subtle body is redesigned, this would be possible on a full time basis not otherwise

Chapter 13
Diet

Food Impact on Celibacy

The celibate effort is related to food consumption. Everything done by the body is done through food energy, both the physical ingredients as well as its subtle counterpart. The quantity of air in the blood stream matters too. Those who absorb a greater percentage of air into their lungs, have more oxygenated blood and less carbon dioxide content proportionately.

There are two types of pranayama breath-infusion practices. One is to increase the oxygen and simultaneously decrease the carbon dioxide and other negative gases. The other is for the reverse effect. Many human beings have a high tolerance for carbon dioxide. These people can work comfortably in places with poor ventilation. Such persons may smoke cigarettes or other smoke producing substances which causes an increase in the carbon dioxide or which infuse carbon monoxide into the blood stream.

For this practice of kundalini self-tantric, the increase in fresh air is required. The ascetic should do breath-infusion which makes the corpuscles be chock full of oxygen with the least amount of carbon dioxide.

This helps celibacy in the long term but it may increase sex desire in the short term. In the beginning when a yogi does breath-infusion, there is rapid movement of oxygenated blood through the body. This causes an enthusiasm among the cells which may cause an increase of sex desire. In the long term however it will result in a reduction of sex desire because the sex hormones will be evenly distributed through the body instead of being concentrated in the genitals. In addition due to the breath-infusion the yogi will learn how to shatter out the bliss content of the sex hormone energy. This will reduce its lust potential.

Semen Distribution

The important achievement is to get the reproductive energy to be distributed elsewhere in the body, anywhere besides the genitals. As nature would have it, the sexual fluids are concentrated and then stored in the genitals. The breath-infusion process is for causing these hormonal energies to be distributed elsewhere in the body, preferably throughout the psyche evenly.

At first the effort is to cause the sexual energy to be combined with oxygen in the blood stream and then to be combined into the kundalini so that it may become aroused and go up the spine into the brain. This is the conventional method of kundalini yoga practice. It is preliminary but it is a big achievement for any yogi.

The movement of this sexual energy up through the spine is known as urdhva reta practice, with urdhva as the Sanskrit for upward and reta that for semen.

kundalini lifeforce explosion in subtle head
buddhi intellect orb is affected

breath-hormone energy arches over
to kundalini lifeforce power central
causing kundalini energy to ascend into the brain
where it explodes into bliss awareness

However in a more advanced state the effort is to lift the energy as it is through the trunk of the subtle body without having it be routed through the genitals. At first it has to be routed through the genitals but as the yogi gains more and more control, he can directly lift the energy without it passing through the genitals. This is not lifted with willpower alone. It is done primarily by doing breath-infusion which makes the energy submissive to willpower. Breath-infusion also vaporizes the energy so that it has a quality which makes it responsive to willpower commands.

Route of Sexual Energy

The yogi must study the route of sexual energy. Then he may take steps to alter the design of energy distribution which was created by the kundalini psychic lifeforce. This is not an easy achievement. It is not done by the flick of a finger. It certainly will not be achieved by willpower or moral opinions.

The natural system is already known to every adult human being who made observations of the digestive system and sexual intercourse activity of his or her body. Here is the listing

- Food is eaten
- Food is digested
- Hormone energy is created from the digested material
- Some hormone energy is used to produce sexual fluids
- Sexual fluids develop a polarity charge
- The kundalini lifeforce is attracted to the sexual charge in the genitals
- Sexual arousal results in the discharge of sexual fluids which is an exciting pleasure event

This natural system was designed by nature. It operates with or without input from the core-self.

The preliminary achievement for kundalini yoga is to cause the sexual charge in the genitals to be attracted to the kundalini lifeforce so that this charge moves to the kundalini as contrasted to the kundalini being attracted to the sex charge. Hence the difference is the direction of movement and the component which makes the first move in the process. While for natural sex participation, the kundalini is attracted and it makes the first move, in conventional kundalini yoga the sex charge becomes attracted and it makes the transit to the kundalini.

I described this as the preliminary part of kundalini yoga but some ascetics think that this is the total objective. The conventional information is that this is the total kundalini yoga, the effort to route the sexual energy to the kundalini which is the reverse of what is normal. Hence some ascetics become fanatical and are against anyone going beyond this stage. However, this is perhaps the first time in modern human history, that anyone divulged stages beyond this.

The final achievement in kundalini yoga is more than just a reversal of the natural passages of the sex energy. It is an effort to eliminate the formation of the sexual hormones. Why manufacture the hormones in the first place? If they are not produced, there would be no concern with how to route them. The effort to do so would be eliminated. In childhood there is no production of sexual fluids. Sex urge is not present and does not have to be accommodated or reformed.

This is mysterious until we consider that sex energy is based on the food digested. If the digested materials are not routed to the reproduction glands, there would be no sexual energy which must be re-routed.

There are two phases in this practice. The first is to lift the sexual energy up through the trunk of the body so that it is not routed to the kundalini and it is also not used in the genitals. That is the preliminary phase of the advanced process.

The second is to lift the digested hormones as soon as they are produced so that they are not routed to the reproductive glands for taking a sex polarity charge. If the digested hormones are lifted up through the trunk of the body before they are routed to the sex glands, there would be no sexual polarity.

Is that possible?

Fortunately it is because each cell of the body has its individual mini-kundalini. The convention described above is based on using spinal kundalini which is massive and compelling compared to the micro kundalini of the individual cells. The first part of kundalini control, the convention kundalini yoga, has to do with the spinal kundalini.

The advance practice uses the micro kundalinis of the cells. Using that one can cause these micro kundalinis to act so that they release their polarity charges upwards. Thus the spinal kundalini loses significance. The system of energy distribution changes. A neutral bliss charge which is lust free is produced in the psyche.

By the grace of the sun-deity, Michael Beloved happened to be the person who became fated to release this information to humanity. It frees human beings so that they can make tremendous advancement in the redesign of the psyche even before they would leave a physical body and reach higher dimensions.

Air as more than having Physical Effects

Air is a physical material but its infusion into the body by the pranayama breath-infusion practices produces positive subtle effects. The increase in the percentage of oxygen in the bloods stream means that there is a decrease of carbon dioxide and related negative gases. Carbon dioxide is displaced by fresh air when one does breath-infusion doing bhastrika or kapalabhati rapid breathing.

The more carbon dioxide that there is in the body, the more materialistically inclined one is likely to be. Conversely the more fresh air is in the body, the more insightful one is likely to be. Carbon dioxide promotes dullness of mind and dependence of passionate energy for motivation. Fresh air promotes clarity of mind and reliance on neutral bliss energy for motivation.

Air Quality in Sexual Fluids

The increase in fresh air in the cells by ingestion of more air through the lungs, means that the sexual fluids will be of a higher quality. Thus even if the yogi does conventional kundalini yoga, his practice will result in a higher state of consciousness when the kundalini is aroused, otherwise the aroused kundalini will cause a duller type of awareness with much less clarity.

When spinal kundalini is struck by breath-infused sexual energy, the resulting state of consciousness is reliant on the quality of the sex energy which mixed with the breath while doing the infusion practice. The yogi should strive to improve the quality of this mixed energy. He does so by making sure the lungs absorb the fresh air while doing breath-infusion.

If for instance one does breath-infusion but the lungs fail to absorb the fresh air, it means that the percentage of carbon dioxide in the blood stream will not be reduced. When this mixed energy strikes the kundalini, its arousal might reach into the brain but it will do so with the result of a low or mediocre state of consciousness.

When the lungs absorb the fresh air which is presented to it, this energy is infused into the blood stream, with the result that when it is mixed with the sex energy and hurled into the kundalini at muladhar chakra, it goes up through the spine into the subtle head and the yogi experiences higher, brighter more insightful states of awareness, with various grades of bliss consciousness, which has less lust content.

Fasting for Celibacy

One can use fasting to assist in the celibacy effort but fasting alone will not contribute to full success. If the body is deprive of food its reproductive capacity will be reduced. This is proven in the case of domestic animals, where they cease reproducing if they are not fed sufficient fodder. Because of bad nutrition human beings in drought stricken areas also suffer from reproductive deficiencies.

It is okay to fast but one should study what to do to decrease the intake of food which is counterproductive to yoga. Assuming that I eat more rice than necessary, say for instance that I eat one cup of rice more than I need on a daily basis. Then after one month on that rice-excess diet, I may cease eating rice for one week or more, to rid my body of the bad effects which the month of extra rice caused.

However suppose I simply stop eating that excess of one cup of rice at each meal, then there would be no need to fast. An ascetic should self-study diet and its effects such that he may fast daily by reducing or eliminating foods which are counterproductive to yoga practice.

Any food which noticeably increases sex desire should be curtailed. Over-eating which results in a distended stomach and in food pressure being applied to the genitals should be discontinued. The time for taking meals should be adjusted so that food processing in the intestines does not interfere with resting of the body. Whatever improves the clarity of mind and fitness of the body should be adopted immediately.

In all respects, the ascetic should take control of his life. He should promptly adjust whatever will cause clarity of consciousness and the sorting of his gender category. Since the core-self is confused as to its identity, it should task itself for being patient while it investigates its true status. In so far as its identity is inflated, it must downsize to find what will be left after it sheds the facets of itself which were caused by its intellect and lifeforce.

Its sexual identity which is a composite based on suggestions and mock-ups done by the lifeforce and intellect should be segregated so that it can access what it truly is.

Food Pressure on Reproductive Organs

The ascetic should determine when to eat and what is the correct quantity. Food should not cause a distended stomach. It should not cause food weight pressure to be on the reproductive organs. Self-observation is necessary so that the ascetic can come to terms with counterproductive habits.

If during rest periods there is distention in the abdomen and pressure on the genitals that would cause excessive sexual thinking which will result in masturbation or sexual intercourse when otherwise that would not be required. Anything which aggravates sex desire, which artificially increases it, should be examined as to the cause and how to remove it.

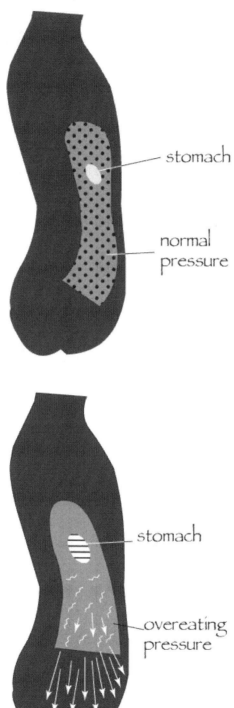

stomach

normal
pressure

stomach

overeating
pressure

Spices, Peppers, High Protein and Oil-Saturated Foods

An ascetic should use bland foods. He should avoid spices and peppers. Chemicals in spices are difficult to assess as to what they do in the body, as to if they interfere with the chemical composition of glands or if they enter the brain and affect nerve junctions and sensitive cells. Peppers are stimulants but they aggravate cell structures by chemical burning. Addiction to peppers is worse than addiction to sexual indulgence but peppers do prompt sex activity because the burning chemicals scorch the genitals and prompt memory of sexual activity.

High protein foods and oil-saturated preparations cause over production of reproduction hormones which in turn cause overwhelming sex urges which no one can resist. Monks who indulge are forced to masturbate but they must do so in private so that they are not discovered. Some adopt homosexual behavior even though they are not homosexual by nature. They do this to protect the monk status because if they procured heterosexual conduct they would lose their positions in the religious institution. The homosexual behavior is hidden. If it was known; that would cause disgrace for the monk order.

In one religious institution in which I served, some men who were not homosexual abused boys homosexually because they had access to the youths in the boarding school of the organization. If females were available they would not have done that. If they procured females publicly they would have lost seniority and saintly status.

Some individuals who become monks are homosexually-inclined and know that they are. Some of these are sincere in the desire to renounce sex interplay completely. However their aspirations have no power to rid them of the need for intercourse with persons of the same sex. Hence while in the monk order, they eventually procure some other monk as a sexual partner. They secretly break the vows. Many of these are never discovered.

Respect for the Digestive Organs

An ascetic should not distend the stomach and intestines by eating more than necessary. Even if one is circumstantially urged to overeat, one should study the situation and make plans to avoid it in the future. It may not be possible to refuse excessive food outright, because it depends on who offered the preparation. However as far as possible, a yogi should distance himself from situations in which one would be pressured to eat excessively.

Even dear friends, even fellow yogins, may encourage one to eat excessively. Thus one must somehow resist. It is best however if one does not live close to any relative, friend or religious associate who is addicted to overeating.

One should respect the digestive organs beginning with the stomach. One should eat as much as it would take not to get a distended stomach and stretched bloated intestines. When one overeats there is discomfort. One feels the stretched stomach, intestine, colon and abdomen. This recognition should be sufficient to alert that something was terribly wrong. One should adjust the behavior so as not to repeat this.

Night Eating Curtailed

A yogi should cease eating at night, but he may do so gradually until it ceases completely. It negatively affects meditation practice if the yogi eats late. It drastically reduces the rest period of the body. Anything which enters the stomach must be processed as soon as it gets in there. This is the natural way. A person's willpower has no effect over this. Digestion is controlled by involuntary impulses which are sent by the kundalini lifeforce.

Once food enters the stomach at night, the body will keep processing the matter until it reached the terminal of the intestinal track which is the bottom end of the colon. This means that some energy will be in use through the night for processing such food matter. This requires muscular actions to shift the food matter through the long winding intestines. This will negatively affect the sleep cycle of the physical body. It will rob the subtle body of energy which is required for objectivity during dreams.

It is important that an ascetic be objective in dream states, but if there is insufficient consciousness energy to support dream notation and memory, the ascetic will not derive the benefit. He will not remember dream events. He will not have objectivity during dream phases. This means that he will not track astral events and will be unable to sort what is imaginative astral states and what is astral reality. He will forget whole dreams and dream sequences. It will be to him as if there was no astral experience when such activity did occur in fact.

The ascetic should over time shift the eating habits so that the main meal is early in the day. This will allow for intestinal operations to be completed during daylight hours and in the early evening. This permits full rest of the digestive and excretory systems during the night. The lifeforce can then dedicate its energies to cell repair and organ readjustment. The astral body would have more consciousness allowing the yogi to make notation of astral experiences.

Food Movement during the Night

To streamline sexual energy, to remove all excess so that one can investigate the gender of the core-self, one has to terminate the excess and then sort the energy to identify the composites. The core-self is not the only contributor. It is not the most influential factor. Apart from ancestral presence, there are adjuncts which are native to the psyche. This psychic equipment must be accounted for.

The primary adjunct involved in reproduction and sexual expression is the kundalini lifeforce. This is not the only adjunct but it is the one which must be brought to order before the core-self can express some control over the current gender designation of the self. The present social gender, even if it reflects the actual gender of the core-self is an artificial mento-emotional construction. Eventually the core-self will eliminate it and adopt its real person-format.

For the time being however the kundalini has the most influence into what the psyche expresses as gender. This is true even if that expression runs contrary to its actual gender.

The kundalini operates on the basis of the evolutionary drive of the life form which it is aligned to. According to the stage of the life form, and according to its needs, the kundalini is induced and is given facility to develop a gender which is based on the current needs of that species. Kundalini is not free to do as it pleases but it seems to be independent when one cannot see that the individual kundalini is merely a micro-part of a larger lifeforce which is an entire species which evolves using available psychic energy.

To get a foothold on the activities of the kundalini one must first remove its excessive activities. Its energy expenditures must be reduced. Then the yogi can focus on the essentials.

Food excess should be eliminated but the reform should be done gradually. Late food eating which results in the intestines having to process food during the night should cease. These actions will free the kundalini from energy expenditure processing food during the night. The saved energy will be donated to the subtle body so that activities in dreams may be noted with more objectivity.

Lifeforce Expenditure

A yogi must study the lifeforce operations to determine how power from the core-self is seized for unnecessary operations which are due to some type of sensual greed. Any energy which the core-self must contribute affects the self's objectivity either to support, increase or decrease it.

If the lifeforce continues its independent decision-making, the core-self must fund the expenditures with the negative result of not being objective due to a lack of insight into kundalini's psychic actions. Food consumption is just one area of lifeforce decision-making which may negatively impact the self.

Food consumption concerns four areas of the body; the stomach, small intestines, colon and anus. A yogi must see to it that none of these organs are overtaxed by overeating or by eating at the wrong times.

Each yogi must decide what to do to achieve this. Without this the core-self will be taxed in excess for energy to maintain the inefficiency. This will result in lower levels of meditation which will negatively impact clarity of mind.

The stomach, mass of intestines and colon, the anus and the pubic floor of the body, come under excessive pressure if there is overeating. These parts of the body are also strained if there is eating at the wrong times. This activity causes the life-force to extract more energy than necessary from the core-self. This energy is passed to the lifeforce in the form of excess attention from the core self. This prevents deep meditation.

No yogi should buy into the philosophy that it does not matter what one does because one can transcend everything and reach higher levels during meditation. This is plain foolishness. Hatha yoga as it was taught by Gorakshnath Mahayogin includes methods for full reform of the kundalini's activity, and with good reason because even though the lifeforce psychic mechanism is not the core self, it is connected to the self in such a manner, that its activities must be sponsored by the self. This sponsorship is both time consuming and distracting for the self.

If the kundalini is not reformed, one cannot transcend its inefficiency. One will have to sponsor its mismanagement even during meditation practice. Hence it makes sense to take responsibility for its activities outright because one will have to pay for its mishaps any which way. That is enforced by the psychic material nature which will force one into situations where one must settle its accounts.

No yogi should be so dishonest as to sit in meditation after overeating and after eating at the wrong time, and then pretend that he is in the highest meditation and that his distended gut and the resulting pressures on the pubic floor has no effect on him.

Ignorance during Dream States

A simple test to see if a compacted gut affects the yogi, is the check on dream recall. Out of so many hours during sleep how many minutes of dream recall can the yogi honestly report?

In addition how much attention does the yogi have to place on the stomach and intestines because there is continuous peristaltic movement during the night as the muscles of the intestines move on and on?

A yogi must reduce these expenditures to the absolute minimum otherwise his meditation practice will never get to a deep level. He will remain forever a mediocre ascetic.

An example of this inefficiency is that if one eats a heavy meal in the afternoon, late afternoon, early evening or later, that food will move through the small intestines during the night. By mere willpower, a yogi cannot compel his body desists from processing this food. The processing is automatically done by involuntary actions within the body. These actions require some attention from the core-self which has to render that attention even if it does not desire to do so. One can use narcotic drugs to shut down the involuntary actions but that would be disadvantageous because such chemicals will impact meditation negatively.

After eating that heavy meal, the yogi's intestines and colon will be moving through the night. This involves movements of vast quantities of blood through the veins and arteries. Ultimately when that food moves down, it will produce a pressure on the lower abdomen and pubic floor. Any extra pressure on the pubic floor will cause the creation of thoughts which relates to urination, evacuation and sexual intercourse. There may be arousal of sexual urge leading to the need for sexual intercourse. This may result in masturbation and/or sexual contact with someone of the same or a different gender.

Fanatics think that it is all about reducing excess sexual stimulation and its resultant compulsions. It is not so. In fact the real energy drain, the real distraction to take into consideration, are the small leaks like for instance, thinking of food, thinking of the muscular actions of the intestines during the night. Such thoughts may be subconscious for the most part which makes them worse than consciously thinking of sexual intercourse. A big leak out of a tank is easy to discover as contrasted to a pin-leak which one is not aware of but which is continuous and undetected.

A sexual urge which arises from overeating or from eating at the wrong time, may be resolved quickly by a sexual intercourse which will be finished once one reaches the climax of the indulgence, while muscular actions in the colon for hours during sleep will be a continuous distraction which will negatively affect dream recall and psychic perception on the astral side of life.

Small Intestine Continuous Action

The small intestine has such a design, that it keeps squeezing and stretching as long as there is food matter in it. It does not relax until every bit of food passes to the large intestines. This means that if there is food matter in the small intestines during the night, it will keep a muscular movement for as long as it takes to get every bit of that food into the colon. That muscular activity requires energy which is supplied by the lifeforce with an interest from the core-self. This interest will be expressed even during sleep. Even if the core-self does not desire its interest to be involved in the digestive process, that interest will be invested because that is an involuntary action of the psyche. Because the core-self cannot terminate this involuntary digestive process at will, the only way to lift the interest is to be sure that during the night there is no food matter in the higher intestine.

It is not unusual for adults to eat a late meal, pass urine and stool if they can, retire to bed, rest a little while discussing the past day's activities, engage in sexual intercourse, then roll over in fatigue and fall asleep.

Much energy is expended during the intercourse but during the sleep phase thereafter, much more energy is given to the process of digestion as the small intestines and/or the colon operate the digestive process.

This causes a greater stupor during sleep but with pain interference which is due to the peristaltic movements of intestinal muscles. There is little or no recall of the astral activities, which means more or less that the person was unconscious or was sleep-walking on the astral planes. Periodically the person's awareness will shift back to the physical body, where the person will experience the discomfort which the physical body is in.

Kundalini Sensual Expression Compared

Kundalini is used for all sensual expression in the psyche and outside of the psyche. In all cases it is the same type of sensation activation but with differences in how the energy is consumed. There are three types of consumption denoted by whether there is exhaustion, neutrality or exhilaration occurring immediately after the sensations are climaxed.

All sensual expressions which terminate in exhaustion, require a restocking of hormonal energy to right the psyche. The most obvious examples are climatic sexual pleasure and drug-induced experience. These use vast amounts of stocked hormonal energy which are consumed to produce the pleasure or perception shifts (hallucinations). In sexual climax experience for instance, the energy is consumed so thoroughly that after the experience there is a depressed state due to lack of energy to maintain even ordinary mental focus. For the purpose of insight consciousness, this use of hormonal energy is discouraged.

Of course from nature's view point there is relief of the sex urge in this experience. There might be the benefit of creation of an embryo. Otherwise it is a wasteful act in terms of the depression which occurs immediately after the experience and which continues for a time but is unnoticed because of the stupor of the person concerned.

There are sensual energy experiences which do not consume the hormonal energy, where that energy is stirred just the same as like in sexual climax experience, and yet the energy is not consumed. Thus there is no exhaustion resulting. This type of experience happens when kundalini is aroused by yogic methods. The primary method for this is breath-infusion practice, where fresh air is compressed into the blood stream through the lungs. This energy surcharges the blood cells. This mix causes a neutral bliss energy to emanate from the cells but it does not consume away the hormonal force as in sexual pleasure operations.

Kundalini arousal by breath-infusion may also produce great exhilaration either on par with or superior to sex pleasure experience and without exhaustion resulting and with no loss of hormonal force. This type of experience comes with insight into the various regions and layouts of the subtle body and the discovery of various means of psychic perception.

Due to its depressive effects thereafter, sexual climax experience is discouraged in kundalini self-tantric. The operation of kundalini arousal using breath-infusion is preferred. It is not a moral issue. It does not involved social comparisons. It is a matter of gender discovery for the individual yogi. It is purely an energy observation and investigation into the best possible pleasure expression within the psyche.

Sexual Climax Trigger Compared

What is the difference between sensual pleasure with resulting exhaustion and such pleasure with resulting exhilaration? It is the way the energy is consumed, the method of generating the pleasure.

Sexual pleasure is generated by operating the touch sensation in the body. This may be done by imagination as well as by actual touching to certain parts of the body. When imagination is used, it stimulates the touch sensation. Sufficient stimulation of that causes the firing of sensation charges which results in the pleasure experience. Just as fuel is used to create fire, and just as the fuel is consumed in doing so, so the energy handled by the touch sensation is consumed in the sexual pleasure experience. Hence that energy cannot be used again because it is consumed in the process. This and this alone is why sexual climax experience is unsuitable for self-gender research.

The consumption of the energy causes a shortage of hormonal boosts in the psyche, which results in a shutdown of many energy operations. This is interpreted by the mind as fatigue. It causes mental stupor and tiredness. It deprives one of insight consciousness.

In contrast to generating this pleasure experience by operating the touch sensation primarily, in kundalini arousal practice using breath-infusion, the pleasure is produced by infusing fresh air breath energy into the hormonal energy. This causes that energy to be touched by the compressed fresh air, which results in pleasure expression, in exhilaration, without the consumption of the hormonal energy. When this experience occurs there is no exhaustion as the result. In fact there is more clarity of perception, more insight consciousness. This is why this method of pleasure generation is preferred.

Female Approach to Sexual Pleasure

The female approach to sexual pleasure is somewhat different to that of the male. This is due to the anatomy of the sexual organs in each case. However the exhaustion after going through a sex experience climax is common to both genders. The challenge is the same; that of achieving pleasure without having a resulting depression. This is achieved by infusing physical and subtle air energy into the psyche. The experience of getting bliss experience without a negative mood resulting is important as factual evidence that there are other types of pleasure which are not based on consumption of energy, where the energy involved expresses bliss feelings but is not consumed during the expression. This prepares the yogi for transit to higher worlds.

Pubic Floor Relief

The pubic floor of the body should not be stressed by overeating. The stomach should not be distended. The abdomen which contains the intestines and colon should not be overworked due to over-eating and eating at late hours. Any stress on the pubic floor may cause increase in sex desire which will cause increase in sex urge with the resulting activity and its depressive result. More serious are the increases in other less-obvious sensual activity like for instance increased snacking, increased thinking, increased focus into the gut because of excessive muscular action, increased unwanted association with persons who indulge in over-eating and decreased energy in the astral body because its allotment of consciousness is reduced as a result of the eating indulgences.

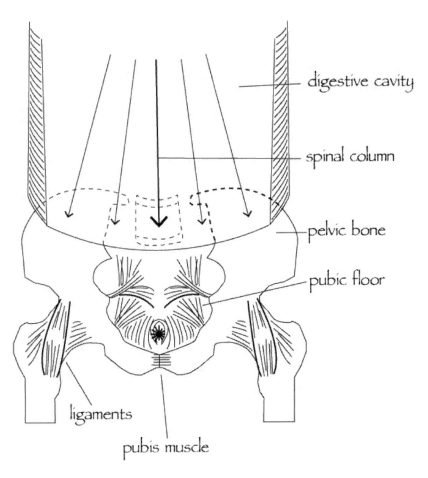

digestive cavity

spinal column

pelvic bone

pubic floor

ligaments

pubis muscle

For sure the pressure on the pubic floor is a material incidence but the cause of the pressure a psychological. This is why I am concerned about it for kundalini self-tantric practice. This pressure comes because of a lack of control of what goes into the mouth, as to the quality and quantity, as to the time of eating, as to the attention which must be invested in these operations and their resultant effects.

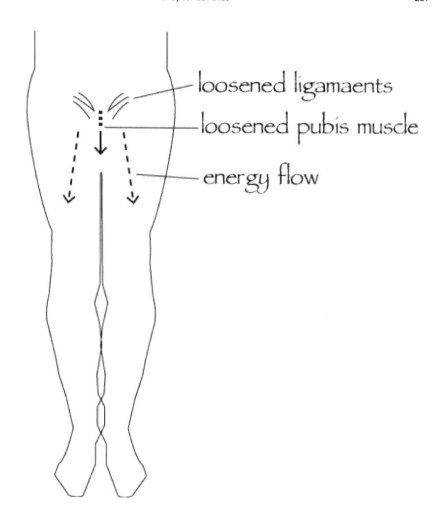

loosened ligamaents

loosened pubis muscle

energy flow

Muscular Lock of Perineum

Yoga celibate practice and dietary control protects the pubis muscle from stretching more than necessary. Inevitably that muscle will stretch at parturition when the mother's body delivers a baby. Otherwise that muscle should not be stretched by overeating and compacting of waste in the colon.

Celibate practice includes several muscular locks, one of which is mulabandha or the contraction of the perineum. That is contracted and pulled upwards into the body. When this practice becomes proficient, it stops energy from being expressed through the sex organ chakra. It restricts the sex chakra on the spine so that energy is not expressed into the genitals.

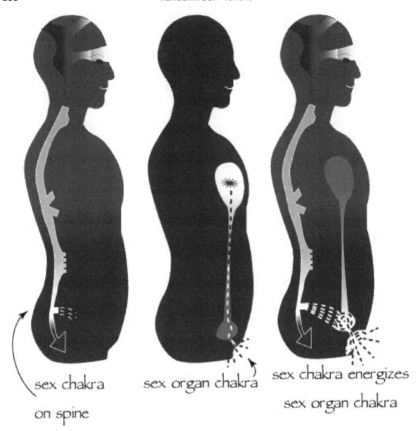

sex chakra   sex organ chakra   sex chakra energizes
on spine   sex organ chakra

The diet should be adjusted. The time of eating should be reformed, so that there is no undue pressure on the pubic floor. Besides pregnancy there is no favorable reason to have an extended abdomen and weight forcing down the pubic area. The bad habit will result in undue attention being given to that area. It will result in less psychic sensitivity, less recall of astral activities and more inner interference during meditation.

Waste Expulsion

Waste expulsion should be prompt. Stools should not linger in the colon and/or rectum. The evacuation of waste results in the removal of one's attention to such matter. Even though the person may have no objective awareness of it, the presence of waste in the colon and rectum is accompanied by the attention to those areas. This extra attention sabotages the meditation efforts because it decreases psychic insight and hampers recall of astral states.

Physical Operations for Digestion

For digestion food may remain in the stomach for one to three (1-3) hours or more before it is transferred to the small intestines. The transit through the long winding passage of the small intestines could take between three to nine (3-9) hours or more. This would mean a minimum of four (4) and a maximum of twelve (12) or more hours before entering the large intestines or colon. The stomach will not enter a state of relaxation except an hour or four after something solid was taken. Liquids are digested faster, especially water which is absorbed through the stomach walls.

Even water, a relatively neutral food, must be processed in the body and will pass through the kidneys sometime after it is taken. This is evidenced by observing men who drink beer, where they frequently void the liquid waste from the kidney in the form of urine. All of this requires attention from the core-self for processing. This negatively affects meditation. It increases attention to the physical side with a corresponding loss of perception of what happens on the psychic plane.

The muscular movements which take place during digestion should occur during the daylight hours for the most part. One should arrange meals to facilitate this. It should not be that one eats the main meal in the late afternoon or evening, because that would mean that during sleep, the stomach and the higher intestines would be operating muscular movements which would require attention from the core-self even during sleep when one should be attentive to astral matters.

If the abdomen has much activity during the night, that will result in less astral objectivity which will decrease psychic insight. That is undesirable. It is not simply a matter of willpower or desiring to be astrally aware. It is not a matter of making a decision to be conscious on the astral side. One has to reduce involuntary activities which sponsors physical awareness during sleep.

Chapter 14
Gender Confusion

Many Gender Configurations

As one moves through lifetimes in various species at various times and places, it is likely that one will assume different linear or complex gender configurations. Which one is the true social role?

It is understandable that in one life, one may be male, then in another female, then in yet another bisexual, then in another asexual. Who or what dictates which gender one will assume? Is the person capable of being every possible linear or complex gender?

Quirks of Destiny

The person is obviously the plaything of providence. Even if it wants to be male, female, neuter or bisexual, it is totally dependent on the facility provided by the psychic material nature. So much in the formation of a gender is dependent on hidden developments which takes place while the person's objectivity is suspended, where nature alone controls what the person will emerge as.

Why is it that someone who identifies as male finds itself to be a female body? Why does the converse happen? If indeed a person identifies as male and has a female body, what agency caused the mismatch? Why did nature not design the body to match the psychology?

Religious Principles

Each culture, ethnicity and religion has moral standards. Each modern government has secular laws. This does not take into account every variation of gender. For kundalini self-tantric, we dismiss the secular, cultural and religious moral codes because these render no clarification about the gender confusion.

Remember that whatever happens in this creation is a possibility of nature, irrespective of who is targeted, or who is the agency to bring it to fruition. An entity who uses a human body, which will last approximately one hundred years, is here after some thirteen billions years of development of the universe. Hence he cannot be the cause of what he does or what he is afflicted with.

A person with memory of only the present life, even if he had multiple past lives in the human and other species, cannot be held accountable for his activities in terms of being the ultimate cause. If anything he is a superficial agent. One who does what we consider to be right or wrong, cannot be the ultimate cause of his activities.

After becoming the body which was expelled from the mother's form, the person cannot be held as the cause of what that body is capable of. There is no sense in saying that after thirteen billion years, someone is born as a human, animal or less and that person is totally responsible for his or her behavior, or that person can make autonomous choices about what should or should not be done.

To get insight into the creation of simple or complex gender configurations, we must begin by considering that the human being cannot be the cause of his or her gender or the lack or confusion of it. We must accept that nature is the cause and that the individual is merely a rendition of one of nature's possibilities. This does not solve the social problems which society faces due to complexities of gender, but it is the truth nevertheless.

Some politicians are concerned with gender simplification of males and females and nothing besides. That would make management of human beings into a simple business for governments. However this is not the reality.

Parental Neglect

Some people feel that sexual orientation is developed during childhood mainly through parental influence or the lack of it. Irrespective of the childhood social pressures which cocoon someone into a specific gender identity, there must first be the potential for that in the psyche of the individual. No matter how much manure one puts on the roots of a plant, that cannot change the essential nature of the vegetation. That will not change the type of fruit which it produces. It could cause more luscious much bigger fruit but it cannot convert an apple into an orange.

We see that horticulturalists may use a lemon stalk as the base for an orange stem, where the produce are oranges with minor lemon tinge but we cannot produce an apple from that lemon base. Hence the possible expressions of a child must be there in its potential, regardless of the influences which prevail from parents, schools, friends, celebrities and media.

Internal Format ~ External Mismatch

Our lives are filled with internal/external mismatches but we ignore these and continue head on for simplicity sake and to decrease the uncertainly which may cripple our ability to function. In meditation however, a yogi should face the realities and not be afraid of discovering that he is on unsure footing or that he will be denied by nature. In a way if one is nothing, one has nothing to lose. If one is a little of something, one has very little to lose. If one has a big stake in this, being a good sport is the way to face misfortune.

It is about self-discovery, as to what is the truth under this. The face of the person, the external format of the body, may or may not match the internal situation. It may look male but it may feel female. It may be contrary. Nature may produce a female form which has for inners, a male profile. What then?

How would it be if we blamed the person for the appearance which nature produced for it, if that production was contrary to the person's gender? If a woman feels sexual love for a woman, what is the origin of that? Why has nature expressed that? Why did nature not prevent the production of that?

Management of Socially Disapproved Behaviors

For kundalini self-tantric, we are not concerned with management of socially-disapproved behaviors. Society has every right to monitor the social conduct of citizens but this does not change the internal profile, even though it may stifle expressions which run contrary to expectation.

Self-tantric means turning inward, facing the truth about the inners of the self and determining what is the underlying gender format. If it is male, so be it. If it is female so be it. If it is neuter, so be it. If it is androgynous, so be it. This does not mean that the ascetic should ignore society's requirements. In fact when dealing socially the ascetic would do well to comply as far as possible otherwise he or she or it may face unfavorable treatment.

What is discovered about one's gender has value in the long term even if one must act contrary for the sake of getting along with society's norms. What is discovered in meditation does not have to be used in the external social world. Its use is in the subtle dimensions where the remnant person-self will function after losing the physical body. Self-tantric is a private practice with hopes for expression elsewhere. The social environment of human beings will never accommodate every production which nature can render. The ascetic should not use his or her time, riling against the rules manufactured by the controlling human beings.

Reincarnation / a Necessary Premise

Reincarnation is a necessary premise in the self-tantric practice. At first it begins with a belief in the possibility of past and future lives. Deep introspection provides direct evidence of reincarnation but for the meditator alone not for anyone else. This experience may be termed as being subjective to physical perception but it is objective within the self.

During deep meditation a yogi will have experiences where he will discover the self to be a person whom one was in a past life, in specific important circumstances of that life. One will perceive others in the environment just as it was, but one will not see one's face, even though one may see the rest of one's body. There will be no mirrors where one can see one's facial features. Incidences experienced in this way will give the yogi insight into his identity, gender role and societal function in the past life.

A yogi will have predispositions towards others in the present life. When these feelings occur, if he is sensitive he will know what relationship he had with numerous persons whom he meets in the present life. This will be revealed to him within his psyche by the emotional and mental disposition which he feels as instinctual feelings towards other persons.

By repeatedly experiencing astral projection and studying dream states, a yogi will get to know what part of the psyche will survive the current physical body. With this experience one can understand how one came to identify with the current body which developed from being a sperm in the father's reproduction apparatus.

Conversion Flexibility of the Subtle Body

The subtle body is a flexible person-content container which can adjust to various specie-configurations and to as many gender variations as nature could produce. This means that just about anything is possible in terms of what the subtle body can adapt to and represent.

The core component which adapts is the kundalini lifeforce. There is a primary core-self in the psyche but that is not the change adapter. To understand the changes a yogi must study his kundalini in its aroused state. Then he will see the possibility and can abandon misconceptions about the potentials. Ideally the core-self should govern the behavior and inner alterations of the psyche but in general practice, this is not the case, for it is the kundalini which primarily governs emotional expressions. The kundalini manufactures variations in states of consciousness to which the core-self is subjected and corralled.

There are many influences which the kundalini takes into account. The primary ones are:
- Genetic information of the particular species
- Desire energy from past lives
- Schematic for physical survival of the species
- Schematic for survival of the subtle body which must transition to another form shortly

The **genetic information** of the particular species is carried in the physical body of living creature forms. For the higher species, the genetic code was developed over millions of year in the mundane evolutionary cycle. It influences the kundalini for its promotion through time. It does not yield to suggestions unless these are in line with its status and would promote or demote it along set lines of biological need.

The **desire energy from past lives** is carried in the subtle body as urges which influence the kundalini to take possession of opportunities which promise fulfillment. These energies may remain unfulfilled for millions of years. Some are altered because of partial fulfillment and feedback in the psyche which reformats them according to recent fulfillment attempts.

The **schematic for species survival** is carried in the cosmic reservoir of energy. From there it becomes divested wherever physical life can be manifested. The subtle forms of the entities occur according to their evolutionary development. These forms become attracted to the psychic creature form potentials. By that alliance physical forms manifest.

The **subtle body also has a schematic** for its survival. It will survive for billions of years but still it will be finished when the subtle energy in the universe collapses in on itself. The subtle body is also obsessed with permanence which is something it cannot attain fully because the psychic material nature is endlessly mutable. The subtle body wants to have permanence. This is why it is drawn into the course for creating the low vibration physical forms, one after the other.

Evolutionary-Acquired Tendencies Asserted

As one transmigrates through various species, over millions of years in the progression of the universe, one acquires tendencies which were native to the specific life forms. These habits cannot be dismissed by desire or willpower actions. The core-self carries these inclinations like barnacles on the back of the whale or bacterial infections in the body of a mammal.

Through meditation, a yogi can discover these tendencies and work on the psychological level to neutralize them. The turn of gender, the way it is manifested, varies from species to species. As such the investigation into the self's gender-identity, means sorting gender feelings and behaviors which were imported into the psyche as it transmigrated through numerous species. What is left after cataloging the gender displays which were acted out because of compelling influences? Who is the core-self in its bare gender definition?

The imprints from various species of life are not present as an objective record of the infestations. The yogi discovers them as subtle subconscious imprints with the potential for forcing the self to act out linear and complex gender roles. The investigation is a search through abstract energy.

Transmigration is Bewildering

Transmigrations even within the same species, even within the same family, is a complex set of abstract movements which are bewildering to the core-self. The psychic material nature makes these movements and the core-self is subjected to them irrespective of if it wants to be traumatized. Some phases of the operation are done within the observing ability of the self but much of it is so abstract as to be non-actions to the self because of the self's inability to comprehend subconscious and unconscious movements.

Even if the person moves from a body in one human family to another body as a relative of the same family, the core-self is unable to track every movement. Instead it shifts involuntarily from stage to stage, some conscious, some unconscious and some subconscious. These psychic movements which are followed by physical changes, occur with or without the core-self's cooperation.

It is ludicrous that religious and social leaders project the idea the person-self can in one life, change his abstract nature, his unconscious and subconscious motivation, by a simplistic religious formula which is nothing but a cosmetic treatment.

It would require deep meditation over many lives, before a yogi can even conceive of the powers which motivate the self's behaviors, what to speak of eliminating such energies, much of which is not visible to the self. For self-tantric, one must move aside from religious oversimplification and tackle this bewildering and knotty complex head on.

Gender Discontent

A person who is dissatisfied with the gender of his or her body, who feels that he or she should be the opposite sex or should be of a neuter orientation may have a valid grievance or be mistaken. In that case, when investigating self-gender, one should consider these aspects:

- Gender of the isolated core-self
- Acquired subtle gender configuration while transmigrating
- Biological gender of the present body

The **gender of the isolated core-self** is the most abstract realization which the yogi could determine. At first he will not figure this because it is too subtle to know. He would have to objectivize the adjuncts like the sense of identity, intellect and kundalini lifeforce. Of these the most subtle is the sense of identity. It takes many lives of meditation for a yogi to achieve the required subtlety to read into the abstract parts of his psychic nature.

The **subtle gender configuration** the yogi currently has is the state of his subtle body's sexual orientation. This is a complexity which shows as a male, female, neuter or androgynous being based on many bewildering formats from countless past lives. Modern astronomers estimate this universe to be about 13 billion years in the making. Assuming that the subtle body was existing since the beginning of this cosmic time, the amount of lives one self used would be countless. It could mean that any gender configuration which the subtle body expresses is actually a complexity even though it appears or feels as a something as simple as male, female, neuter or androgynous. The task of sorting this is tremendous. One would have to be a super-yogi, a siddha perfected being, to self-clarify this.

The **biological gender** of the present body is to an extent obvious. However there are cases where infants are born with male and female organs or with the absence of either. Why does this happen?

If I am born with a male body, and feel myself to be a female or neuter being, how do I reconcile that? Should I live and function as a male even though it is contrary to my feelings? Before the modern era, many persons did just that. They were circumstantially forced to do so because of pressing social mores which were enforced even by threat of death.

But what would be done by a self-tantric yogi to solve his dilemma if indeed he was born with a male body but felt female or neuter?

In that case he would begin the investigation with the clear cut very obvious factor which is the male body. He should try to get a clear cut definition of what that male body is in regards to what material nature intended for it to be. For this investigation he may have to function as a male in a heterosexual or homosexual relationship according to his orientation and by whatever opportunities he finds himself to be in.

Viewing the experiences objectively, not trying to enjoy them, allowing the pleasure in them to happen without craving these, he should study the function of his body and how nature uses it. Being satisfied to see what the male body is capable of, he should form conclusions about the advantages and disadvantages of that gender. With this information he should move inwards to investigate the more complex issue which is the gender configuration he acquired in many previous births.

While transmigrating, one may gain a result which is quite different to what one experiences most of the time. One who has a certain gender of subtle body may have had the opposite gender in the past life. We cannot assume that a certain gender of the subtle body means that during the transmigrations that person always had that sexual orientation.

The research into the gender orientation of the subtle body takes years of meditation sensitivity to determine how the person assumed the present body on the basis of a series of similar or dissimilar subtle body orientations.

Birth Environment

The birth environment which is a combination of the father, mother and others may be a primary influence in the gender of the body or in the gender preference which is different to that of the body. A child with a male body, may become so attached to its mother that the child mimics the mother's attitudes, moods and postures. After sexual maturity when the maleness of the child's body becomes very evident, the psychological absorption may cause the child to be at odds with the physical needs of its body.

It could happen that when it enters its would-be parent's environment, a deceased person with a male profile is influenced to adopt the female gender. Its subtle body may molt into a female configuration, but its physical form may assume a male profile due to fated genetic influences which persists on its own.

Species Adaptation

The core-self can adapt to any life form but each is limited according to the sensual and motor facilities the form affords. Some lower species have one or more superior sensual or motor skills. Overall the human species has the most advanced performance equipment.

This causes the human to experiment with its sensuality and motor abilities but with the risk of developing habits which may cause descent into lower species. In so far as a behavior mimics the specialty of a lower species, its use may cause the psyche to mutate to that lower form? When transmigrating some routes go from a lower species to a higher one or from one species to the same type but there can be reversals from a higher species to a lower one.

Changing of Gender in the Same Body

Modern medical techniques allow someone to change the gender of the body. Surgeons can remove a male organ and design apparent female entry instead. Female ones can be sealed and apparent male appendages added. As medical science advances, this will become more commonplace.

The use of hormone therapy allows persons whose bodies are male to feel female. This provides relief for persons who report that their psychology is female which makes the male body contrary to their emotional states. Those whose bodies are female and who have male moods may use hormone therapy to switch their female body feelings to that of a male.

Sex Change in Puranic Literature

In the Puranic literature, there are examples of persons who had sex changes. One history is that of King Shudyuman. He was the son of Manu. Shudyuman was to be a male child but due to a mistake in the parental request, it happened to be a female child. This was because the father's desire for a son was superseded by the mother's for a daughter. The departed soul who was to be Shudyuman had a male gender designation of subtle body but by the influence of the mother, this gender did not prevail. The result was that a male departed soul was born as a female baby.

After this male person was born as a female, the father consulted the mystic priest who conducted the conception ceremony. The priest explained that one of his assistants was influenced by the mother to format a daughter instead. Manu then asked the priest if there was no possibility of reversing the child's gender. The priest petitioned a deity and the body of the infant changed to that of a male child.

As fate would have it, after this child grew up, he became the king. Once this King Shudyuman rode on horseback and entered into an enchanted forest. As soon as he entered his gender changed to that of a sexually-mature female. There were ministers and officials with him. It happened to each of them. The stallions they rode also experienced the gender change. This place was enchanted by the Goddess Durga, the personification of material nature.

King Shudyuman was born as a girl named Ila. His infant body was female but his subtle body was that of a male. At the request of his father, a magical priest changed the female infant into a male. Later in his adult life, Shudyuman experienced a sex change where his body reverted to female.

When this happened, the king was surprised to experience it. Soon after, as a beautiful woman, she fell in love with a man named Budha. She had a child for that man. Later this transformed woman appealed to a mystic priest to change the female body to a male one. The motive was that she could not function as a king while using a female form. The mystic said he would assist but with the condition that Shudyuman would be a man for a month and then a woman for a month alternating.

This is a case of a person experiencing the full range of male experience for one month and then experiencing that of female for the next month. This is rare because that person was put in a position to objectively compare the facilities offered to each.

But this person's subtle body had a male designation. If we catalog this we still could not determine the gender of the core-self of this person, because a male subtle body does not prove that the person is male as a core-self.

A male subtle body, does not prove that the subtle body is actually male either because that configuration may be due to pressures applied to the subtle body while it transmigrated.

Affection is Convertible

Affection which is the lubricant of positive relationships is convertible. This is why liking a person may vary from one type of feeling to another, from a neutral emotion to a loving one or from an endearing mood to indifference.

The investigation into self-tantric roots up the expressions of affection to find the underlying basic feeling which ultimately sponsors the variations. From one mood to another, which relationship is the source feeling?

Social morality is applicable when it is supported by the society which surrounds the individual. As soon as those props are absent, things change, where in one life one may be the brother of someone and in the next life the spouse of that person. Which of these relationships is the underlying one?

Displeasure is the reverse of affection. For those who enjoy tension it is the choice lubricant. For those who detest conflict it is an obstructive material.

Gender Neutrality

Unless the core-self is completely segregated from its adjuncts, especially from the kundalini life force, that self cannot realize its gender. In combination with the kundalini life force the core-self assumes the gender configuration of the life force even though this design changes from time to time. It changes when the core-self is in a non-observational position. The self has no leverage in the matter and must comply with the development. This means that the self may be in a neuter, male, female, bisexual or any combination or alteration of gender.

It stands to reason that if the self can assume any simple, altered or combined gender or alteration or combination of gender, then it must be neutral to the core. However this line of reasoning has no value in this discussion. The psychic material nature may or may not override the base-gender of the self. One cannot assume anything about the base-gender on the basis of the self's assumption of a sexual configuration which is drummed up by material nature.

The only thing we know for sure about the self, is that its energies are used in the operations of the life-force. It does not have to be neutral to sponsor the behavior of the kundalini.

Chapter 15
Core-Self Segregation

Duality as a Permanent Reality

Duality which means that the core-self should develop itself and simultaneously aid in the development of material nature, is a permanent challenge for any yogi. In one consideration subscribing to material nature is for the most part against the core-self. In another view, the effort to isolate and see to the needs of the self is permitted only in a limited way within material nature. This means that to an extent the core-self must comply with material nature and simultaneously see to the self's interest.

There is no choice in the matter because currently the core-self does not have the power to extract itself fully. The psychic material nature in the form of the personal kundalini lifeforce clings to the core-self the way a leech clings to a mammal it encounters. Removing this parasite will not be easy. In the meantime, the core-self must serve some needs of the material nature and simultaneously pursue its own interest.

In terms of gender, this means that the self must be what nature stipulates by genetic design and it should simultaneously research its actual gender which is apart from the expressions which come out of the kundalini physical life-force. Only very deep meditation can give the required insight.

Reducing Media Influence

A yogi must reduce media influence, so that his psyche is not forced to live out gender designations and roles which are suggested through the viewing of videos, photos, art, literature and music. Self-gender investigation concerns the bare core-self with reference to the influence of its adjuncts. If there are fresh inputs from media, the research will be more complicated. It will take a longer period of time to complete.

The yogi already has trillions of sensual impressions which are logged in memory. These will assail him to become the gender configurations which were lodged in his consciousness in the past. He does not need to add more impressions.

To activate the past impressions, the yogi should meditate. This will allow even the subconscious memories to percolate into mento-emotional feelings and visions which the yogi can sort and then eliminate. In time the yogi will tap into the gender of the bare core-self.

Kundalini Lifeforce as Repository of Tendencies

The kundalini lifeforce which one has in this life, was the same energy repository which one had in previous lives during the development of this universe. It will remain with the particular self for the duration of universal time. This means that all tendencies exhibited by that lifeforce are present in it at all times. Its full potential is present as well. According to the time and place, a tendency may be manifested. In this respect there is no good or bad behaviors, no right or wrong ones. All tendencies, the desirable and unpleasant ones are part of the gamut of possibilities.

By shifting the psyche to a higher level of existence, the yogi limits what expressions the kundalini can exhibit and what potentials it can aspire towards. He may go to a realm in which there are no undesirable experiences merely because in that place such displays do not occur.

Limitless Expression of Sexual Variation

The kundalini psychic lifeforce is capable of limitless expression of sexual variation in different degrees and combinations of gender. This begs the question as to which one is the true one for a particular core-self. Does the kundalini mirror the gender of the self? Which of the kundalini's expression is the mirror image of the sexuality of the self?

For self-tantric, the yogi must segment the core-self from its psychic adjuncts, the kundalini being one of these operations. Unless the self is segregated it cannot determine its gender. Otherwise it will identify with the variations which the kundalini creates, feeling it is this, then it is that and then again it is some other male, female, androgynous or neuter being.

Core-Self Struggles to Isolate Itself

Because of the adhesive power in the psyche, the core-self will struggle to separate itself from its adjuncts. Each self must execute mystic actions to free itself so that it can experience itself apart from the adjuncts. At first this will be an experience of itself with reduced influence from the adjuncts.

The kundalini psychic lifeforce permeates the psyche such that the core-self is boxed in by it and must withdraw itself from the sensual addictions before it can get an idea of a differentiation between itself and the adjuncts.

By itself, does the self experience itself as a certain gender? Is the self-confused by the gender configurations which are produced by the kundalini lifeforce, where that self cannot free itself due to being sensually hypnotized?

Core-Self Segregation from the Supernatural Sociology

In a local sense, the heart of the problem of self-gender may be solved if the self isolates itself from its adjuncts. However because the self is limited, this segregation may reveal to it, a new complexity which is that there is a supernatural sociology which has an impacting influence.

When all is said and done, when the yogi manages to isolate the core-self from its adjuncts, he or she will face the supernatural community to determine its requirements and influences.

Because the self with adjuncts or the self without adjuncts is not an absolute unto itself, it must take into account supernatural influences which over-ride even its basic gender configuration.

If we begin with a neuter self which comes in the range of influence of the psychic material nature, that neuter person may find itself to be something other than neuter. The same would occur, if the self were to part away from the psychic material nature and absorb the influence of a supernatural community, which was outside of the influence of material nature. The self is left as something for adaptation, either to the psychic material nature or to something higher.

The Investigation

The investigation into self-gender has three major phases with many minor researches throughout. The major ones are:

- Parting the core-self from its adjuncts
- Becoming stabilized in the segregated core-self
- Facing supernatural influences which are beyond the psychic material nature from which the adjuncts emerged

The task of **parting the core-self from its adjuncts** is achieved through yogic meditation. The yogi must first turn the psyche inwards, damping down on its extrovert tendencies. There are various ways of achieving this but the yogic procedure is to use asana postures and pranayama breath-infusion which is followed by pratyahar sensual energy withdrawal. Postures and breath-infusion accelerate the effort to internalize the interest of the self but some ascetics make the effort without doing postures or breath-energization.

When the psyche is internalized enough, it develops an interest in its inners. This leads to clarity where the unified subtle self is realized as a core-self with adjuncts. The adjuncts are:

- Sense of identity
- Intellect which thinks and imagines
- Kundalini lifeforce with senses outlay

- Memories which are compressed experience-information

Becoming stabilized in the segregated core-self makes it possible to sort the core-self from its adjuncts. Once the self realizes itself in segregation, it may plan to reduce the influence of the adjuncts. This leads to proficiency in silencing the adjuncts. The core-self can then spend time alone (kaivalyam) to get used to being itself without adjuncts.

Many years of meditation are required before the self can **become stabilized as the segregated self**. When this is achieved, the self may study its gender and check to see how its base energy is used by the kundalini lifeforce to create other gender configurations, some of which are similar to that of the core-self and others which are vastly different.

After it segregates itself from its adjuncts and has discovered its bare gender, the core-self must turn to **face supernatural influences which are beyond the psychic material nature**. The realization about self-gender, the freedom to be alone without the adjuncts, does not turn the limited self into an unlimited absolute feature. In fact the clarity the ascetic gains from discovering its self-gender, reveals through insight consciousness that the self has to adjust to deity influences. It needs a relationship with the deity to whom it is attracted.

Ancestor Use of Gender Potential

Spirituality aside, species life in material existence has survival and reproduction of life forms as the priority. No matter what the ascetic realizes, no matter his level of gender differentiation, there is ancestral pressure which bears down on every side. That influence is ever present.

The aspirations of the core-self which run contrary to the needs of its adjuncts cannot override every contrary behavior of the body. The body was created by and in material nature with intentions which have nothing to do with the highest desires of the self. This means that the self cannot make the body serve in every respect. There will be occasions when the body will act to the contrary.

To be honest, the yogi must be aware of this and simultaneously pursue the discovery of core-gender. This means that one may have to serve the gender purpose of the current body. Doing so should not deter the internal investigation. The question remains as to who owns the body. Who can compel the body to act in a detrimental or beneficial way?

Is the body the exclusive property of the yogi? Do the ancestors have the right to force the body into contrary behavior? How does the ascetic proceed with gender investigation while simultaneously managing contrary behavior of the body?

The ascetic notes when the body act in manners which run contrary to the interest of self-discovery. This is a list of influences which prevail on the body:

- The body's genetic disposition
- The body's ancestral influence
- The adjuncts' influences
- The social absorption
- The core-self's enforcement
- The susceptibility to a deity

The **physical body's genetic disposition** is so powerful that it may force the body to act in a way which is the opposite of the core-self's base-gender. Suppose the ascetic accurately determines that he or she is a female gender to the core, then this does not mean that the physical body used is female necessarily. It may be male. In that case the genetic influence of the body will force it to operate in masculinity. This will continue at least until the physical body dies. Then however the subtle body may continue to mimic this other behavior.

The **physical body's ancestral influence** may force it to act in a gender role which is in opposition to that of the core-self. Suppose the core self is neuter to the core, then it might find that its body acts as male or female as dictated by ancestral influence. We observed where male goats who would normally mount nanny goats, ride the buttocks of other male goats and masturbate. This happens when there are no accommodating female goats available. This homosexual behavior is driven by ancestral needs which motivate the male goats to ejaculate sexual fluids.

The **adjuncts' influences** may force the body to act in a way that is contrary to the core-self's gender. Any of the adjuncts or a combination of two or more may cause an undesirable behavior. The sense of identity when it comes under the influence of any other adjuncts may reinforce that other influence, forcing the body to act in a contrary way. The intellect when it is charmed by sensations may overpower the psyche and cause it to act in a contrary way. The kundalini psychic lifeforce when it is empowered by nutrition may overcome the psyche and cause it to act for reproducing the species.

The **social absorption of influences** from other bodies may cause the sensual energy in the psyche to demand that the body act in a way which is contrary to the core-self. This can be resisted on some occasions but not in all.

The **core-self's enforcement** of its desire to be its basic gender may cause the body to exhibit a behavior which is consistent. This will happen on occasion but not in every case. The body has priorities. It has the ability to be resistant to the needs of the self. The self must reserve itself so that if it gets the opportunity, it can relocated out of the psychic material nature into a dimension in which its true gender is expressed as its total self.

The **susceptibility to a deity** may cause the body to act in a way which is different to anything the self or its adjuncts may dictate. This will happen if the deity's influence is expressed directly on the psyche. The yogi should have sufficient insight to know when the psyche is commandeered by a deity.

Ultimately for the purpose of self-gender, the yogi should be happy in discovering the true gender and in knowing the influence of a deity which alters the gender to facilitate divine relationship. This deity influence is a fantastic bliss rendering experience.

Ancestral Possession of a Descendant

It is imperative that a yogi should study how from a disembodied state one acquires an embryo. What is the view in the hereafter when one first makes contact with potential parents? Should the ascetic wait until he becomes deceased to know this?

Splitting off from the adjuncts includes understanding how they function both while one has a physical form and when that form is no longer available. By isolating the core-self during meditation, the ascetic may curtail other influences. Yet, he must also develop insight into how the adjuncts execute their compulsions. If the ascetic fails to perceive how the adjuncts carry out their behests, he will be unable to stop the operations. Recognition of the movements of the adjuncts during their early stages is paramount in the quest to shut down their operations.

The adept must also perceive the various alliances formed by two or more adjuncts when they reinforce one another and thus form a conspiracy which the core-self is powerless to stop. By understanding every detail of how the energies are initiated, developed and expressed, the ascetic would have the ability to shut down most of the unwanted features. Those which he cannot stop, which are destined to occur come what may, will not suppress his insight if he can perceive their initiation, development and expression.

Enjoyment as Flow of Affection through Gender

One of the most baffling experiences to dissect is enjoyment. If it is intense and blissful, it is near impossible to analyze. In fact enjoyment has within it a discouraging energy which causes a lack of investigative concern. It dampens any tendency for analysis. It promotes a lack of objectivity.

The flow of affection is experienced as enjoyment. It has many formats one of which is gender. Usually a human being cannot be discriminant when he or she experiences intense pleasure. For discovering the self's gender, one must sort between the base gender, the affection, the source and target of a flow. The ascetic may simultaneously experience the enjoyment and be insightful about its constituents.

Sex Organs in Gender Research

Though prominent in sex experience, the sex organs have little importance in gender research. For this we are concerned with the whole being not with its sexual focus. This research is more about introspection into gender and less about sexual expression. If the organs are involved in this research, partners will be useful but that is not the aim of this practice. This is an investigation about the base-gender of the core-self. This is not about having or not having a partner. It is about turning inwards, flashing off the adjuncts, experiencing the isolated core-self and determining gender profile or the lack thereof.

If a deity is evident after the base-gender is realized for the isolated, non-partnered self, then the self should observe what develops as the new gender face. But that will occur in a spiritual dimension, on the other side of the psychic material nature, not here in the astral existence which one experiences in dreams.

Sexual Pleasure is an Expression of Gender

One convention is that sexual pleasure is at the heart of failure to achieve freedom from rebirth. This is because indulgence is the main vice for a human being. It is the most intense biological pleasure.

However, despite the alarm about sex, it is still not the source of the need for rebirth. Sex is an expression for gender and so are many other features of relationship. Pleasure is a complex array of energies which the ascetic should sort to see the parts and their sources.

Gender research is the object of this inquiry because gender is the source from which relationships and potentials are formed. The ascetic should meditate going back into the source core-self. This is much further than its pleasurable or undesirable expressions.

Gender is not sex pleasure

Even though sex pleasure is an aspect in its own right, it is not the source of gender. It is an outcome from gender, just as a mango pulp is a production which forms after planting a mango seed. A study of the pulp, no matter how detailed will give very little information about the seed.

To understand the self, one must leave aside its expressions and its involvements in the expressions of its adjuncts. The study of a mango seed is a world apart from the study of flavors in mango pulp. Indulging in mango eating, or not indulging, does not give insight into the mango seed.

An occupation or aversion with sex pleasure will not give insight into gender. It is a fact however that those who are spell-bound by sex pleasure cannot complete the investigation into gender. Their occupation with the pleasure deprives them of the interest into the gender. These persons will mistake the format of pleasure as the gender.

For one who abhors the pleasure, he will not have the power to research the gender. In the effort to comprehend gender he will at some stage be confronted with the pleasure and must face it head on to get to its sources. This does not mean indulgence with a partner. It involves self-study with or without a partner.

Sex Pleasure is a Composite Energy

The interpretation of sex stimulation and indulgence as a pleasure source is a free conclusion afforded to human beings. Free as it is, it is untrue. Why would nature indulge us with fibs? Who knows?

Some ascetics are of the opinion that dual tantric practice with sex indulgence will clear up the issue as to the composite parts of sexual pleasure. These yogis are fools. The best method of researching sexual pleasure is not indulgence with a partner but rather, observation of the composite parts of the most minute slightest sex urge which arises in the psyche of the investigator.

As soon as there is partner involvements, its gets so complicated that it is near impossible to gain insight. Each partner is himself or herself a composite. That alone destroys any idea about singular celibacy through social behavior.

There is no one person in the psyche of a sex indulgent person. Others are present in that single psyche. The only thing single about it is the fact that it is one psyche or one psychic housing compartment. Besides that there must be more than one core-self in the subtle form. The investigation must admit this initially.

Sex Climax Trigger

The sex climax trigger is an electrical mechanism but it is so designed and the core-self is so situated in reference to it, that the self regards the trigger and its electrical spread of energy, as pure pleasure. The climax experience is so dominant over the core-self that it has difficulty sorting the energies. The self mistakes the pleasure as enjoyment.

After much meditation, after isolating the core-self from its adjuncts, especially from the sensual range of the kundalini lifeforce, it becomes possible to objectively regard these electrical experiences to gain the insight into how they can be interpreted as sensual pleasure.

The conversion of a bio-electrical experience into being a bliss pleasure is done by the connecting medium between the kundalini sensuality and the core-self. This linkage is the buddhi intellect analytical mechanism. Meditation is the method for perceiving how this operates.

From the conventional perspective, it will still remain a pleasure experience even for the yogi but he will have the additional insight which will afford objectivity during the occurrence. He will be simultaneously experiencing it as a pleasure and as merely a bio-electrical charge of energy.

When a certified mechanic drives a car, he experiences the ride just as any non-mechanic would but he also has more insight into exactly how the vehicle operates. In one way he is similar to a normal driver, but from another perspective he does not identify with the convenience of the vehicle.

Sexual Exposure Reduces Introspection

To discover one's base-gender much introspection is required. Any object or activity which causes a reduction in introspection, and which invests the self into what is external to its core, is counterproductive to core-gender research.

Sexual exposure can result in internalization either for the exposed person or for the victim. However this type of internalization supports viewing the experience as pleasure and not as a research into self-gender. Such experience does not award objectivity to the core self. Instead it leaves the self as an involver with no insight into the constituent parts of the experience.

Core-Self Stripped of Adjuncts

When the core-self is stripped of adjuncts, it is likely to discover itself as being gender-neutral. This does not permanently free it from other influences. As soon as the meditation is over, the self will again have to accept suggestions of the adjuncts. It will again come to identity itself with the sensuality of the kundalini psychic lifeforce.

However when the self is in a meditative state, where it experiences itself as being distinct from its adjuncts, it can gain insight into its spiritual gender potential, as to whether its neutrality may be expressed as male or female and whether this development happens because of the proximity of a deity, a person-God who is the hub of relationships.

How will the neutral self convert into being male or female in association with a deity and in an environment where the adjuncts are no longer present to express an influence for this or that gender?

Change of Gender

There is history of persons changing from one gender to the next during the lifetime of one physical body. Modern medical procedures and hormonal treatments demonstrate this. There is history in the Puranas and in some other ancient texts of change in gender over the use of more than one body, whereby in one life a person is one gender, and then in another that person is in the opposite or some other classification.

This may suggest that for some the psyche has the possibility of any gender. The word psyche however does not mean one psychic existential factor. This is because there is a core-self, a sense of identity, an intellect, a kundalini lifeforce, actuating memories and focal and unfocal sensuality in a psyche. Each psyche may be influenced by some other psyche but in addition each psyche has components.

When the psyche assumes a gender configuration that does not mean that the core-self is actually that lifeform. It does however mean that the self will be subjected to the experiences which that form exhibits.

Each gender exhibition is a complexity. None of it is a simple mix of influences and energies. For instance in a childhood body, there is little or no access to the sexual memories. This means that even if the person used a specific gender of the body before, it cannot recall that past experience. It cannot access memories which would consciously affirm or deny that sexuality. It may be influenced to react according to subconscious memories but those would be involuntary instincts.

Due to the length of time this universe was being displayed, (thirteen billion years), we can assume that there cannot be an original or first gender configuration for anyone at this time. Each person must display genders which are affected by memories of the past. None of this is original but the loss of memory makes it appear to be newly created formats.

Core-Self Gender Undisplayed Here

The core-self's gender cannot be displayed in the physical or psychic material creation. This variety-world is separate from the spiritual level where the core-self could exhibit itself without being a power supply for adjuncts. This information however does not free the self from being involved in gender displays here. It may motivate the self to endeavor for transfer to the spiritual plane. This spiritual level is not the psychic energy. It is not the subtle world in which our dream and fantasy bodies function.

From these physical and psychic planes the core-self can learn much about gender potential and expression. That information is useful in giving the hint about gender and relationship. It will not show the spiritual relationship which the self may have if it is translated to the spiritual level. It will however make the self understand that gender and relationship will be experienced if the translation happened. Still the self should not indulge in speculation or wishful thinking. It should patiently wait in meditation for revelation.

There is no need to think about what one's gender would be in a purely spiritual world. There is no need to imagine what it should be. There is no need to wish that it be this or that gender. One should meditate and wait for revelation. Attempts to determine the spiritual gender before it is revealed contribute to a greater delay in the revelation.

Physical Gender Potential of the Next Body

A yogi should always aim to cultivate habits which are in line with what he or she would prefer in the next body. Some say that the yogi should not plan to have another material form. Hence he should not harbor conceptions about what type of physical body he may have after the present one. However to be realistic, I recommend that a yogi should cultivate habits which are conducive to taking the next body with a gender which is agreeable.

The next physical body is not based on the present physical form but on tendencies which the subtle form retains as content. Some tendencies were developed in the present body. Some were adopted from past physical forms. Since a limited being cannot stipulate what his next body will be, one cannot know for sure how one will be positioned by fate. Nevertheless, one should adopt a lifestyle which is supportive of the type of gender one prefers. All the same in meditation one should know that the gender of the core-self is not determined by anything on this side of existence. It will be based on energies from the exclusive spiritual plane.

A yogi should simultaneously be reserved and open-minded about spiritual gender, while being selective about subtle body sex configuration. Both outlooks are necessary for success in maneuvering through material existence and being prepared for spiritual translation.

It is not a matter of becoming a celibate because that is meaningless except for beings who are absolute and who can command what the psychic material nature will do. A yogi should be prepared to be sexually involved because participation in the reproductive process is necessary if one will take a new body. A celibate cannot get a new body without being involved in the sexual energy of the potential parents. Hence one should not be foolishly idealistic, pretending that one can be totally aloof from sexual engagement.

This does not mean that the ascetic should crave sexual connections. In fact the ascetic must practice kundalini self-tantric for discovering the gender of the bare core-self. That practice does not involve a partner. One cannot get the insight through sex involvements. It can only be done in deep meditation.

Subtle Body Features

The subtle body is very important for a yogi. The physical body is only problematic because some of its features may affect the subtle one. The physical form can influence what the subtle body will do even after the subtle one leaves the physical one at death. This is why it is important to track and reform the subtle body's behavior in dreams experiences.

The idea that the subtle body does not matter, just as the physical one is irrelevant to the spiritual aspects of the self, is not ascribed in this book. A yogi must take the subtle body seriously because that is the medium through which he will transmigrate to some other subtle existence and also back into physical history according to the decree of fate.

There are verses in the Bhagavad Gita which should be considered:

ममैवांशो जीवलोके

जीवभूतः सनातनः ।

मनःषष्ठानीन्द्रियाणि

प्रकृतिस्थानि कर्षति ॥ १५.७ ॥

mamaivāṁśo jīvaloke
jīvabhūtaḥ sanātanaḥ
manaḥṣaṣṭhānīndriyāṇi
prakṛtisthāni karṣati (15.7)

mamaivāṁśaḥ = mama — my + eva — indeed + aṁśaḥ — partner; jīvaloke = jīva — individualized conditioned being + loke — in the world; jīvabhūtaḥ individual soul; sanātanaḥ — eternal; manaḥ — mind; ṣaṣṭhānīndriyāṇi = saṣṭhāni — sixth + indriyāṇi — sense, detection device; prakṛtisthāni — mundane; karṣati — draws

My partner is in this world of individualized conditioned beings. He is an eternal individual soul but he draws to himself the mundane senses of which the mind is the sixth detection device. (Bhagavad Gita 15.7)

शरीरं यदवाप्नोति

यच्चाप्युत्क्रामतीश्वरः ।

गृहीत्वैतानि संयाति

वायुर्गन्धानिवाशयात् ॥ १५.८ ॥

śarīraṁ yadavāpnoti

yaccāpyutkrāmatīśvaraḥ
gṛhītvaitāni saṁyāti
vāyurgandhānivāśayāt (15.8)

śarīraṁ — by body; yad — which; avāpnoti — he acquires; yat — which;
cāpi — and also; utkrāmatīśvaraḥ = utkrāmati — departs from + īśvaraḥ —
master; gṛhītvaitāni = gṛhītvā — taking + etāni — these; saṁyāti — he goes;
vāyuḥ — wind; gandhān — perfumes; ivāśayāt = ivā — just as + āśayāt —
from source

*Regardless of whichever body that master acquires, or whichever one he departs from, he
goes taking these senses along, just as the wind goes with the perfumes from their source.
(Bhagavad Gita 15.8)*

श्रोत्रं चक्षुः स्पर्शनं च

रसनं घ्राणमेव च ।

अधिष्ठाय मनश्चायं

विषयानुपसेवते ॥ १५.९ ॥

śrotraṁ cakṣuḥ sparśanaṁ ca
rasanaṁ ghrāṇameva ca
adhiṣṭhāya manaścāyaṁ
viṣayānupasevate (15.9)

śrotraṁ — hearing; cakṣuḥ — vision; sparśanaṁ — sense of touch; ca —
and; rasanaṁ — taste; ghrāṇam — smell; eva — indeed; ca — and;
adhiṣṭhāya — governing ; manaścāyaṁ = manaḥ — mind;-- ca — and +
ayaṁ — this; viṣayān — attractive objects; upasevate — becomes addicted

*While governing the sense of hearing, the vision, the sense of touch, the sense of taste, the
sense of smell and the mind. My partner becomes addicted to the attractive objects.
(Bhagavad Gita 15.9)*

Krishna, the self-portrayed Supreme Being, identified the core-self as his
partner but he does not list a gender. It is left open. This is why we suggest
that the student of kundalini self-tantric not try to create or imagine a self-
gender. One should wait for revelation about this.

The psyche is defined by Krishna as a composite something, which
consists of an individual eternal self along with six senses. By convention
there are five senses but collectively these are housed in the mind which is
rated as the sixth sense. The psyche has the individual limited self which is
eternal along with the five senses and the mind which uses the five senses to
make deliberations. This mind is known to us as the intellect, the psychic
faculty which imagines and analyses.

Irrespective of whichever body that the self acquires, or whichever one it departs from, it goes taking the senses, just as the wind goes with the perfumes from their sources. The aspect which goes is the psyche of which the individual self is part of its contents. The senses and the mind or intellect is packaged with the self. Together these transmigrate to another body after the present one is finished.

The senses and the mind do not change with the death of the body. Whatever condition the sense and mind are in at the time of death, that same condition remains as in the astral state hereafter. Hence whatever habits the psyche adopted during the physical life, it will assume because the subtle body retains the behaviors.

The individual self is supposed to govern the sense of hearing, the vision, the sense of touch, the sense of taste, the sense of smell and the mind, but the association with the information which the senses provide causes the self to become addicted to the attractive objects. This produces a force of habit which may degrade the psyche in terms of causing it to adopt lower behaviors. Lower habits may cause the self to be drawn into births in lower species in which those lower habits are amply exploited. Thus a yogi should take care to protect the subtle body from becoming accustomed to behaviors which will cause the psyche to be adaptive to lower lifeforms.

Core-Self Adaptability

A yogi should study the adaptability of the core-self; not its immediate coordination with gender and species but its connection to the adjuncts which were supplied by the psychic material nature.

There are two adaptations to consider. Only one, the simplest, concerns the core-self. The more elaborate one concerns the subtle body as a whole but with the main controlling element being the kundalini psychic lifeforce.

The subtle body is the adapter to the various species of life and to the gender configuration which one may assume in any species. That is mistaken by many ascetics as an adaption of the core-self but it is not that. The subtle body is not the core-self but it is a container which houses the core-self and other psychic operations.

The adaptation of the core-self is its acceptance of a sense of identity which is a neutral energy which is affected or tarnished by the proximity of the intellect. The intellect psychic instrument is in turn affected by the kundalini lifeforce, a repository of tendencies, which collects data through the senses which it designed as five orifices on the subtle skin of the psyche.

It is important to sort the components of the psyche in meditation. As long as one feels the unity of the self where one cannot discern, the core-self, sense of identity, intellect, kundalini lifeforce, memory and senses, one cannot know which functions are native to which parts of the individual being.

The discovery about the bare core-self is that it is genderless. It is of a neutral being, without a gender tendency in its present configuration. This does not mean that it has no gender but it does mean that under the present conditions even if it has gender, it cannot display itself in these dimensions of the physical and psychic material nature.

Both the core-self and the sense of identity which is fused to it are of a neutral flavor. The intellect is biased or colored because of its affiliation with the kundalini psychic lifeforce which in turn is biased or colored by memories and sensual data. That in a gist is the present existential situation.

Core-Self Tagged Falsely

Presently, the core-self is tagged falsely as its subtle body. It must simultaneously recognize the tag, function as the tag and also know that it is transcendental to the influences which created the subtle body's gender format. That format varies from life form to life form, from this gender in a life form to that other gender in the same or different species. And yet, the core-self bears the responsibility to segregate itself even though it must experience the features of the particular configuration its subtle body assumes.

I declared above that the core-self is neuter gender or genderless. That will be its discovery in meditation if it can totally segregate itself from the adjuncts. However this does not mean that it is actually genderless. It may or may not be. The meaning is that in this creation it can only be displayed as a genderless wonder. To find out what it would be elsewhere, it would have to transit across an existential divide into a purely spiritual dimension.

Core-Self Learning through the Subtle Body

One develops supernatural perception at the most advanced stage of meditation practice. Before that the ascetic has insight some of the time and must practice with little psychic perception most of the time.

The core-self for its part is dependent on the adjuncts for information about the realities it encounters in the physical and psychic material existence. The self learns through the subtle body. It does not learn directly from physical experiences but these occurrences, in so far as the subtle body is involved in them, serves as a learning experience for the self.

The teaching in this book concerns the core-self's gender. From the gender expressions of the subtle body, the core-self gets an idea about the conversion of gender neutrality in multiple roles in varied species of life with stress on reproduction and focus for pleasure indulgence. From this library of experiences, the self may determine to discover its bare gender and open itself to expression on the spiritual plane.

Subtle Body Gender Contrast

The core-self should observe the contrast if any between what is expressed as physical gender and what is felt in the subtle body as its gender. When these feelings match exactly, it should be observed. When it is contrary, it should be noted. When it is partially matched and partially unmatched, that should be checked. The yogi must track to discover where each energy type originates. He should not assume that it is one energy with one single origin.

According to the Yoga Sutras, the cause of our association with the material nature is ignorance. That is removed by experience which is properly analyzed. Curiosity which must be satisfied is terminated by full experience of the incidence, after one has seen it for what it is worth.

स्वस्वामिशक्त्योः स्वरूपोपलब्धिहेतुः संयोगः ॥ २३ ॥

sva svāmiśaktyoḥ svarūpa upalabdhi hetuḥ saṁyogaḥ

sva – own nature, own psyche; svāmi – the master, the individual self; saktyoḥ – of the potency of the two; svarūpa – essential form; upalabdhi – obtaining experience; hetuḥ – cause, reason; saṁyogaḥ – conjunction.

There is a reason for the conjunction of the individual self and its psychological energies. It is for obtaining the experience of its essential form. (Yoga Sutras 2.23)

तस्य हेतुरविद्या ॥ २४ ॥

tasya hetuḥ avidyā

tasya – of it; hetuḥ – cause; avidyā – spiritual ignorance.

The cause of the conjunction is spiritual ignorance. (Yoga Sutras 2.24)

तदभावात्संयोगाभावो हानं तद्दृशेः कैवल्यम् ॥ २५ ॥

tad abhāvāt saṁyogā abhāvaḥ
hānaṁ taddṛśeḥ kaivalyam

tad = tat – that spiritual ignorance; abhāvāt – resulting from the elimination; saṁyogā – conjunction; abhāvaḥ – disappearance, elimination; hānaṁ – withdrawal, escape; tad = tat – that; dṛśeḥ – of the perceiver; kaivalyam – total separation from the mundane psychology.

The elimination of the conjunction which results from the elimination of that spiritual ignorance is the withdrawal that is the total separation of the perceiver from the mundane psychology. (Yoga Sutras 2.25)

विवेकख्यातिरविप्लवा हानोपायः ॥ २६ ॥

vivekakhyātiḥ aviplavā hānopāyaḥ

viveka – discrimination; khyātiḥ – insight; aviplavā – unbroken, continuous; hānopāyaḥ = hana – avoidance + upāyaḥ – means, method.

The method for avoiding that spiritual ignorance is the establishment of continuous discriminative insight. (Yoga Sutras 2.26)

Gender Experience Choices

One may be in a body which is disinclined completely from every relationship other than the heterosexual one. However someone else or oneself even in some other life, may be in a body which is inclined in a bisexual, lesbian or homosexual way. This posits the question as to which experience to pursue.

Each experience contains responsibilities and liabilities. None is free of consequences. Some experiences are approved by society but even these carry reactions. What is the worth of an experience? How frequently should one indulge?

When the ascetic becomes free from society's standards, he or she should still observe these if for no other reason but to get along with the socio-political situation. Freedom from society's moral markings allows the ascetic to gain insight into the judgements of the psychic material nature, which is a super-sensitive mechanism that awards or penalizes in the process of time.

Features of Experience

Experience is complex, making it a challenge about selecting a facet for focus. Can the person even select? Is the experience so forceful that the participant is compelled to endure it? The bewildering array of feelings within an experience makes it difficult even for the serious ascetic to know which aspect he or she should observe and which one deserves a detached coordination.

Why is the core-self accommodating to a particular part of an experience? What determines if the core-self will be withdrawn from participation?

Chapter 16
Celibacy as a Status

Is celibacy a realistic attainment? Is it something hoped for because of reacting to a lack of control during sexual relationships?

The effort at celibacy is considered to be the cure for sexual involvement but that is mostly a feature which is highlighted by male ascetics. Why then are the females not as concerned about celibacy as a solution to the problems of life in material existence?

From a realistic view point, celibacy is not a permanent attainment but a state which one might achieve if one is supported by providence, such that one has a body which has no sex drive or one has a body with sex drive in which one effectively suppresses sexual lust.

Social usefulness is required, but in what way, in what role, functioning as what? The convention is that a celibate priest has some use to society. But we find that most priests are not celibate through and through. Many masturbate. Some have sexual relations in private and continue serving the clergy without being discovered.

The issue about sexual indulgence being the bane of spirituality, has to do with the lack of resistance to sex pleasure. If a human being could be objective to it, the taboo about sex as being the cause of the fall of man would not hold. The stubborn feature about sex is the intensity of its pleasure and the inability of the self to withstand the enjoyment.

However this is based on the design of the nervous system in the physical body and the nadi energy channels in the subtle form. Unless the ascetic could guarantee that he or she will have a body which is designed to allow the self to be larger than the pleasure of sex, he or she cannot be certain that sex will be reduced to being a non-overpowering force.

Supernatural Power Considered

An ascetic must take supernatural power into account. It is not merely the one self who endeavors for liberation. There are others wanting to be free of physical and psychic trauma. Some influences which are higher contribute to the self's being held captive for sexual participation. Some other influences assist the releasing actions of the self.

The influences must be sorted by the yogi. He should recognize those lowly influences which prevent his ascent and those compulsory ones from higher powers which he cannot upset.

Underneath the ascetic in the astral world are the ancestors. They wield considerable power over the body of the ascetic. They can force him to allow the body to indulge sexually even if the ascetic avowed celibacy. That vow applies to the self of the yogi and not to the selves of the ancestors. A yogi cannot take a vow of celibacy on behalf of ancestors who need physical bodies. That would be contradictory. If perchance the yogi does take that view, and if he is lucky, then perhaps the ancestors may not express their rebirth-desire influence through his body, in which case he may uphold the vow.

Above the ascetic in the astral world are supernatural beings who wield powers which supersede him. The supernaturals can force his body to indulge even if he took the vow. Even though the supernaturals do not have service-shares in the body of the ascetic, their influence may prevail. It may upset his celibate aspirations. If he is lucky supernatural influences may not cause his body to desist from celibate behavior. However a yogi should not project ideas about what the ancestors or the supernatural beings may require. He should do his best if they influence him to the contrary or he should proceed rapidly if they do not.

Dormancy of Sexual Prowess

In the womb of the mother, each material body begins as a sexless mechanism. As it develops some gender is expressed with a female having a lower entry and a male having a lower protrusion. Even so the infant has no sexual expression to speak of. In the beginning the sexual organ has no sexual operation. It does not have feelings of eroticism until the body reaches sexual maturity.

This indicates that there is a reservoir or sexual potency which sponsors the sexual development so that at puberty it can be expressed fully. This reservoir is in the subtle body.

Each physical form is manufactured in the mother's body on the basis of full sexuality in the subtle form. The reduced sexual ability in an infant or elderly body does not in any way remove the full sexual potential in the subtle form. As soon as another human body can accommodate the subtle potency, the same individual who lacked sexual interest in infancy or elderly years, will display sexual enthusiasm.

An ascetic who uses an elderly body, should not become proud or confident of not having sex desire. The need is present in the subtle body. A yogi who uses a prepubescent form as an adolescent should also not be proud about his lack of interest in sexual intercourse. He should know that the potential is present in the subtle body which will take control of the sexual organs as soon as those facilities are more developed after puberty. The actuation potential is in the subtle body.

Sexual Neutrality of the Physical Body

Sexual neutrality of the physical body is no indication of the core-self's gender. It is a mistake, and a serious one, to assume that any gender one feels as a material body is the gender of the core-self. For the core-self, there is no correlation of gender which the material or subtle body may exhibit. One has to get these silly ideas out of the mind. However it is necessary for the ascetic to study the gender potential of the physical body and subtle form. He should understand how it is formulated, express and retracted.

It is a matter of energy expenditure from the core-self to the kundalini psychic lifeforce mechanism, whereby when the lifeforce displays a neuter gender a certain amount of power from the core-self is extracted. The observation of this energy trace leads to an understanding of what the core-self would be if it were disconnected from the psychic adjuncts.

How much power from the core-self is required to run a neuter, male or female gender configuration? That is the inquiry. Which one would extract the least energy from the core-self? Which one is preferred? But this has nothing to do with the sex of the core-self. It is a financial energy decision only, not a sex-gender determination.

Elimination of gender configuration

In yoga practice there is a system of curbing the kundalini psychic lifeforce. When the yogi is proficient in that practice, it becomes possible to conceive of eliminating the gender configuration of the physical or subtle body. The focus is the subtle form but the yogi may begin using techniques on the physical system and then transfer the skill into investigating the subtle body.

This process reduces the energy expenditure of the core-self where it can retain most of its effulgence and engage in self-study to determine its gender in isolation from the demanding adjuncts.

The folding up of the gender tools in the psyche, their in-compression, their kundalini yield and their elimination is done by yogis who are on the verge of becoming siddha perfected beings. Such ascetics are on the path of kundalini self-tantric for discovering the relationship posture of their core-selves.

Shedding the adjuncts does not occur by desire or by thinking that the adjuncts are superfluous and taxing. It happens by shifting them to higher planes, so that they ingest higher energies. This reduces the clinging tendencies of the adjuncts. It allows the core-self to relax and focus on itself.

Sexual Life in a Spiritual World

Some religious systems discuss sexual life in a spiritual world. Some deny it vehemently. If there is a spiritual world it stands to reason that any transit from this side of existence would be done with compromises on this side only. A spiritual world would be a higher energy which would not yield to the demands formulated from this physio-psychic material existence. The foundation here cannot undermine anything there. Nothing from this side besides the bare core-self would be transferred there. Hence a person who feels he can influence what he will be when he translates over to that spiritual place is being silly.

If there is sexual life in that spiritual world, we should have an open mind about it. We should not formulate or guess what it is or would be. Even if someone came from that place and described it to us, we would be foolish to think that our related understanding would be relevant because our reference here has no footing there.

It does not matter if there is or is no sexual life in the spiritual world, because if there is it will have no counterpart here which we could match it to. Hence for the time being it is best to assume that the spiritual world is gender neutral. This will allow us to have an open mind which will allow a revelation about the truth there.

Referencing Tales of Radha and Krishna

Some aspiring celibates aspire for life in a spiritual world where Radha and Krishna engage in love affairs. These celibates plan to participate in those love adventures. Some even though they use male bodies in this life, aspire to be female lovers of Krishna based on advisories which were written by devotional masters.

In a way these aspirations are irrational because the format being used to drum up these ideas is that of the present material or subtle body. These two forms are not based on anything which happens in the spiritual world of Radha and Krishna. The material body has a gender exhibition based on ancestral influences. The subtle body has a gender potential which is based on its kundalini lifeforce formulation.

Just the idea of planning to be in the world of Radha and Krishna is ludicrous because no limited mind from this side of existence can influence what takes place in a spiritual world. It is self-conceit which sponsors the idea that one can be drafted into the world of Radha and Krishna, what to speak of planning which gender role one would have if one were to enter such a place.

Krishna's Spiritual Body

I will share an experience I had during the year of 1995 while I lived in Hattiesburg, Mississippi. I was not living in an ashram at the time. I was employed at a United Methodist Church as a maintenance employee. At the time without supervision of a religious sect, I was doing breath-infusion practice, meditation and Krishna ritual worship on my own.

In the ritual worship, I used to offer prayers and worship paraphernalia to two stone forms of Krishna and Balarama. These procedures were derived from the Vaishnava Sect which was founded by Srila Bhaktivedanta Swami Prabhupada.

I used to rest around noon in a storage room which was part of the set of buildings I was employed to maintain. It was normal for me to astral project or to have some mystic perceptions during these naps which usually lasted for about thirty minutes. Once when resting I found myself as a super-body, a spiritual body. Before me was Lord Krishna lying on the floor as a glowing iridescent form. Within this lifetime, I had one such similar experience before. That was the four-handed form of the Padmanabha Vishnu deity, who appeared at a great distance from me.

In the storage room experience Krishna was two-handed and very close to me. The dimension we were in was pitch black with darkness but his body glowed like a radioactive mineral glowing in the dark. Seeing Krishna lying there so near to me, I felt to awaken him. I considered that he laid on the bare floor and should be on a luxurious bed.

Without thinking and without noting that I was a spiritual body and that Krishna was too, I began to move towards him. I thought:

"O my! O my! It is Krishna. He has no couch, no bed, no blanket, nothing. He should stand. I will call him."

Somehow information from my subtle body and physical form was available. On that basis I began to say this prayer which is directed to Krishna:

नमो ब्रह्मण्य देवाय गोब्राह्मण हिताय च ।

जगत् हिताय कृष्णाय गोविन्दाय नमो नमः ॥

namo brahmanya-devāya
go-brāhmaṇa-hitāya ca
jagad-dhitāya kṛṣṇāya
govindāya namo namaḥ
(Viṣṇu Purāṇa 1.19.65)

When I began to recite the second line of the prayer, Lord Krishna in that iridescent glowing deep blue body, began to say in Sanskrit language that he was not the person I addressed. Translated in English he said this, "That is not me. I am not Balarama. No! I am not the person whom you address."

Saying this he got up, faced me and gradually moved further and further away until I could see him no longer. I awakened on this side of existence. It was the most wonderful experience I had of Lord Krishna in this lifetime.

I remember clearly that when he stood, I saw His full form standing before me. He smiled and allowed me to touch his body visually. He was about twelve feet away from me. My consciousness reached forward and made contact with his body. Every part of his form was all spiritual feelings. Every part was delicate and fully of transcendental feeling. At the time a thought flashed of how the gopis were worried about Krishna's lotus feet being pierced and pricked in the forest and some residents of Ayodhya cried to see Rama walking bare-feet when he was banished.

The gender of the spiritual form which I found myself to be in that experience was male but its maleness was completely different to the maleness experienced using the current physical and subtle bodies. There was no genital consciousness in that body. There was no special part of it or part which was capable of more sensations in reference to other parts. Every part of that body had the intense sensations equally.

Body Comparison

From that experience, I concluded that the spiritual body is full of feelings in every part of it. In the human body, the intense feelings are usually experienced in the chest, head and genitals. When the body is harmed there are sharp compulsory feelings in the wound but in a transcendental form intense feelings are everywhere. There is no dulling energy or lust impetus.

The conditioning we get from the psychic material nature at large and from the kundalini psychic lifeforce individually, is that pleasure is intense in only certain parts of the body. This conditioning forces us to develop in a way which reinforces the design of the kundalini which invents varying genders for the subtle and physical bodies.

To break this hypnosis, one should practice meditation to change the distribution of energy in the psyche so that it mirrors the design of a spiritual form. Without experiencing the spiritual body with limbs and senses, one is left only with a neuter sense of the spiritual form as a spark-like entity who is sex-less. One should however keep in mind what I described as my experience of a gender-designed spiritual form.

Romance is not Spiritual Love

Romance and conjugal love in the material world using either a physical body or a subtle one or both, is not spiritual love. This statement solves no problems. It does not in any way berate romance between material bodies or subtle forms. It only expresses a truth that romance using these bodies is not spiritual love.

For spiritual love on this level, there has to be sharing of character experiences not sexual organ participation or deep feelings of emotions. The lifeforce and the core-self are two different realities. One is not the other. If and when these energies coincide, unless we sort one from the other, our assumptions about them will be mistaken.

An ascetic who is engaged in a romantic or conjugal love, must continually sort the energies so that he or she does not mistake one for the other. Yes, one may service these relationship but one should be alert as to the portions which are conducted by the kundalini psychic lifeforce and those which have to do with the core-self specifically.

The attraction of one kundalini to that of another kundalini is an attraction. In fact it can be a very powerful and assertive convincing energy but it is still not the attraction of a core-self to another core-self.

Purification of the Kundalini Psychic Lifeforce

Even though the kundalini is not the core-self and even though the kundalini has its own lay out which is completely separate from that of the core-self, still the self has an obligation to purify the kundalini.

If the kundalini is not purified the core-self will be unable to conserve its energy. Which means that the core-self will remain extroverted to a degree and will be unable to introspect fully on itself. So long as it is connected to a kundalini psyche lifeforce, the condition of that lifeforce in terms of efficient of transfer of energy, will have an impact on the realization of the core-self.

The kundalini is fed by breath energy and food nutrition. Breath energy is absorbed through the lungs. The foodstuffs are absorbed through the stomach and the intestines mainly. The entire gut system should be reformed. Eventually a yogi should eliminate the need for physical food. It is the subtle body which needs the physical foodstuffs, this is why a physical body is created for the subtle form in the first place. Hence curbing the digestive process and the breath ingestion system will affect the status of the subtle body.

Subtle Body Changes Required

Even though the subtle body is not the spiritual form, one cannot experience the spiritual form unless somehow the subtle body is purified and reaches its highest energy level. Let us say for example that a person is graced by a deity such that this person's subtle form reaches its highest energy level. That person may experience the spiritual form. The method of how the subtle body will reach its highest energy level is not a contention. Whichever method will do is acceptable.

It may be proposed that someone would reach the highest level of the subtle body by the grace of a deity or by the mystic action (shaktipat) of a powerful yogi. That is not denied. The point is that if the yogi can reach there by his efforts or by grace of a powerful person, either is satisfactory.

When there is an infusion by a deity, the person may transit through the levels of the subtle body so rapidly that it appears to be instantaneous. In fact the person may not perceive the transformation and may only recall himself or herself, as a physical being, who somehow or the other was suddenly translated to being a spiritual person.

The yogic system for doing this is to upgrade the subtle body by using asana postures, breathing infusion and compression and then practice internalization. When the murky energy in the subtle body is removed, the subtle body will jump into its highest frequency, from which the transit to a spiritual body may occur.

Reduction of Sexual Complexity

To study self-gender, a yogi must reduce his sexual complexity and hope that by the grace of God and nature, he is not confronted with sexual propositions which he would not be able to resist. Providence is powerful. A yogi, limited as he or she is, cannot side-step it always. Hence one may hope that somehow or the other one does not have to be challenged sexually by anyone who is irresistible.

However all the same, since from our relative position fate is unreliable, since it is no man's pawn, since it controls and manipulates all, a yogi should have a method whereby he can proceed with self-tantric practice and also comply with the challenges fate places before him, even those circumstances which deter the practice.

By all means one should try to reduce the sexual complexities. When they flare up one should take steps to reduce their glare step by step and with patience.

A yogi should cherish isolation and should keep his whereabouts as out of view as is possible, otherwise many complications of destiny which otherwise one would avoid will be forced into one's experience, causing many complications which one just cannot bring to a yogic conclusion.

Vigilance of Dream States and Psychic Transmissions

A yogi must be vigilant during dream states and may be aware of psychic transmission, even the slightest ones. Lack of objectivity during sleeping conditions is the bane of yoga practice. One cannot be a yogi if one is not conscious of the activities of the subtle body during sleeping phases. It is a matter of curtailing the power-draw from the core-self for the operations of the subtle body, especially of the kundalini psychic lifeforce which is present in both the subtle and physical forms.

When the two bodies are in synchronization, the lifeforce is situated in both of the forms with the physical one being the commanding presence. When the two are out of synchronization, as for instance during sleep of the physical one, the kundalini for the most part remains as its command center in the physical one but it releases a portion of its controlling energy with the subtle one. A yogi must study how this occurs so that he can monitor the leakage of energy from the core-self to the kundalini psychic lifeforce. That expenditure of the core-self should be reduced to the very minimum.

The core-self remains centered in the brain of the physical system during waking hours but it is involuntarily shifted into the subtle body during sleep. Its presence there can be with objectivity or without it.

The greater the draw of energy from the core-self the less objectivity that self has and the more it will be unable to understand what its participation is in the execution of the lifeforce's plans.

Even though the core-self is not the kundalini psychic life-force, that self is affected negatively by large draws of its energy which go to the life-force, hence it is paramount that the core-self monitor the lifeforce to reduce this energy expenditure.

Yoga Postures and Breath-Infusion Practice is Useful

Yoga postures and breath-infusion practice are useful in the quest to reduce the energy-draw from the core-self. Control of thinking energy is another method which in the ashtanga yoga system is termed as pratyahar sensual energy withdrawal. That is an introspective process of shutting down interest in thinking operations which are counterproductive to deep meditation.

Vow of Celibacy

No limited being should take a vow of celibacy because there is no guarantee that one will be supported by nature in the commitment. However every ascetic should aspire for celibacy even though the reality is that one may not be able to absolutely honor the aspiration.

It does not matter if a yogi can absolutely be celibate, what is important is that he or she practices with the understanding that the bodies are joint enterprises in which ancestors may use the body for their own purposes which are contrary to one's aims. As such the yogi has to be sure that his portion of the energy is dedicated in the desired way, but that does not mean that he can force the ancestors into his commitment.

Genetic Tendency of the Physical Body

The genetic tendency of the physical form can only be changed permanently in very rare cases and by steep austerities only. In some cases there is a change and then the form unexpectedly reverts to unwanted behaviors. This is because the ancestors have shares in the form. The desire to change it does not give the ascetic the right to abolish the ancestral influence. Hence if those people relax their desire to use the form for some time, and if that relaxation of their influence coincides with the aspiration of the ascetic, he will find that for a time the form does not exhibit what is unwanted. Then suddenly when the ancestors again desire to use the form, it will resume behaviors which the ascetic felt certain were eliminated.

The genetic tendencies are there in their own right. No ascetic can abolish them forever. They developed over many millions of years through evolutionary adaptation. They will remain in place for as long as physical life is current. Ascetics come and go but the physical and psychic material nature along with its biological layout will continue to eternity, at least until the physical creation pans out.

Monk/Nun Theory

The theory regarding celibacy is that once a person takes the vow, he or she should be strong-willed and should remain confined in the monastery.

There are two groups of these monks. One group accepts reincarnation as a fact. Another set denies reincarnation outright or say that it has no relevance. Some monks have no idea about genetic influence. Some others have no idea that ancestors have rights to use their bodies for sexual purposes.

Due to this ignorance and due also to arrogance about willpower, the institutions for celibacy are mostly farces. Who can account for his or her subtle sexual activities even if he or she has absolutely no physical breaches? Unless the ascetic has clear astral perception during dreams he or she cannot honestly state if there is a breach by the subtle body.

Anyone who masturbates, regardless of whether he or she is discovered, is not celibate. Anyone who fantasizes about sex is not celibate. Anyone who flirts with anyone else is not celibate. Even if a sexual arousal peters out, anyone who experiences that is not celibate. This does not devalue the effort for celibacy. The attempt to be celibate is praiseworthy, except for the ignorance about the rights of the ancestors to use the body sexually regardless of the sincerity of the monk or nun concerned.

This book does not say that one should not be a monk or nun. In fact this book appreciates anyone who aspires to be or who is a monk or nun but we want you to admit the reality of the genetic influence of the body. Beware of the ancestral rights and the swipes of fate, which may force you to engage sexually even when you feel that it is not in your interest.

The subtle body is a sensuous form, even more so than the physical system. For that matter the sensations experienced in the physical body have their origin in the subtle form. To make the claim that the subtle body is celibate is a daring thing to say. Yes, a yoga siddha body is celibate, as we hear of it from the ancient yogic texts. All the same most entities who use or used material bodies do not have yoga-siddha forms. They use regular subtle bodies which are prone to all types of unrestricted sensuality.

For those who are deceased, the big attraction which they feel towards material existence is sex indulgence, not so much for the pleasure of it but for the opportunity to take an embryo. Hence for them celibacy is unwanted. The whole concept of celibacy is revolting to the psychic and physical material nature. Against that where does the puny willpower of the ascetic stand? For the living it is the sexual pleasure which they are after for the most part. For the dearly departed it is the reproduction potential which holds their interest. Hence the inconvenience of celibacy.

Chapter 17
Kundalini Sensations

Willpower versus Tendency

In the battle between willpower and tendency, willpower will lose most of the time. It is not what an ascetic decides to do but rather what his sensuality favors. The sensuality is expressed by the kundalini lifeforce psychic mechanism which maintains the subtle and physical forms and which creates the urges and actions which motivates the forms.

The willpower of the yogi is real but it does not have the amount of power which the kundalini exhibits. Any pledge which depends on willpower may be subjected to reversal if the kundalini wants the contrary.

Can the ascetic stop over-rating the willpower? Can the ascetic come to terms with the kundalini by curbing its interests, so that it always supports the willpower? The answer to this is that the ascetic can reform the kundalini but only to a degree. Even the kundalini is a joint enterprise with the ancestors. The ascetic may curb his portion of it but he cannot fully control the portion which belongs to those who are departed. Hence celibacy is up in the air because of these loopholes in autonomy of the self.

Kundalini Survival Mechanism

Putting aside the negative and very mandatory impact of the ancestors, one has to deal with the kundalini. That energy is not geared to support the interest of the core-self. The kundalini life force is a survival mechanism for transit through the various levels and dimensions of the physical and psychic material energy. It is not designed for the benefit of the core-self. Instead it uses energy from the self to support its operations.

The self should gage its lack of control of the kundalini. It is not a question of the influence from others, not even from the ancestors. It is a matter of shifting the kundalini to a higher level and causing it to abandon its survival game focus.

Kundalini Operates Sensation Transfers

The kundalini operates multiple sensation transfers, using one or a combination of sensual approaches. It can undermine anything that a celibate is determined to do. The kundalini has the full range of sensation potential at its disposal. For that matter the nervous system in the physical body was created by the kundalini on the basis of its layout in the subtle form.

The core-self mistakes the sensation developed and expressed by the kundalini as self's sentiency. This causes the self to willingly endorse the majority of the kundalini's enterprises but at the expense of the self which enjoys or suffers according to the consequence which nature gives. A yogi is tasked to sort the core-self original ideas from those of the kundalini. At first the core-self must be detached from the kundalini. Then it can begin to see its action in contrast to what is drummed up by the kundalini.

Sexuality of Kundalini Misleading

The sexuality of the kundalini is misleading because the core-self mistakes its gender for whatever is expressed by the kundalini. The self must honor the kundalini's sex outlay to some degree but that does not mean that it should identify itself as that exhibition of gender. A yogi must simultaneously do what is a forced impulsion and also remain in the know about its core-self and its kundalini sensation outlay.

Those who fail to sort the core-self from the kundalini must begin the investigation with the information provided in this and other similar literature. Over time while meditating and also observing the components of the psyche, the yogi will see this directly. The yogi will live as the kundalini would have it and simultaneously there will be insight into what is the self's format and what is the kundalini's sensation constructions.

Extraction from the Sense of Reason

Extraction from the sense of reason is comparatively easier than detaching the core-self from sensations. In the toss-up between sensations and analytical thoughts, sensations will be proven to be the majority force in the psyche. The core-self even in alliance with the sense of reason rarely overpowers the sensations.

This means that any core-self which by nature is sensation driven is likely to be prejudiced for the kundalini psyche lifeforce which would make it near impossible for that self to have objectivity. That self-will frequently sides with sensation which will make it near impossible for it to be feelings-resistant.

Sexual arousal, though overpowering and intense is only one type of sensation. There are many minor feelings which overpower the self. Since these are hardly noticed, the self under-rates their influence. Instead it looks for big events and considers that if these were suppressed, the self would be victorious over its adjuncts. However this line of reasoning is flawed.

It is more important to squelch the minor sensations than it is to challenge the intense expanded ones. Even the obvious feelings begin with tiny hardly noticeable sensations. If these initial impressions were confronted and disempowered, not supported, the self would gain more autonomy over the psyche.

Upgrading the Kundalini

It is important to upgrade the kundalini psychic lifeforce, so that it is on a level whereby its operations allow more insight for the core-self. If to operate its adjuncts the self dishes out energy in an inefficient and haphazard way, that self will be unable to monitor its permissions for kundalini operations. The result of this is that at its expense the self will subscribe to operations to which it has no insight.

It is necessary for the self to curb the kundalini and to cause it to operate on a higher level. It is not enough for the self to force itself into being detached, because it cannot be detached when the kundalini operates from a low level. To make the correct decisions and to have the power to command the psyche, the self must retain the majority of its power and not dish out energies to sponsor a low grade kundalini.

Social or Pseudo-Spiritual Roles of Celibacy

True celibacy has little to do with the social or pseudo-spiritual role a person exhibits. If someone is a monk or nun, and if that person has overt or covert breaches, he or she is not celibate. Religious institutions establish pseudo-spiritual gender roles not real ones. However if someone has a partner and if that person practices austerities which result in a greater degree of sexual abstinence, then that person has a foothold in celibacy.

The format of gender as a monk or nun is pseudo-spiritual because it is based mostly on the concept that the sexual format of the material body can feedback to and affect the spiritual posture of the core-self. This is totally false.

The method however of aspiring for this pseudo-spiritual sexual or asexual role has value as a stop-gap method for lessening the current interest in sexual relationship, so that the monk or nun can focus on sensual restraint and further imbibe the doctrine of the religious sect.

In the long term however the effort will be proven to be meaningless because the kundalini will again resume its sensual interest, and the core-self will be helpless to put a stop to this.

External Social Format is Useless

The external social format of gender is useless for giving the indication of the progress with self-gender discovery. This does not mean that the yogi should be careless or reckless socially. But he must remember at all times that the external format is not helpful with the internal features. The best way to deal with the internal format is to do introspection where the core-self is isolated from the kundalini psychic lifeforce and the intellect. The disconnection from the adjuncts leaves the core-self with no social access, making the social definition irrelevant.

For peace sake the ascetic should observe social norms but he or she should get away from society whenever possible so as to be free of having to be bogged down playing the social game. Instead of buttoning up to get social approval, it is best to spend the time introspecting so that the core-self can know itself in distinction from its adjuncts.

Suppression of Kundalini Sex-Desire

In the monk/nun syndrome there is the constant threat that the individual will vie for political control. This is because the kundalini has to express or vent itself in some way. If it is not allowed sexual expression, its energy will inflate some other feature of sensuality in such a forceful way as to make an oblong growth on the psyche which will cause the ascetic to become blind to sexual opportunities but to be visually aware of some other area in which he or she can take social privilege.

Sex expressions is about giving facility to one's ancestors but there are other ways of doing that especially political avenues, where one can influence others to engage in sex and give opportunity to one's ancestors in other families without one having to be bogged down with the domestic tasks which result. Many monks and nuns master some kundalini sexual restraint in the exact proportion to which they express political power over other human beings in the religious institution.

Again the spread of the kundalini's gender expression has nothing to do with the core-self sexual orientation. Hence it is important to sort the core-self from its adjuncts.

Suppression of Sexual Energy

Apart from the components of sexual energy, the suppression of it is dangerous for an ascetic. He should discover a method for expressing it so that it does not accumulate into an irresistible force which must be expressed either in masturbation or in sexual participation.

This has nothing to do with the gender of the core-self. It is purely a kundalini incidence but it should not be ignored because if the kundalini is stressed that will cause it to draw more energy from the core-self which will in turn cause the self to lose self-focus.

The most effective means of dissipating the sexual energy is by the use of asana postures and pranayama breath-infusion. At first the ascetic should practice to dissipate the sexual energies which accumulate in the groin area of the body. Later he should work to dissipate hormonal energy which is extracted from digested food. If the hormonal energy is diffused as soon as it is formulated, there would be no concentration of it for use as sexual energy. This is how one purifies the kundalini which in turns causes it to extract less energy from the core-self. This results in more self-focus and less attraction between the self and its adjuncts.

Dissection of the Psyche

A one-size-fits-all policy will not work except in a superficial way. A yogi must dissect the psyche if he really wants to derive a celibate formula which will work through the various levels of his persona. The idea of celibacy by vow, determination or force of pride is worthless because it does not take in account the separate parts of the psyche which are required to participate for full success.

Celibacy as a whole for the psyche of the individual where every part of the self agrees to comply with it, is a fantastic concept but it is hardly practical for any limited person.

A limited person cannot command his or her kundalini to change its evolutionary urges. Except for wishful thinking and being propped up temporarily by nature there is no such thing as a celibate kundalini. The very nature of the kundalini is to reproduce. It cannot do that without cell division in very primitive forms and sexual interplay with cell splitting in complex life forms.

Another issue is the intellect analytical organ which is a psychic operation in the head of the subtle body. Unless the ascetic forces that instrument to give up its fondness for the kundalini psychic lifeforce, he cannot rely on it to permanently focus on a celibate condition. The intellect will side with the kundalini as soon as the core-self relaxes focus.

Yet another issue is memory information which is another automatic psychic operation in the subtle body. The ascetic cannot change memories which are lodged in the subconscious mind. These are from millions of years of experience having to do with creature existence in the physio-psychic material world. These just cannot support absolute celibacy. The conclusion is that celibacy as an ideal is hard to pin down.

Celibacy as Applied to Males and Females

Celibacy is such that it has a different approach for males and females. A method used by males may not be suitable for females. The very construction of the sex organ equipment of each gender is different. The function of each is also very specifically different. The formation of the sexual hormonal energy in each is totally different.

To oversimply the two approaches and present them as a similar system is sheer foolishness. The construction of emotions in males and females is diverse. This denies a simplistic approach to any attempt at celibacy in either gender.

Methods used by males over the centuries will not be suitable to females. Over the centuries there were more males in monasteries than females in nunneries. There is more information about yogic efforts at celibacy for males than there is for females. Both are a complexity which makes a laughing stock of simplistic morality.

Free of the Kundalini Gender Preference

A yogi or yogini must aspire to be free of the kundalini's gender preference. There must be an effective way to breach the influence of the kundalini, so that the core-self can realize itself separately. This is not an easy achievement because as it is the core-self is connected to the kundalini by a powerful psychic adhesive force. One might imagine the self to be separated but that is not the same as actually being apart from the kundalini.

Yogis have several methods of breaking away from the lifeforce. One which I recommend is to become absorbed into the naad sound resonance which is heard at the back of the head during meditation.

Some yogis use the method of first energizing the kundalini psychic lifeforce so that the kundalini moves up the spine into the brain and penetrates either the brow or crown chakra. This causes the core-self to float or be immerged in the highest level of energy of the kundalini. This also gives the self some objectivity in regards to the kundalini because then the energy of the kundalini loses interest in its gender preferences.

Regardless of how a person separates the kundalini from the core-self, it is absolutely necessary that the ascetic does this, otherwise he or she will never get to realize the core-self's gender.

Celibacy is a Limited Solution

Celibacy is a limited solution. It will not cause the self to realize its gender in isolation. Celibacy of a physical body if it can be attained even, or celibacy of a subtle form if that is possible, does not in any way clarify the core-self's gender. There must be a complete break-away of the core-self from its physical and subtle bodies before it can know its gender. The gender expression of the physical and subtle forms or the lack of such expression does not reward the core-self with experience of its isolated gender.

Physical or subtle sexual involvement is bewildering but so is all sensual expression, sex being just one of the sensual applications. If celibacy of either the physical or subtle body will inspire the self to discover its isolated gender, then celibacy would be useful in the quest. The ascetic must deal with his or her fated social interactions so that regardless of full or partial celibacy, he or she can realize the core-self in isolation. The self's gender must be realized regardless of the self's celibate or non-celibate social means.

Focus on reforming the present gender configurations and its challenges has value in yoga practice but on the high end of yoga, it has little use, because the reformation and redesign of the kundalini must be left aside, or a full face examination of the core-self without respect to any of the potentials of the kundalini, must be achieved.

Reformat of the kundalini by the core-self does not do anything to reveal the gender of the core-self even though it does make it easy to carry out that investigation. Kundalini redesign is an achievement for a yogi but it does not directly yield the clarity about the gender of the bare self.

Reproduction is On-Going

No matter what, reproduction is an on-going need. Those who are departed and who are not transferred to suitable existences elsewhere are fully reliant on sexual intercourse for getting the next body. That is their priority. From every side we are bombarded with the need for reproduction. On this plane of existence, no one can banish this all-pervasive energy.

Regardless of if one is celibate or not, if one requires a human body one is compelled to contribute to a sexual intercourse. Hence celibacy as an ideal has its practical limitations.

Perhaps the most threatening aspect to full celibacy is the presence of ancestors. Their rights into the life of the body is a potential upset. At any moment an ancestor could discard a monk's or nun's vow because the commitment uses parts of the psyche which belong to the ancestor. Thus there is uncertainty about a non-sexual commitment.

Deities of Sexual Organs

I discussed the influence of the ancestors. Another personal force to contend with are the deities of the sexual organs. These are supernatural beings who have psychic register just as the ancestors have a subtle impact in the life of an ascetic who uses a body to which they contributed services.

In some meditations the ancestors are seen. In some the deities are perceived. Yogis see these deities in certain meditative states. Sometimes a deity leaves an organ and another deity takes possession of it. This happens when the vibration of the organ is lowered or upgraded.

The possession of an organ by a deity ups the ante on whether the self can fully control the organ. If for instance, the deity flushes that organ with much supernatural power, the ascetic may be unable to control it. He or she will be forced to indulge it. Hence celibacy as an absolute principle is unrealistic.

Since the organ has tendencies of its own which may on occasion confiscate the governing position of the self, the organ itself is a threat to celibacy. One's sexual organ may be avaricious for sexual participation. The force of this may be more than one could contain.

Reduce Kundalini's Sexual Needs

By all means a yogi should reduce the kundalini's sexual needs but for reasons other than morality, other than status in a religious society, other than for pride in thinking that celibacy is or can be achieved.

The reduction of the kundalini's sexual outlays results in conservation of energy of the core-self which will allow that self to complete more in-focus on itself to determine its gender without respect to the adjuncts which are its functional means in the physical and psychic material existence.

For the self to realize its nature in isolation, it requires full conservation of energy during meditation. If any of its energy is used by the kundalini for any reason, sexual or otherwise, the self will be unable to make a thorough research. This is the why it should curtail the expenditure of energy which is extracted from it by an adjunct.

The kundalini has its own energy generation and stockpiling system. Besides that it extracts energy from the core-self. Our concern here is the extracted energy. That must be reduced considerably and then in meditation, that should cease for a time. This is in compliance with Patanjali's declaration in the Yoga Sutras about the termination of the mento-emotional energy:

योगश्चित्तवृत्तिनिरोधः ॥ २ ॥

yogaḥcittavṛtti nirodhaḥ

yogaḥ – the skill of yoga; cittavṛtti = citta – mento-emotional energy + vṛtti – vibrational mode; nirodhaḥ – cessation, restraint, non-operation.

The skill of yoga is demonstrated by the conscious non-operation of the vibrational modes of the mento-emotional energy. (Yoga Sutras 1.2)

Locating a Perfect Celibate

The quest for celibacy is laced with difficulties on two counts:
- The psyche is by nature gender-adaptable
- Most teachers who pass as celibates are frauds

Reliance on the psyche for celibacy is a misnomer. The psyche itself is gender-adaptable according to what facilities it is afforded by the psychic and physical material nature. At any stage, according to how it is shifted here or there in the mundane evolutionary cycle, a male psyche can display female qualities and a female psyche can do the contrary. Hence the core-self is tasked with a serious problem which is that besides itself, every part of its current psychology is flexible.

Finding a celibate teacher is quite a task. At any time in history, there may be no expert within geographic reach. This means that the only access may be psychic, either to reach the person by mystic communication or to attend the person on the astral planes. There is also the problem of accuracy of intuition of the student. Finding the teacher psychically may involve communication distortions such that even if the teacher can render valid methods, the student can neither understand nor implement these.

Reduction of Romantic Notions

Reason is important in yoga practice, as to the motive for a certain discipline. Any restraint which has the wrong basis will result in failure in the long term. Romantic notions should be voluntarily reduced so that the core-self energy allotments to the kundalini is curtailed. It is not the romance which is the problem but the resulting mandatory energy drain.

When there is sensual activity, the self cannot stop the involuntary power extraction of the kundalini. Hence the way to curtail it is to pressure the kundalini into ceasing excessive sensual outlays. These include sexual expressions.

This is not about morality. It is about energy efficiency so that the core-self is not forcibly involved in power extractions to run excessive sensual operations. All romantic notions should be reduced. For introspection in on itself, the core-self must first reduce the amount of energy which flows from itself to the kundalini.

Reduction of Sexual Pleasure Interest

The ascetic must reduce sexual interest because the core-self's sexuality cannot be discovered through kundalini-sponsored sexual expressions. Nature's sexual expressions even if they are considered to be moral, do not show the core-self's gender. The yogi has to reduce nature's expressions so that in isolation the core-self can be understood.

Whatever is fated to occur will happen irrespective of the disciplinary desires of the self but it should not think that it is responsible for everything that happens. Even obviously degrading behaviors need not foreshadow the core-self because its accounts are totally separate from that of the kundalini. However unless the ascetic transferred focus to the core-self, he or she will feel despondent when the kundalini does things which run contrary.

Instead of focusing on the contrary behaviors, the self should focus on the energy drainage which supports the actions. It is not what is done but how it is sponsored.

Assistance Required

A yogi needs assistance from advanced ascetics who reached higher planes and mastered the techniques which the yogi aspires to be proficient in. There must be reliance on some environment and on some advanced persons? The yogi cannot be so independent that he does not require assistance. Association will be there. Influence will penetrate his nature from time to time. It is a matter of which association is preferred and which level of existence is suitable for discovering the gender of the self.

By reducing lower associations, a yogi automatically gravitates to higher company. He does not rely on physical presence of great persons. He can connect with great people through psychic communication.

Over time, a yogi should from within the mind, gradually choke out the need for his psyche to be receptive to and to participate in the life of people who are focused on lower objectives, who have little or no interest in returning the focus of the self into itself.

Diverting the Kundalini Lifeforce

Kundalini yoga practice is useful both in the bid for celibacy and in the self-tantric practice. Even though both use kundalini arousal as an assistance method, the efforts are different. In celibacy the objective is to derail the original plan of the kundalini lifeforce which is to use sex hormone energy for sexual expression with intentions to reproduce lifeforms.

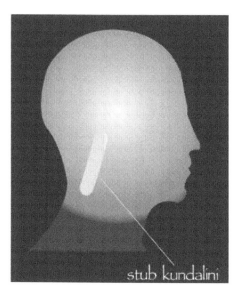
stub kundalini

In the self-tantric effort, the kundalini lifeforce is relocated into the head so that the micro-cells of the system no longer contribute hormonal power to the grand kundalini at the base of the spinal column. This reduces the accumulation of sexual hormonal energy which in turn causes the kundalini to lose interest in sex indulgence.

For the celibacy effort, the yogi should influence the life force to replace sex procurement with interest of higher states of consciousness. For this the kundalini must cease its keen interest in sex energy and begin aggressively locating non-sex-charged bliss energy in the psyche.

Energy Distribution Efficiency

To increase efficiency, so as to decease the energy which the kundalini draws from the core-self, it is necessary to practice asana postures and pranayama breath-infusion, which are the third and fourth stages of the ashtanga yoga system explained by Patanjali. It is not a matter of morality. This concerns energy consumption so that whatever causes a power draw out of the core-self is reduced. Even some moral aspects may be reduced if they inefficiently draw current from the self.

In kundalini yoga the effort should be made to reduce the carbon dioxide in the body so that there is a relative increase in fresh air in the cells of the body. This translates to a proportionate increase in positive astral energy in the subtle body. The carbon dioxide in the physical body and its counterpart in the subtle form, should be extracted using breath-infusion. This diagram shows where these energies usually concentrate:

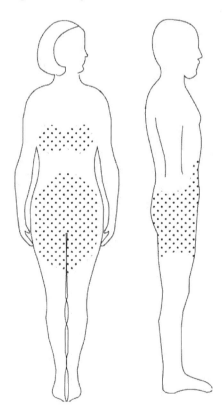

Design of the Psyche

Even though the core-self is not the psyche, and it is not its adjuncts, still unless it understands the designs of the components, it cannot consistently curtail their influence. This means that the self will be ruled by the adjuncts for the most part. Someone by chance, or with the help of a deity, may transcend the adjuncts for a short time but in the long term that person will fail in the quest for self-control.

Understanding the designs in the psyche is the beginning because that in itself even though it is a plus for the self is not sufficient to cause the self to supersede the authority of the adjuncts. The psyche was designed by the kundalini just for the purpose of fulfilling the lifeforce's objectives. Thus anytime the self relaxes its authority, whatever little control it exhibited will be reduced automatically.

Arrogance of the Self

The arrogance of the self is based on its ignorance, its assumption that it was and should be in a governing position in the psyche. The question remains: When was the self dominant?

The answer is that since the formation of the psyche, the self was not the autocratic ruler of the senses. It was a power supply for the operations of the kundalini which was the governor. The intellect fauns itself as the defacto ruler of opinions and the core-self pretending that it is in charge, crouches under the intellect.

A yogi must break apart these falsities, face up to being a stooge for the adjuncts, develop insight into how to tip the table in the favor of the self and earn ownership in the future with the adjuncts under tight supervision.

Competing Interests in the Psyche

Within the psyche at any given time in any given internal/external circumstance there are competing and allied interests between the adjuncts one to another and between a specific adjunct and the core-self. There is a permanent escortship of the core-self by the sense of identity. There is a standard alignment between the sense of identity and the intellect. There is a general pattern of cooperation between the intellect and the kundalini lifeforce. This is a conspiracy for the most part which undermines the ideas for autonomy of the core-self. There is a passing of information from the memories to the intellect with the memories doing so to assist the kundalini for the most part and to bamboozle the core-self.

The senses are obedient servants of the kundalini. They procure information about sense objects and engage in the business of mining pleasures and displeasures in the form of experiences which afflict the core-self.

These competing interest are baffling such that without deep contemplation, the core-self cannot understand the operations. It is at a loss to know how to gain more say in the affairs of the psyche.

Sensual Perception as a Conjoint Enterprise

Sensual perception is a conjoint enterprise, where the core-self and the adjuncts procure information from sense objects. These subtle impressions are digested in the psyche. In any sensual pursuit each of the adjuncts may have differing or similar interest. This is like when vendors take a trip up a river into the remote parts to buy items on the cheap for retail at a profit later. Each vendor has interest in particular products which he or she can peddle in the city later.

Even though the boat makes one journey to a remote destination, still once the boat arrives, each vendor is attracted to a specific product with a specific bargain in mind. When the boat departs from that place, each vendors will have items which were packed in specific containers. It is one ferry which docked at one remote terminal but with varied interest of varied vendors fulfilled or unfulfilled according to what was available.

One vendor may be depressed because the items he wanted were not present or were available at too high of a price. Another vendor may be elated because he purchased choice items at a reasonable price which will bring profits in the city. And yet another vendor who purchased items might be worried that he may get insufficient profit.

Each adjunct has particular interest in any sensual experience. In fact one adjunct, or the core-self even, may be disinterested and may have to tag along in the pursuit of a sense object. The intellect may crave a particular type of enjoyment which the core-self wants to evade. The kundalini may shun an interest of the intellect. A memory might be reluctant to accept the impressions of a certain sensual experience which it finds to be depressing. The eye may want an experience which the nose dislikes intensely. In some experience the core-self and the adjuncts may crave the experience so much that they cooperate in procuring it.

Psychic Perception Necessary

Psychic perception is necessary for all phases of self-realization. A person without psychic perception, who is not clairvoyant or clairaudient cannot be successful in celibacy. He or she is without perception of what his or her subtle body does in dreams and astral projection experiences. His or her mind does not have the sensitivity to register psychic contact which occurs when using a physical body even. This disqualifies that person for advanced spiritual practice.

If one cannot perceive the psychic communications which flash across this environment, one cannot make adjustments either to cease the communications or to enhance them. Of course the mind will still be subjected to those abstract influences. It will still be affected. It will still act impulsively according to how it absorbs these. But the person will have no clarity about the impulsions.

Chapter 18
Crazed Subtle Body

Passion is an enthusiasm energy. It is necessarily to use it in this creation. It is bewildering because it uses haste as its motor power. Due to rapidity, it dodges censorship by the core-self. Any sensual pursuit has passion as one of its ingredients but the quantity of passion is what determines if an experience will be a compulsion or not. The greater the quantity of passion, the more compulsive an experience is, with the core-self yielding to the activity.

Passion operates as an emergency power which extracts energy from the core-self for operations which may be traumatic. To curtail passion the yogi must developed a foothold in the clarifying energy such that when an enthusiasm begins, he can monitor it in his interest.

There is an attraction between the core-self and passion, such that the self feels compelled to link with passion. As soon as this linkage is completed the core-self loses objectivity and cannot discern the mission of the passion. This puts the core-self at a disadvantage. On one hand, it has to sponsor a power drain. On the other hand it is liable for the use of the power which is extracted. If however the self can position itself in the clarifying energy, it could know the mission of the passionate energy and determine whether to support it or not.

Passion Recruits the Intellect

The passion energy enlists the intellect for supportive justifications. In every passionate act, there is assistance provided by the intellect. The psyche is designed for cooperation between the kundalini lifeforce and the intellect, with the latter being an accomplice.

The core-self has a task of perceiving how the kundalini prejudices the intellect and causes it to endorse whatever schemes for exploitation the kundalini creates. Once the intellect is influenced, it obediently induces the core-self to allow the passage of energy to the kundalini. If the core-self is reluctant to cooperate, the intellect increases the pressure until the core-self yields or until the core-self generates enough resistance to shut down the intellect's suggestions.

Core-Self's Conquest of the Intellect

Nature provided no check valve between the core-self and the intellect. This means that the core-self is at a disadvantage and has no failsafe way to disconnect itself from thought rationalizations. Since the connection with the intellect functions simultaneously as an energy conduit, the core-self is drained of energy continuously because it is always hitched to the intellect. The method to break this connection is to be remote from the intellect.

The ability of the core-self to disconnect itself from the intellect is an earned proficiency. It is not a nature-given skill. In meditation, the yogi must located both the core-self and the intellect. Then by relocating the core-self to the back of the subtle head, he must create a chasm between the two. This distancing of the self causes it to develop a power to reject the propositions of the intellect. In time the core-self silences the intellect so that its natural power over the self is greatly reduced.

Because the kundalini and the intellect are perpetually in cahoots, the core-self's rejection of the intellectual propositions may be ineffective. In other words, the core-self's command for the intellect to abandon the kundalini, may be rejected by the intellect. It may go ahead with supporting the kundalini even after the core-self instructs it not to cooperate. However if the yogi practices distancing the core-self from the intellect and if he upgrades the kundalini, the self will find that suddenly the intellect becomes obedient to the core-self. It abandons its alliance with the kundalini.

This will leave the kundalini in a powerless position, where it cannot act freely as it did before. The flow of energy it once got from the core-self through the intellect ceases.

Moods are supported

Moods are supported or they diminish to nothing. The three mood collectives are:
- Lethargy
- Enthusiasm
- Clarification

Each mood must be supported by energy intake and consumption. As soon as there is no support a mood vanishes. The kundalini is the mistress of moods. It uses these to control the body. Its primary concern is survival. It secondary interest is reproduction so that it can leave a dead body and procure residence in or as another life accommodation.

Its purpose for surviving is to exploit animate and inanimate resources. This is the sum and substance of our situation. The core-self may have other objectives but regardless the kundalini usually rules the day, with the self edging in fulfillments when it is permitted.

Lethargy though undesirable for the most part, is used by the kundalini to put the body into a state of stupor. This can be constructive or destructive. One usefulness of lethargy is to cause cells of the body to rest while the kundalini repairs another part of the system. The core-self is put out of commission when the energy of lethargy is scattered through the body. It may be decommissioned fully or partially as an unconscious condition or as a drowsy feeling.

In an unconscious state the core-self is drained of so much energy that it loses objectivity. It continues existing but subjectively only. It is deprived of its witnessing ability and has no recall after the condition is terminated.

Enthusiasm is a desire energy. It is experienced as encouragement. The self can hardly resist it. This encouragement draws much energy from the core-self which is induced to sponsor it.

Clarification is an insight energy which gives the core-self the option to permit or deny behaviors of the intellect and kundalini. The self has the most autonomy when it is supported by the clarification energy.

Moods have Patron Deities

Even though moods are experienced as the feelings of a person, the moods themselves have patron deities. All pleasurable and displeasurable feelings have patron deities. Normally a human being is unaware of the deities because of their being in different dimensions. In 1995 when I studied the Sanskrit language, I met many Sanskrit experts during astral projections to India. Many of these were yogis. Some were valid celibates who practiced breath-infusion and who were isolated from the public. I learnt many related yogic techniques from these persons.

Once in the astral existence, I was studying Sanskrit from a teacher with whom I did a correspondence course. There was no confusion of mind as there is in some astral encounters. Everything was clearly perceived. I sat at a table with this teacher, when suddenly a woman appeared in the distance. There was a sickly glow of light in her eyes. She smiled as she came down an isle where I sat.

Instinctively I wanted to move but I found that I could not. As I sat there and as the woman approached nearer, I kept thinking that I certainly did not want her to touch me. She was far away at the time, about forty or fifty feet, but I could tell that she wanted to greet me as one would welcome a long lost friend.

She acted as if she knew me. I was certain that she was no acquaintance. However when she was within about ten feet, the Sanskrit teacher suddenly disappeared as if to say, "This is your concern. Take care of it as you can."

When the teacher disappeared, I suddenly realized that against my will the woman would touch me. Previously, the celibate masters whom I knew in the astral existence had warned me about being touched by someone who had sexual intentions. I wanted to honor their idea. I said to the woman "You can pass but do not touch me."

I kept repeating that but the woman came closer and closer and touched nevertheless. After doing that she held my body and put her head on the genital area. When she did that energy left my body. My lifeforce shivered the body as if the body would continue shaking forever. It began impulsively and I could do nothing about it. After about five seconds, the woman removed her head. She said, "I will miss you. But there are others. Every day they come. I meet them regularly. I will go away."

At first when the woman was about to put her head on my genital area, she said, "Let us dance. Let us dance." Afterwards her head rested on my body which shivered in an awful way.

After transferring back to the physical existence, I clearly remembered that the woman has a sickly elderly body but she was in a happy mood. She was afflicted with a sickly white-yellowish color as if she lost youth and vigor. I realized that she was the witch named Jaraa, the deity for old age. She is involved with cold viruses, pneumonia, bronchitis, constipation, kidney failure, colon rot, vaginal cancer, prostate cancer and venereal disease.

Jaraa is a deity for the lethargy which springs from sexual enthusiasm. Usually enthusiasm springs from desire for sensual pleasure. Once the pleasure is experienced, the mood converts into lethargy. Then Jaraa takes control of the psyche. She bargains with the person promising social seniority. For this privilege she awards infirmity.

Sex Organs have Deities

The sex organs have presiding deities. One deity may leave the organ while another assumes predominance over it. This depends on the level of energy which the organ consumes. A lower energy attracts a low level deity. A high energy attracts the corresponding deity.

These deities enjoy the pleasure afforded by the organ. However all of the sensual orifices of the body have deities, not just the sexual ones. This means that besides the ancestors who can independently enjoy an organ, a predominating deity can enjoy one as well.

Dietary Distractions

To make the investigation into self-gender, there must be a reduction in all expenditures of the kundalini lifeforce. One must understand that if the core-self is forever preoccupied supplying energy at the whim of the lifeforce it cannot self-focus efficiently to discover anything about itself.

One such area is diet. Sex and everything else is supported by diet which is the fuel which with air intake energizes the entire body. Diet is an important part of the sensual energy. This means content of diet and timing as well. The wrong diet as well as the wrong time of meals may ruin the effort at gender discovery. The connection of diet is twofold: one concerns the type of food and the other concerns how the food is processed in the body. Food is digested by chemical and physical heat which is produced directly and indirectly by the lifeforce. Chemical heat is produce by chemical reaction when gastric juices and enzymes are mixed with the food ingested. This chemical heat changes the food into a mush which in turn is mashed and pressed through the upper intestines so that nutrients are extracted from it.

An ascetic should select the right food for eating. Certain foods promote lethargy. Other foods promote enthusiasm. Yet other foods promote clarity. A yogi should restrict himself to foods which support clarity. Depending on how they are prepared and when they are eaten, some foods can support a different mood. Take rice or wheat for example. These cereals are rated as life-sustaining foods. They participated in man's struggle for existence for thousands of years. They have awards for contributing to our survival. Depending on how they are prepared they could contribute to clarity of mind, enthusiasm for exploitation and stupor.

If one mixes rice, water and sugar and allow that to ferment, wine or vinegar may be produced. This would contribute to the lethargic mood with the possibility of enthusiasm for certain sensual pursuits.

Sugarcane may be exhilarating but if it is fermented it may induce a stunned condition. The ascetic should study food effects so that he can select those which promote clarity and insight consciousness. This will give the core-self the upper hand so that it can better govern the psyche.

Time of Eating

The time of eating is important

Besides the food selection, the time of digestion must be observed. A simple food like milk has varying effects according to the time of consumption. If one drinks it at nine at night, it will not give as good a result as if it is taken at nine in the morning. Some of the milk turns to curd in the stomach. If one drinks milk at nine at night, the curd produced will be pressed through the intestines during the night. This results in energy expenditure in the physical body, while the subtle body was shifted out of it during sleep. The effects of this is that the subtle body has less energy for objective participation and dream recall on the astral side.

If one eats late at night, one cannot stop the food from being processed in the physical system which means that energy will be extracted from the core-self to operate the digestion in the physical body. This will result in less dream recall, lack of objectivity during astral encounters and some pain in the physical system as it works to process the food through the night.

Useful Repulsive Foods

Some foods which the mouth is repulsed from have medicinal value. If prepared in a certain way, these render health in the body. A lemon is sour to taste and contributes to a lack of enthusiasm. Still one may use it to cure a cold or to increase the body's immunity to certain diseases. This would put it in the clarifying mood. Even liquor which is rated as lethargic may serve the body for clarity if it is used as a mouthwash for instance or as a disinfectant to wounds.

Reversive Foods

Some foods are regarded as nutritious and have served mankind with sustenance for thousands of years, and yet if prepared in a certain way such foods may cause stupor or ill health. Foods like butter for instance sustain our bodies, but if taken to excess it causes obesity and vascular disease. It may cause uncontrollable passionate urges and ignorant moods. A yogi must consider the effect of the food, the time eaten and the quantity taken.

Lack of Protein

Lack of protein contributes to celibacy because protein is a boost for the reproductive glands. Anyone who is subject to a poor protein diet will find that sex drive decreases. This however does not mean that it is lost forever. As soon as protein meals are resumed the libido will manifest with full force. A yogi understands the part protein plays in kundalini gender display. Food is part of the composition of sex energy. It is not just the person or the glands or the sensual interest, there are other contributing factors. An ascetic should if he can reduce protein intake so that he is not over-stimulated by sex desire but he should not mistake a lack of protein impetus as true celibacy for it is not.

Foods which Promote Overeating

An ascetic should identify foods which promoted overeating and cease or reduce that diet. In all respects a yogi should reduce the expenditure of energy which is required by the kundalini lifeforce. All operations of the kundalini calls into play the routing of energy from the core-self. This energy expression reduces the core-self's introspective ability which deprives it of self-insight.

For an example of a food which promotes overeating, let us take the example of sugar. When sugar is tasted in a food that produces a desire to have more sweet taste which in turn means that more food is eaten just for the sake of having more taste. This is overeating.

For instance if one is offered bread one may eat say about two slices but if it is a sweet bread one may eat four or more slices. The sugar in sweet bread induces the tasting sense to demand more sugar. The only way to get that is to eat more. The tasting sense causes the hands of the body to acquire more bread just for tasting more sugar. This is the way in which one sense, in this case the tasting sense, can enslave another sense to indulge an unwanted behavior.

Fasting which Produces Overeating

Fasting is supposed to control eating but if it is done haphazardly, it promotes overeating. Most people who do religious fasts and those who curtail eating for reducing obesity, resume overeating as soon as the restraint is concluded. This is because the lifeforce is resistant to curtailment of its food acquisition habits.

Usually fasting plans do not take into account the attitude of the lifeforce. Instead, a fasting regime might be to satisfy a cultural or religious requirement. However despite the gravity of ethnic habits and religious demands, the kundalini effectively resists the disciplines.

Even if the person completes the fast still the kundalini if it did not agree to the deprivation will strike back and cause overeating as soon as the observation served its cultural purpose.

Subtle Body is a Sensual Operation

The subtle body is a sensual operation as a whole but it has singular and multiple sensual pursuits and absorptions. The confusion about whether the core-self is the subtle body or if it is expressed as the subtle body does not go away easily. It takes years and years of meditation to get to the bottom of this.

Knowledge about the subtle body (sukshma sharira) and the core-self (atma) regarding their distinction is not enough to cause realization. Many persons reason that the core-self must not be the subtle body, just as the core-self cannot be the physical system which it uses, and yet that analysis is not the realization.

To understand clearly and distinctly that the core-self is not the physical form, the person has to experience distinction in astral projections but then it means that he or she identifies as the subtle body. Astral projection is the way to distinguish oneself as a subtle body which is distinct from the physical form. Once the yogi experiences the self as the astral body in an astral world which is distinct from the physical body in the physical world, he or she can declare to one and all that he knows for sure that he is not the physical system. Yet, this does not mean that he or she has realized the core-self.

The core-self is not the subtle body but the paradox here is that even though it is not that, it is one of the components which is in the subtle form. There are many components under the hood of a car and yet none of these is itself the car. But the engine which is only one component is the most important part of the car.

The subtle body is similar to a car but in that subtle form there is a core-self which is the essential component. Functionally this is contradicted because the kundalini psychic lifeforce is the most active component in the car. It might be compared to a transmission which converts the energy of the engine to varying rates of speed for the vehicle.

Once the ascetic has many astral projection experiences in which the subtle body is known all by itself without it being influence by the physical system, that yogi can begin the inquiry into the form of the core-self.

Step number one is that one should realize the self as the subtle body which is distinct from the physical form. Step number two is that one should realize that the subtle body is a container in which the core-self is housed.

As a sensation formation, the subtle body is primarily an expression of the kundalini psychic lifeforce. This makes it to be a sensitive apparatus. The self is lured by this sensitivity.

Subtle Body as the Format for Sense Pleasure

The subtle body is the format for sense pleasure. As such the core-self is attracted to its sensations. However this attraction causes the core-self to be a power-supply for the lifeforce. For the experience of sense pleasure, the core-self all but sells itself to the kundalini psychic lifeforce.

The kundalini, not the core-self, is the primary manipulator of the subtle body. It manipulates the form in mining pleasures. However in the process it is forced to mine displeasures as well. This is because the psychic material nature has balanced reversals for whatever is pleasurable. The core-self for its part is attracted to the pleasures and it is held fast for corresponding displeasures.

The yogi should work in meditation to rupture the core-self's attraction to the kundalini, so that there is a check point through which the self can terminate any of the kundalini's mining operations.

The trigger connection between the core-self and the kundalini is the intellect psychic mechanism. The core-self must develop a method of instant disconnection or connection with the intellect but at the core's mere whim not at the intellect's or the kundalini's behest.

Subtle Body as Enemy of Physical Restraint

The subtle body is the release valve for any pressure which is created in the psyche because of inordinate physical restraints. If the kundalini has a desire, or it is in the process of developing one, and an action is taken to physically snuff out that expression, the subtle body acts as a vent to further develop that same desire which was squelched on the physical plane.

A common example of this is a monk who feels a sex desire towards someone, and who takes steps to disassociate with the desire physically. Even if he does so successfully, he may have a wet dream or some other astral development for fulfillment of the desire using the subtle body.

Physical celibacy is a keynote for subtle breaches of the same because the kundalini disrespects the limits imposed by the core-self. When the self is focused on physical morality and other methods of discipline on the physical plane, the kundalini if it is unable to influence the self for contrary behaviors, will shift to the astral level where it has more autonomy. Because the core-self does not supervise the energy expenditures, the kundalini which is the defacto controller simply ignores the core-self and finds some other level for expression of its desires.

Physical Exhibition of Restraint

For the practice of self-gender discovery, the physical level is misleading because whatever is achieved physically is no indication about subtle control. An ascetic must keep the physical in order but he should not feel that what he achieves there leaps over into all subtle planes. The main focus in this practice is the subtle and super-subtle activities.

One cannot rely on social approval because that is based primarily on the actions of the physical body. An ascetic cannot rely on status or social recognition. He has to go inside the psyche to get an understanding of his condition. It is in the privacy of the mind that the ascetic should face up to his faults and find methods of redesigning the psyche.

Monk Status as Advantageous

Being a monk may be advantageous in the quest for discovering the gender of the core-self in distinction to the profiles which are adopted by the kundalini as it transmigrates through numerous physical life forms. All the same being a monk may be disadvantageous. There is no hard and fast rule. Each ascetic must be regarded individually.

If for instance being a monk causes the person to rely more on the physical side of sensuality, then that monk status would be the cause of failure. Each yogi must research this individually to find out what is best in the long term. Ultimately it is the review of the subtle body which counts.

Morality as a Physical Body Objective is Superficial

Though necessary for the sake of social peace-of-mind, morality as a physical body objective is superficial. It has no lasting impact on the subtle form. For a time it may scare off the kundalini but in the long term, the kundalini will breach it. The ascetic must shift the focus to the subtle body and must directly study how the kundalini operates to procure sensual stuffs.

To be clear the ascetic should heed the physical morality in so far as he or she can but with that there should be a clear understanding that physical restraint is limited. If the ascetic breaches social norms, he will find that conflicts with society utilize valuable time which is better spend in meditative states. Thus a yogi should be morally inclined according to the definitions in society but he must also be aware that this compliance does not eliminate the unwanted behaviors of the subtle body.

Subtle Body is Sensually Crazed

The subtle body is all about sensations, very acute thrilling ones. This is why the hope of total detachment from sensual life in the physical or psychic material existences is practically nil. The system is set against anyone getting free of being sensually wired. There are only two ways to beat this system. One is self-effort. Unless there is self-effort there is no hope because the system is designed to do what is natural, which is to use the core-self's power to run the operations of the kundalini lifeforce. If something is natural, and if one requires to change it, one has to commit sustained effort.

The second method of beating the system is to have a powerful agent or agency extract one from it. This means that some deity or some more powerful agency has to link to oneself and transit one to a better environment. Many human beings rely on deities to extract them from this situation but in general that method is impractical.

The two methods of extraction are listed:

- Self-effort
- Extraction by a powerful agent or agency

I feel that both methods are necessary and must simultaneously be applied in the life of the ascetic. Self-effort alone cannot work because from this side of existence one will not get all the necessarily impetus to get out. Grace of a powerful agent or grace energy from a powerful agency cannot work alone either because before the grace can have a matching subject to elevate, the individual has to upgrade himself or herself from within the psyche.

Because the subtle body craves sensual variation, it is of little assistance to the core-self in its bid for self-discovery. The operations of the senses result in direct energy consumption from the core-self. This energy drainage causes a loss of objectivity. Somehow the core has to shift so that the sensually craved subtle body cannot extract energy from the self. That will cause the self to introspect effectively.

Chapter 19
Energy Budget

In the practice of discovering the gender of the core-self, morality has value but not as it is regarded conventionally. A yogi has no use for the conventional meaning of morality but he may comply with it for peace-sake, so that he is not inconvenienced or resented by human society. A yogi should not interfere with the conventions of the world but he must also not allow those stipulations to define his conduct fully.

For this practice, the reason for any type of sense restraint is to cause more efficient energy use and less power extraction from the core-self. This reduction in energy consumption from the self results in more introspection.

An increase in sensual expenditure causes an increase in energy extraction from the self, which in turn causes more extrovert interests. This is against the practice. A decrease in sensual pursuits and expressions causes a decrease in energy extraction from the self, which in turn causes more introvert awareness. This promotes practice.

There are various types of sense consumptions. Some take a little energy such that they are usually ignored. Some take a median amount of energy. These are barely noticed by the self but they are costly nevertheless. Some others being energy intensive consume large quantities of energy. These are the obvious vices. Sex pleasure is regarded as such.

Traditionally celibacy is pinned down as number one achievement for a yogi. Sex indulgence is target as an unwanted behavior. It is such an energy burn that it stands out as a bane of yogis. And yet because it is such an obvious tax it is one of the easiest aspects to isolate. The only stubbornness about sex indulgence is that nature has it as part of the mandatory reproduction process for creature survival. It is an intense attention-consuming process. If the ascetic bisects it, he would understand its composites and can deal with each, step by step.

Other forms of sensuality, especially the minor ones which are hardly observed may be more of a problem than what is objective. Even though their take is tiny, the less-obvious sensual pursuits pilfer energy just the same. Tiny is one thing, continuously being extracted is different. A pin hole in a tank can evacuate the tank if it remains draining continuously.

Sensual Conservation Necessary

Conservation of sensual energy is necessary, otherwise the core-self will not experience insight consciousness. It will be unable to reach deep states in meditation. Since the subtle body craves sensations, the conservation of sensual energy is unnatural to it. Hence the yogi has an uphill struggle in the discovery of self-gender.

Any type of sensual restraint could be good and that includes celibacy. However the ascetic must be aware than applications of restraint may carry an unwanted backlash of increased indulgence at a later date. This happens if the kundalini psychic lifeforce is disagreeable to a discipline which is imposed on it.

It does not matter which sensual orifice is restrained, if the kundalini wants to indulge through that facility, it will note the restraint and apply pressure for the indulgence at the same or at some other time.

There are five sensual means with variations of these as well as with mixtures of two or more of these. If one is restricted the kundalini might sulk about it, in which case, it will resume the banned indulgence as soon as it gets the upper hand over the core-self. Sex indulgence is only one such need which the kundalini would resume. It could be a pleasing sound, a pleasing feeling, a pleasing flavor, a pleasing color or a pleasing odor. It could be a sensation which more than one sense simultaneously appreciates.

The ascetic should never over-rate short-term disciplines. Why should he cease an expression for which he invested heavily already and which nature will not retract. Why should he attempt to cease an activity which is an ancestor's compulsory use of his mind and/or body? The ascetic should have insight to perceive the components of an activity as to if it can be curbed without the kundalini re-enacting it at a later date.

Sometimes it is necessary to fight a losing battle but one should do so with the understanding that it is a waste of time nevertheless. One should not do so with the feeling that one will achieve much. One should have the proper insight and not live on vain hopes and an overestimation of the impact of the core-self's preferences. If the kundalini is more powerful than the core-self and will insists on unwanted behaviors, then at least the self should be aware of this. In the meantime it can study the ways and means of the kundalini to determine how to undermine it in the future.

Benefits of Sensual Conservation

Sensual conservation has such benefits, that the lack of it is detrimental to the progress of an ascetic in terms of his introspecting to get information about the core-self. It is not only sexual conservation of energies. All types of sensuality must be brought to heels. All holes in a leaky tank should be sealed, not just the obvious ones.

Those who focus on sex and other overpowering sensations and who think that the matter ends there, are wishfully thinking themselves into failure. It is sensuality which is the problem not sexuality. Sexuality will continue on and on until the end of time, at least until there are no more animal bodies to beget. Sensuality will continue as well. The ascetic should curtail it, step by step, reducing all outlays sufficiently to proportionately increase the ability to introspect.

The operation of extroversion is based on the core-self's interest in phenomena which is outside of its psyche, as well as interest in information within its psyche which relates to the outdoors of the psyche. The self is both an internal and external investor. It cannot be merely an internal concern. It also cannot be just an external seeker. However in this situation, when it has more external interest than internal concern, it becomes psychotic and cannot properly settle within itself.

The ascetic should gradually reduce sensual pursuits so that there is conservation of the energy which leaks from the core-self to sponsor such activities. There must be a reduction in the small and large leaks as well as the sensation and non-sensational participation. Every type of sensual outreach should be examined for ways to curtail for the sake of increasing the self power which is to be invested in turning the interest of the self back into itself. The self needs to know itself intimately. It must use its interest energy to discover itself. It should sensually investigate itself with the same eagerness which it uses to exploit the outdoor environments.

In common speech self means the person but in this yoga investigation, self means the psyche which is a container in which there is a core-self with adjuncts. This must be sorted. It can only be discovered by conservation of sensual energies. It is not sexual activity which is the key but the commerce between the core-self and its thinking-imagination faculty. These two compatriots have a close relationship which must be splintered. When these two are separated, the core-self will develop insight into itself and will understand how it is connect with and hypnotized by the imagination faculty. Over time in meditation, the core-self will realize itself with a new power so that it can forcibly separate itself from its adjuncts.

Reduction of Sensual Interest Attracts Negativity

A yogi should not expect only positive feelings from others. Reduction of sensual interest, if it is detected by others may cause in some persons resentment and loneliness. A yogi should be ready for negative returns from people who realize that he reduced the sensual participation.

For one who is mostly extrovert, the introvert attitude of a yogi is threatening. The best way is for the yogi to be isolated. This will affect others in the least possible way and will bring much less hard feelings. A yogi, for peace sake, may pretend that he is extrovert. He may pretend that he is interested in worldly existence. But inside his mind, he should have no genuine interest in it.

The Satisfaction Factor

Each sensual experience, sexual intercourse included, has a climatic aspect whereby a person feels satisfied only after having so much of the sensation. In sex experience it is obvious as to there being a climactic moment and there being a subsiding of the pleasure until the psyche courses down to a neutral or dulling state.

Each gender may interpret the same experience in different ways. All sensual experiences have their satisfaction quotient but only in the very sensational ones is it obvious. This means that the less-sensational experiences are more demanding than the obvious ones, because the less-sensational events have vague satisfaction points in reference to if they were concluded.

This is why even if a person is a perfect celibate on the physical side, that someone may become degraded even without being a sexual deviant. Some small incidence might cause that person to assume a lower behavior.

A yogi musts train his nature so that even if there is no satisfaction or if a satisfaction is not concluded, the nature does not hanker for climatic indulgence. The adjunct which is involved with this is the kundalini psychic lifeforce. It relies on complete satisfaction in every type of sensual outreach. If the satisfaction is not gained, it creates a memory for completion. This memory will haunt the self until the satisfaction is realized.

Isolation of Core-Self

The core-self so long as it is unified with or adheres to the kundalini lifeforce, cannot determine what is particular to itself. Hence it becomes confused and identifies with whatever arises as a matter of course. The self assumes responsibility for whatever the kundalini pursues sensually. To change this arrangement, to give the core-self the ability to terminate or freely authorize an activity of the psyche, it has to become isolated. This is not as easy as it sounds because the natural connection between the core-self and the kundalini is through two other adjuncts which are the sense of identity and the intellect analytical mystic tool. Each of these have an influence over the core-self. Each combines with the other in some way to bring the core-self under subjugation.

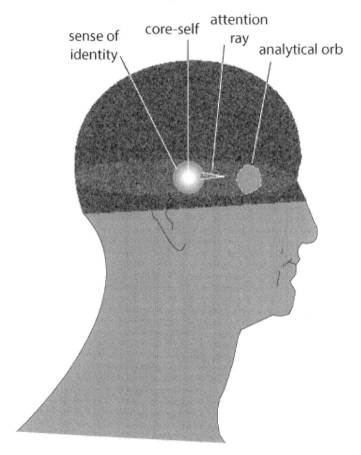

sense of identity   core-self   attention ray   analytical orb

default locations of core-self and
psychic adjuncts in head of subtle body.
kundalini which is in subtle trunk
is not represented

There are simple, semi-complex and super-complex sensations which are either enjoyed or disavowed by the core-self. In all respect the self should sort these to isolate which components are involved in the experiences. Self-segregation is required for the core-self but if the situation is complex the core-self requires more insight, more meditation and a greater degree of mystic accuracy to determine it.

The sense of identity is the adjunct which is closest in vibration to the core-self. It surrounds the core-self spherically but it is a neutral energy which has one function; that of focus. The object of the sense of identity's focus is the intellect which is a psychic technology in the head of the subtle body.

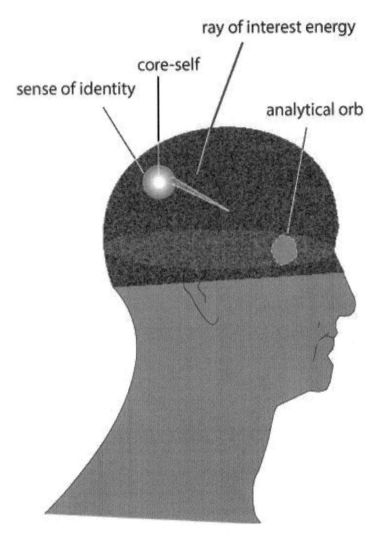

To discover the intellect, the core-self has to isolate itself from thinking and imaging. The psychic organ which imagines and reasons is the intellect. It is the focus of the sense of identity. When the sense of identity makes contact with the intellect, sensual data is made available to the core-self, which it appreciates.

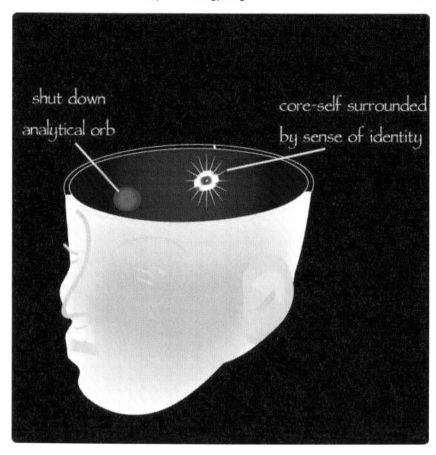

shut down
analytical orb

core-self surrounded
by sense of identity

The intellect for its part is focused on the kundalini psychic lifeforce but it does so in a variety of ways, primarily through the five senses. Besides these there are memory chambers which regard the intellect as their focus. Whenever a memory is activated it leaves the memory chambers and passes through the psyche until it pierces the intellect which displays that information to the sense of identity which in turn, causes the core-self to perceive the data.

In a complex operation, all the adjuncts may be involved such that the core-self becomes bewildered trying to sort the experience. It becomes hypnotized and cannot objectify itself to make an independent decision. The mere awareness of these operations causes energy to flow from the core-self to the adjuncts which in turn further entertains the core-self at its expense.

Separation of the intellect and the kundalini occurs through upgrading the energy level of the kundalini. So long as the kundalini is on a lower level, the intellect cannot separate from it, which means in practical terms that the core-self will be influenced to sponsor undesirable activities. To elevate the kundalini a yogi should do breath-infusion so that the kundalini gets a higher grade of subtle energy which in turn will cause the kundalini to shine brightly, illuminating any psychic area through which it traverses. This will have a direct impact on the intellect such that it will lose interest in low-level operations and will provide the self with data about higher states.

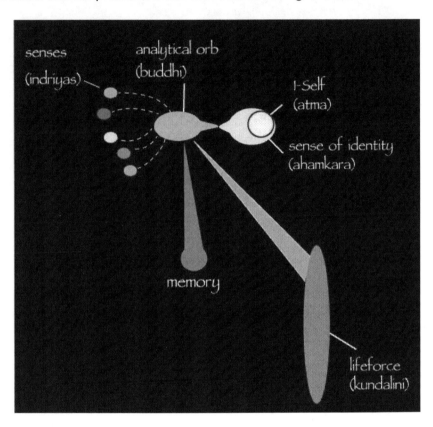

Self-Gender Discovery is a Mystic Process

Physical disciplines, moral actions and any other austerity which has a physical register for the most part, is useless to give the yogi information about self-gender. If he lacks psychic perception, the ascetic should begin with physical practice. Gradually over time, he should transfer focus to the subtle level. Then he can begin to segregate the core-self from its adjuncts and make headway with core-self research.

There is a way to begin with physical practice and then to switch to subtle perception. A yogi should learn this and proceed. Whatever is necessary on the physical plane should be enacted but with the understanding that in the final analysis only the subtle perception counts.

Chapter 20
Lifeforce Independent Operations

It may be considered to be a convenience, a free service, but the lifeforce's creation and maintenance of the physical and subtle bodies is not in the interest of the core-self. Nevertheless no matter how we scream and shout about his, the fact remains that the core-self has to learn lessons from the lifeforce. The core-self must also assist the lifeforce in its maintenance chores and must cooperate with it, even after realizing that the lifeforce does not like to submit to the self.

To what extent should the core-self cooperate with the lifeforce? What routine task of bodily maintenance, should the core-self confiscate from the lifeforce?

As it is, as his material body was created in the parents' bodies, the kundalini is the primary manager. In fact the core-self was ill-equipped to do the duties which the kundalini effortlessly performs. This arrangement is not for benefiting the core-self, and still the core-self may derive some advantage from it. By observing the work ethic of the kundalini, the core-self can determine the changes it would have to make if it were to take control of the psyche.

Hormone Conservation

In the traditional celibate practice hormone conservation is recommended. From the angle of not using hormones for sexual pleasure participation, it makes sense to conserve sexual energy. However when we consider that any energy which is conserved has to be used in one way or the other, it does not make sense to conserve the hormones. The formula for self-gender practice is that as soon as hormone energy is generated in the body it should be used immediately.

If there is no energy conserved, there will be no accumulated energy which may force the ascetic to indulgence in whatever pleasure that energy sponsors. The system is created so that digested food is used to form liquid concentrates in the body. These are the hormonal energies. These serve specific purposes like for instance sex hormones which produce sex interest or libido. However nature's ultimate use of sex hormones is not pleasure but progeny generation. If however the ascetic will not participate in progeny creation, then it is best if his body does not formulate sex hormones.

If there are no such hormones, there will be no sexual interest resulting, there will be no sexual polarity charge which would produce irresistible urges. The question is however:

Is it possible to shut down hormone production?

To be practical, it is best to assume that it can never be totally quieted but it can be reduced. Reduction in food intake, efficient distribution of breath energy, mastership of special asana postures, mind control in terms of reducing focus on sex related objects, would cause reduction in hormone production. The less produced, the more likely it will be for the ascetic to be free of urges.

If one does breath-infusion, food which is processed in the stomach and higher intestines, would be mixed with fresh air. This energy would normally go to certain glands. In those organs it would be concentrated. What if this energy were used before it was concentrated or just when it was concentrated but before it was transported to the organ?

Use of Herbs or Drugs

Gender experience can be altered by using herbs or drugs. These are mostly kundalini alterations which happen because of the influence of chemicals. The kundalini is not the core-self. Its expression of gender is no indication of the core-self's reality.

It is necessary to study the kundalini but it is best to do so without using herbs or drugs. If anything an ascetic who finds it necessary to use the substances, should astutely observe their effects to understand how they shift the level of perception in relation to changes according to the substance which the kundalini consumes. The best method is pranayama breath-infusion. I recommend that for surcharging the psyche with fresh air and subtle pranic energy. This energizes the kundalini and shifts it to a higher plane from which insightful meditation is gained.

Kundalini Arousal

The kundalini is not the core-self. It is not the intellect which imagines and constructs thoughts. It is not the sense of identity which gives the core-self a focusing impulse. The kundalini is neither of the five senses even though it produced those senses. It is not the memory chamber, even though it has memory imprints which operate as instincts. And yet the yogi must arouse the kundalini because its elevation is the preferred method of elevating its behavior.

Remaining on low levels of the kundalini and reforming it from the habits which are native to it, is not the foolproof way of altering it. When one forces the kundalini to behave in a more exalted way, it will resume its lowly behavior as soon as one relaxes the discipline. This will happen time and again because what is natural on any level cannot be permanently removed from that plane by anyone.

To have a permanent change one has to relocate the kundalini to a higher level in which its natural behavior is suitable. Then it cannot resume

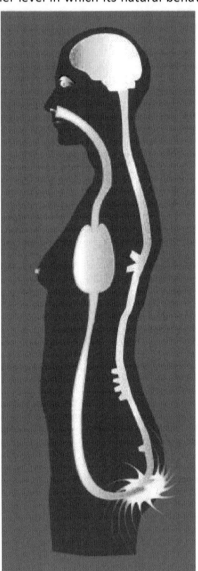

an old behavior unless it is lowered to the level where such is the convention.

Kundalini arousal may happen by chance, every once in a while. One person may have no recall of its arousal except in sexual pleasure experience. For yogis the sure method to daily raise kundalini is the kundalini yoga process of using breath-infusion, particular kapalabhati or bhastrika pranayama, which are rapid breathing systems with focus in the psyche, using compressions, contractions, postures, gestures and mental in-focus.

If the kundalini is raised on a daily basis once or twice per day, eventually it will remain in an aroused condition. Initially it becomes aroused by breath-infusion and then soon after it resumes its lodging at the muladhar base chakra. But from steady practice, it may remain above the neck of the subtle body, continuously energizing the brow and crown chakras which are in the head of the form.

The influence of the brow chakra will in time forge its way to the crown chakra, so that they remain connected at all times in an aroused state. This gives the yogi continuous insight consciousness which is regarded as a type of samadhi elevated perception.

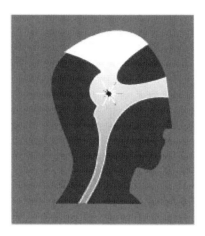

Sense of Belief

The sense of belief, confidence, and faith is a permanent part of the psyche. Everyone exists with this sense. For a yogi, it must be replaced by experience of various dimensional states. To experience higher states, one begins by energizing the kundalini so that its sensations become more sensitive and can more accurately determine objects and environments.

A yogi should strive to shift focus from the physical to the subtle existence, so that more and more he is perceptive of what happens on the subtle plane, and less and less he is focused on making physical history. More and more he should be perceptive of subtle bodies, those of ancestors, those of higher beings and those of yoga teachers.

Breath-Infusion Required

Breath-infusion is beneficial for a yogi because it attacks the heavy hormonal energy, causing it become less dense and making it spread evenly through the physical and subtle forms.

Due to gravity heavy hormonal energy takes a downward route such that it lodges in the lower trunk, thighs, legs and feet. This contributes to a grosser awareness. It reduced the chances of one having insight consciousness.

Initially the ascetic should do breath-infusion aggressively. When he fragments the dense hormones he should pull that lighter energy through the neck into the head of the subtle body.

This causes the kundalini to extract less energy from the core-self which is a perpetual energy producing reality. The reduction in energy extraction from the core-self results in more introspective focus with increase in psychic perception and sensitivity.

Lifeforce Prone to Sensuality

The kundalini lifeforce is addicted to sensuality. This is natural for it because the lifeforce is a sensation-producing psychic mechanism. The life force uses sensation to express itself and to receive energy from other sources. Because the self is unable to self-analyze itself when it is occupied with sensuality, that occupation is negative for the core-self.

When the kundalini is aroused through the spine into the brain, one experiences more clarity of perception as well as detachment from the lower habits of the kundalini. It is as if the lower planes no longer exist. However the lower levels remain in place and are experienced again as soon as the kundalini loses support for the higher levels.

To escape sensual dominance, the core-self must elevate the kundalini by causing it to transit to a higher plane. Then the core-self becomes free of having to be attentive to lower habits of the kundalini energy.

Lifeforce Energy Generation

How the lifeforce generates energy is a process that must be studied by the yogi. Failure to examine this process in detail means that the yogi is not serious about reducing the expenditure of energy which is extracted from the core-self for kundalini operations.

It is a waste of time to think that one can rely on willpower and desire to control the lifeforce because the nature process is such that the conduit of energy from the core-self to the lifeforce is involuntary. Certain operations of energy transfer from the core-self to the kundalini or from the kundalini to the core-self transcends the willpower and desire apparatus. Hence to deal with these issues one has to curtail their energy derivation process by changing the level from which the kundalini operates. It cannot be changed by a command from the core-self because the energy will flow regardless and there is no control-valve which could be shut by a willpower or desire command.

Instead of trying to curtail the energy-flow between the core-self and the kundalini, the ascetic should control the level the kundalini functions from, so that it operates from a plane of awareness which renders insight for the energy it consumes. Though useful, morality and other social checks do not play a part in dealing with the intimacy of the lifeforce and the core-self because the intercourse between the two are not externally social.

Physical Actions which Count

There are physical actions which count but these only count indirectly. The ascetic must not think that physical actions have direct impact. They simply do not because it is the impacts within the subtle body which have a tally in terms of the energies which radiate from the core-self.

The core is a perpetual energy source. Its problem is that it cannot absolutely control the use of every bit of the energy it generates. Adjuncts like the kundalini tap into its energy regardless of whether the core desires to contribute or not. Self-disciplinary procedures are for restricting the flow of energy from the core-self to an adjunct but unfortunately, the core-self cannot restrict every bit of this flow.

It is not a matter of judgement about the social value of physical or psychic actions. Here our interest is on checking the energy transfers which empower the adjuncts. Then we check to see if we can eliminate those transfers. The only method for doing that is to relocate the adjuncts to a level of consciousness in which they no longer require the energy.

If one remains on a level where it is natural for an adjunct to draw energy from the core-self for undesirable behaviors, then no amount of discipline will permanently stop the flow of the energy, even though some disciplines will do so temporarily. The secret is to relocate the adjunct to a plane of consciousness where it has no need for that undesirable behavior and does not make an endeavor to fund it.

We may however permanently reduce some behaviors which we cannot totally eliminate on a plane of consciousness which we must function on either because we have a physical body or a subtle one. Yes, one should certainly reduce such habits and should do so permanently if that is possible. But all the same one should realize that a reduction is not an elimination. Thus again, one is faced with the task of relocation if not in the present, then in the future, to a higher plane in which the behavior is not performed by the adjunct.

The understanding is that until one can relocate the adjunct to a plane where the undesirable behavior is unnatural for it. Any restrictive method will be incomplete because the adjunct will resume the behavior even if it is temporarily suspended by a disciplinary action. There is a revealing statement made by Krishna to Arjuna about this:

विषया विनिवर्तन्ते

निराहारस्य देहिनः।

रसवर्जं रसोऽप्यस्य

परं दृष्ट्वा निवर्तते ॥ २.५९ ॥

viṣayā vinivartante
nirāhārasya dehinaḥ
rasavarjaṁ raso'pyasya
paraṁ dṛṣṭvā nivartate (2.59)

viṣayā = viṣayāḥ — temptations; vinivartante — turn away; nirāhārasya — from(without) indulgence; dehinaḥ — of the embodied soul; rasavarjaṁ = rasa — memory or mental flavor of past indulgences + varjaṁ — except for, besides; raso = rasah — memories (mental flavors); 'pyasya = apyasya = apy (api) — even + asya — of him; paraṁ — higher stage; dṛṣṭvā — having experienced; nivartate — leaves

The temptations themselves turn away from the disciplinary attitude of an ascetic, but the memory of previous indulgences remain with him. When he experiences higher stages, those memories leave him. (Bhagavad Gita 2.59)

Even though for a powerful ascetic, the pressure to indulge becomes manageable, it only does so under certain conditions and only temporarily under those circumstances. And certainly, the psyche will keep trying to resume the behaviors because stored memories and instincts will repeatedly produce urges for the fulfillments. It is only if the ascetic reaches a higher plane where those behaviors do not occur, that he will experience permanent relief.

Even though on lower planes, his effort for permanent change will undoubtedly fail, the ascetic should endeavor for control regardless, but with the understanding that it is not possible to bring the undesirable behavior to a complete termination. In the meantime however he should strive to relocate the adjunct to a higher level where it does not have such impulsions or to a higher plane where that adjunct and its urges does not exist.

Simple Bad Habits

Many simple habits contribute negatively to spiritual practice. These may be behaviors with indirect impact. The yogi should realize these and either curtail or eliminate them. Let us take the habit of eating fried rice. This is a material substance with impact on the material body.

First of all the human gut system is designed to process foods which have a liquefied state. The intestines need a mush of food which is liquefied, if one eats something dry then the intestines must first liquefy that substance before it can be digested. This means that eating dried foods is unfavorable.

If one eats fried rice and does not take a liquid, dhal or soup along with it, the body will struggle to process it. The digestion will take much longer than it should, than say if one were to use rice which is liquid-saturated.

Once fried rice is used, the intestines must squeeze it through the long winding track. If the rice is dried it will quickly become compacted which means that it will take longer to transit the intestines and colon. This means that the lifeforce must procure energy to operate the muscular action of the intestines and colon for extracting nutrients from the rice.

This is where the core-self is involved because whenever the lifeforce must expend itself, it will extract some of the required energy from the core-self. This extraction causes the core-self to lose insight consciousness and to be more extrovert. It is not the rice or the digestive process which causes the core-self to be negatively involved. Directly, it is the extra draw of energy from the core-self which the kundalini requires because it has to process a dry food when the intestinal track is not designed to do so.

Once he realizes this, the ascetic should either cease eating fried rice, or reduce consumption of it. If he ceases the habit, he will have to deal with the torment of memories about the pleasurable side of eating the rice. These memories will haunt him relentlessly until he abandons the discipline and resumes eating it or he switched to another level where the kundalini no longer feels a need for that fried food.

Lifestyle

Lifestyle means the methods of the material body, as to how it manages in this material existence. An ascetic should be prepared to adjust the lifestyle on and on, day by day, just to facilitate fate and the yoga practice.

Fate is not always agreeable to yoga practice but that has to be accepted by the yogi. He should negotiate fate regardless of if it is favorable or unfavorable. An ascetic should not aggravate destiny but should do whatever can be done to facilitate it. All the while given the opportunity one should always resume yoga practice and the lifestyle which accelerates it.

A smart yogi should hold no resentment against fate but should realize that whatever fate takes rightfully belongs to it. The yogi is an individual limited person in this existence. He should not expect to gain anything unless fate grants it willingly.

Subtle Body Efficiency

Even though the ultimate objective of this practice is the core-self's gender which is not related to either the subtle body's expression or the physical body's sex alignment, still the physical and subtle systems need to be reined in so that the energy invested in them by the core-self is reduced considerably.

If an ascetic could abolish the physical or subtle body with the flick of a finger or with a wish, then there would be no need to study those bodies and find methods for reining in their sensuality. A yogi must be realistic and should not indulge in wishful thinking and imaginative schemes which the kundalini just will not align itself with.

A simple matter such as strenuous work of the physical body could indirectly impact the meditations one may do for core-self gender discovery. This is because if the actions of the physical or subtle systems cause the kundalini to extract energy from the core-self, the self will be unable to do undistracted introspection due to the energy drainage. As it is, if there is drainage of energy from the core-self, its attention will follow that energy. Stated more precisely the sense of identity which surrounds the core-self follows the focal interest of the kundalini and in doing so causes a leakage of energy from the core-self.

If for instance one works strenuously, it will use up much hormonal energy from the body, so much that the cells may be starved of this energy. The kundalini will then take steps to get for itself a larger quota of energy from the self. This will cause the self to be more extrovert in terms of focusing itself on the kundalini. This focus will act as a large conduit to transmit much energy from the core self. In turn, any effort to meditate will be frustrated because the self will find that it cannot fully internalize.

A yogi must carefully observe these operations, so that he can reduce energy consumption, otherwise his wish to enter deep meditations will be frustrated. The self will find itself to be extrovert either seeking mundane things outside of the psyche or subtle mundane things within the psyche.

Physical/Subtle Bodies Relationship

It is necessary that a yogi should have detailed insight into the operations of the physical and subtle bodies, as well as how one relates to and is affected by the other.

These bodies are related to each other through the kundalini psychic lifeforce. It controls and maintains the bodies with little supervisory assistance from the core-self but with extracting energy from the self. While the physical body is alive, the kundalini resides primarily in the physical form at the base of the spinal column but when the physical body dies, the kundalini transfers itself into the subtle form and remains there until another physical body develops. The embryo develops around the influence of the kundalini and in that sense it is identical with the kundalini but at death this apparent unity is cancelled.

The core-self is stationed in the subtle body. It is never based primarily in the physical form. However it is aware of the physical system through its connection with the kundalini lifeforce. Through sensations which are emitted by the kundalini, the core-self gets some idea about physicality.

In dream states, the physical system usually sleeps while the subtle one either acts on the subtle planes or acts within the imagination faculty. In conscious astral projections, the core-self along with the imagination faculty (intellect) functions socially in the astral world, while the physical body remains asleep or mimics the subtle activities (sleep acting).

If both the physical and subtle systems rest, that may happen with both being interspaced or with one displaced from the other. Rest activities of the physical system are conducted by the kundalini psyche lifeforce's actions or by substances which affect the kundalini by putting it to sleep, decommissioning it so that it has no activity except that of remaining in existence.

Physical Celibacy out of the Question

There should be no reliance on physical celibacy as a sign of advancement for an ascetic. Unless a person can detail his subtle activities as being sex-free in total, a claim to celibacy is ludicrous. Most of it is self-dishonesty. For the social purpose, it may be beneficial to be physically celibate but for the spiritual advancement the result must show on the subtle side. Which ascetic has full objective view on the subtle side at all times, when the subtle and physical forms are interspaced and when they are temporarily separated from each other?

Physical celibacy has value in the social world but it is limited otherwise and should not cause the ascetic to develop pride in it as a spiritual achievement. The whole sensual outlay of the psyche must be examined. Any part of it, sexual or otherwise could betray the core-self. One should have a comprehensive austerity.

Negativity towards Sexual Indulgence is Ineffective

Some ascetics carry a negativity towards sexual indulgence and/or to other forms of sensuality. This approach converts into their undoing because the only way out of sensual victimization is to face up to the truth about each type of vice which one has or which one may develop.

There are two sides to a vice. One concerns the obvious pleasure it yields. The other side concerns its negative aspect which is billed to the enjoyer as the long-ranged undesirable result. An example is the overeating of sugar. Much sugar is sweet to taste. That is the pleasure yield. However in the long term it causes tooth decay and organ deterioration resulting in diabetes.

Apart from that there is addiction for sweet taste. That causes over-eating. Over-eating results in compounded problems for the body. If merely on its negative returns one ceases eating sugar, one will never confront the self in relation to the positive aspects such as the sweet taste which is desirable.

Condemning sexual indulgence or any other sensual vice merely on its negative consequences cannot remove the habit entirely. One must also review the positives and deal with that head on with a decision to forgo that to free the self.

One side of the discussion is to show the negative aspects but the other side concerns evaluating the enjoyment yield and then deciding to forgo it. Even then however the issue is not resolved because one will still be in a realm where that pleasure is available. At any moment according to circumstantial pressure, one may have to resume the habit. Hence after considering the negative and positive aspects, the ascetic must comb through existence to find a place where the vice is absent. All tensions are permanently relieved for the yogi who relocates to some place which does not offer that vice as an experience.

New Psyche Design

The solution to the problem of vices is to redesign the subtle body or to derive another type of subtle form which does not have the vices as a possible experience. Unless it provides a new psyche which has none of the unwanted experiences within it, morality or austerity is an unreliable method.

There is no question of sitting doing absolutely nothing. Until the ascetic can assume a different psyche or can get the current one redesigned, he should take steps to reduce sensual incidences which cause the core-self to go in an extrovert direction. But he should always be aware that a dimensional shift will be necessary.

The present dimension is pressing upon the ascetic day and night. He must make a concerted effort to manage this using morality and austerity but he must also develop insight into how he can transit away from this plane eventually. What is required is a dimension in which the core-self does not have to supply energy to an independent survival-mechanism or kundalini.

Reactionary Methods of Sensual Rejection

Sensual pleasure rejection because of having a bad experience does not serve the purpose to remove the ascetic from having to again participate in the rejected experience. This is because the psyche was designed to accommodate the event. Regardless of if the person wants the pleasure or not, the psyche has the potential for re-enacting the circumstance. In fact it will again pursue and develop within itself the experience.

Reactionary methods are based on hasty conclusions, which will not serve the purpose to delete the unwanted habits. The ascetic should have a scientific approach which includes careful analysis of the formation of the urge. Can it be totally removed? Will it go into dormancy and then reappear later when the ascetic does not have the power to prevent it?

Pleasure Starvation Causes Retrogression of Austerity

The psyche is not the core-self which means that some undesirable needs of the psyche must be fulfilled even when the core-self will be worse off for it. An ascetic must consider this and relate how to reduce undesirable experiences to the minimum while simultaneously locating a dimension in which such experiences are not manifest.

Starving the psyche of pleasures which it feels it should have, results in suppression for the time being with expression in full force at a later day. The ascetic suppresses a tendency or urge and deprives the psyche of fulfilment but only for a time. Eventually the suppressed energy accumulates a massive force, which commandeers the psyche and causes it to indulge in the condemned behavior. Then the core-self is helpless to stop the experience.

I recommend that an ascetic should if he can suppress what is unwanted but with the understanding that the suppression causes a disadvantage in the form of dormant energy which is made more and more powerful with each passing day. Hence along with suppression the ascetic should search for a level where the unwanted feature is never manifested. He should develop a method of transit to that plane.

Isolation is required

Persons doing this yoga practice for discovery of self-gender must by all means become isolated, or as isolated as fate would permit. If one fails to do this, one will have difficult consolidating the progress and penetrating within to the core-self. Any distraction for any reason results in extrovert tendencies to be again awakened which means that in meditation, some time will be used to counteract the outward-going energy. This will happen with any type of sensuality not just with sexuality. Any small or large incursion upon meditation is undesirable. Nothing passes the test if it interferes with meditation even in the smallest way.

To consolidate on internalization of the psyche, one must not regress from day to day, otherwise one will be like Sisyphus who in the myth lost grip of the boulder before he reached the summit and had to begin rolling it up the hill again. It does happen that one makes leaps and bounds in meditation and then due to a small or large incursion one finds that the progress was erased.

The environment is such that there are many triggers for interaction. Any of these can cause the ascetic to become involved for social participation. The ascetic should remain out of sight so as to reduce the incidences.

On the basis of interactions in past lives, every being has potential for interaction with some other being but an ascetic should remain out of sight so that nature is not prompted to activate unfinished business from past lives. Consider going elsewhere and leaving all of this behind. One does not have to settle every difference, compensate for every wrong-doing or be available for every good return from past actions. This can all be left as is, unclaimed.

Ancestral Influence Uproots the Celibate Effort

Ancestral influence effectively uproots the celibate effort, making it near impossible for anyone to be fully celibate. So long as a body has ancestors, and so long as they require embryos, the idea of celibacy is to be questioned. The question arises repeatedly as to who owns the body.

Does the ascetic own it?

Is the spiritual aspirations of the ascetic enough to effectively offset the need of the ancestors for embryos?

Are we saying that the celibacy of a monk thoroughly cancels the contribution of the ancestors to the formation of the monk's body?

The presence of ancestors is proof that the ascetic does not own his body and cannot disenfranchise the ancestors without negative consequence. Of course if the ascetic escapes to another dimension, he or she might avoid the reaction.

Spiritual Body Unknown

Knowing the gender of the core-self as it would be if the self were to realize itself as a spiritual being in an imperishable body-format, is an off-limits subject except for those ascetic who experienced the self in a spiritual environment during meditation states. Everyone else is better off not imagining what that spiritual gender would be.

The immediate realization of the core-self gender under its present circumstances in the presence of its adjuncts is that of neuter configuration. Its shape is particle-like with spiritual light emanating from it spherically. It is realized as such in the existential center of the head of the subtle body.

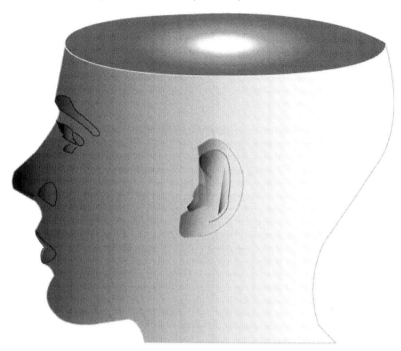

An individual spirit may or may not be neuter but regardless, in this creation the realization is that it is neuter because this place does not accommodate any other spiritual configuration of it. Thus a spiritual body besides a particle-like form is unknown here.

Aggressive Physio-Psychic Practice

To increase the efficiency of energy used and to reduce to the minimum the energy which is extracted from the core-self, a yogi should practice physio-psychic techniques which target the physical and subtle bodies. Their consumption of attention from the core-self should be reduced considerably.

It is not the activity we are concerned with but its energy consumption. Ultimately the ascetic must jump to other dimensions in which a certain necessary activity which is an inefficient energy consumption behavior, is absent. In the meantime until the full transit is made, the yogi should reduce consumption of any sensual expression which drains energy from the core-self for physical or subtle acts which give the core-self no clarity but instead provide it with increased bewilderment.

Hatha Yoga

Hatha yoga as it was taught by Gorakshnath Mahayogin and detailed by Swatmarama in his book *Hatha Yoga Pradipika* is the process for doing aggressive physio-psychic practice. It consist of altering the behavior of the physical and subtle bodies by targeting the kundalini to make it less resistant to the core-self and more accommodating for increasing the self's autonomy.

The kundalini is a wayward energy which has intelligence. It is naturally framed to act independent of the core-self. By using hatha yoga, a yogi can rein in the kundalini so that its sensual quest is curtailed giving the core-self more objectivity. One should study *Hatha Yoga Pradipika*. I penned a detailed explanation which is titled *Kundalini Hatha Yoga Pradipika*. That texts charts the physio-psychic practice.

Asana Postures

Hatha yoga begins with asana postures which are stretches and relaxation of muscles and tendons in the physical body. As this is done the yogi should share focus over into the subtle form. The energy consumption for maintaining the physical and subtle system for their basic upkeep should be more efficient and should be reduced. Asana postures results in a reduction.

If the kundalini psychic lifeforce has to increase its maintenance functions it will extract more energy from the core-self. The self will be unable to stop this extraction. The increase will cause more impulsive extroversion and contribute to the inability of the person to meditate. Hatha yoga, even the physical parts of the practice have relevance in this process of kundalini self-tantric.

Pranayama Breath-Infusion

The second feature of hatha yoga is breath-infusion. This is done separately or is combined with the asana postures. The postures with the contraction and relaxation of parts of the body, cause the release of toxins in the cells and bloodstream. Some will travel to the lungs where it will be expelled in the normal course of breathing. Some however recombine into the cells and tissues. If one does asana postures and does not do pranayama breath-infusion, much of the released toxins will recombine into the body.

The big value of breath-infusion in this regard is that it draws out the released toxins causing it to be transited to the lungs where it is expelled from the body in the form of pollutant gases. Pranayama breath-infusion can be done as a separate practice just after doing the asana postures, but it is best to combine the two practices, so that as soon as toxins are released while doing a stretch, those gases are transported to the lungs for expulsion. This will result in the added benefit of infusing fresh air into the blood stream every time any negative gases are expelled.

There are several pranayama process but the two recommended in this publication are kapalabhati and bhastrika. Bhastrika is the advanced stage of kapalabhati practice. The different is that in kapalabhati stress is placed on the exhale with the inhale occurring reflexively, while for bhastrika both the inhale and exhale are stressed. Both are monitored. After a series of rapid breaths in a certain posture, the yogi ceases the breathing on an inhale or exhale, usually on an inhale. He applies compression locks on the body and then observes within the psyche the movement of the infused breath energy.

Breath-Infusion Affects the Subtle Body

Breath-infusion is simultaneously a subtle and physical process but so is just about anything one may do with a physical body. It is a matter of focus. Initially when someone begins to do asana postures and pranayama breath-infusion, it happens as a purely physical motion. Later when the physical side is not stressed, when that becomes routine, the focus switches to the subtle body. This begins by focusing on the feelings in the nervous system. It shifts into the emotional sensations which arise during the maneuvers of practice. By tracking the sensations, a yogi perceives the format of the subtle body.

Breath-infusion is for detecting, analyzing and adjusting the subtle body. The most sensational force within the subtle form is the kundalini. When it is breath-infused sufficiently, it becomes aroused, causing rapid energy movements and upgraded consciousness which provides insight into higher states.

Muscular Contractions / Locks

There are five primary muscular contractions which are known otherwise as locks or bandhas. These are done in different postures with or without breath-infusion. It is preferred however that these be used with infusion. There are many more locks but the five primary ones are:

- Anus lock
- Sex lock
- Navel lock
- Neck lock
- Mind lock

The **anus lock** is also known as ashwini mudra or the action of a horse's rectum where it presses outward and then is withdrawn inwards. This entails pulling up the anal sphincter muscles. The anus terminates into a circular muscle which relaxes in a contracted condition like a rubber band.

The circular anal muscle is pulled upwards in a strong steady way and then it is gradually released. This is how it is applied for asana postures. The student pulls up and relaxes or pulls up then pushes out then relaxes, or does the pull up and push out several times then relaxes. It is also done in specific postures.

For beginners the **sex lock** is a double lock where the urinary and perineum muscles are applied simultaneously. At first a student cannot sort the two muscles. Later after contracting that conjoint muscle, the student will find that there are two distinct actions which can be segregated, so that he can contract and relax the urinary muscle or do the same with the perineum. These muscles are pulled up and back simultaneously. They are contracted repeatedly for a set number in various postures. The key action concerns the perineum or sex organ muscle. This is the one of interest in this practice. Once a yogi can sort that muscle, he can when doing certain postures, apply the contraction and then relax it repeatedly until it reacts instantly to a willpower command.

The **navel lock** is for arresting the colon, higher intestines and stomach. This may serve to compress the subtle energy. This causes a further breakup of the brick-like pranic energy which comprises the gut. Eventually the ascetic could change the gut by eliminating the need for it in the subtle body. This frees the yogi from the need for taking an embryo after the physical system dies.

The **neck lock** is for supervising the movement of energy from the trunk of the subtle body into the head of the form. At first the objective is to cause kundalini to be aroused up the spine and guide it through the sushumna nadi central spinal passage. Once this is achieved, he should aim to pull up energy which would otherwise be channeled to glands for hormone production. Instead of creating hormones from the energy which is extracted from the stomach and intestine, the yogi should redesign the system so that the energy extracted goes upwards through the neck and does not form into a hormonal force which has to be infused and redirected or be directed through glands and then be re-routed as desired.

The **mind lock** is done in the head of the subtle body. It concerns keeping the attention and interest centralized and being vigilant to know the whereabouts of any energy which enters the head so that the yogi can supervise its transit.

Chapter 21
Kundalini Control

Anyone who aspires for complete celibacy of the subtle body aims at something which is near impossible. Such a person fights a losing battle because the psychic material nature is dead set against this. Everyone in the universe is polarized one way or the other. It is not one homogenous whole something. There is variety in every direction, with attractions, repulsions and neutralities in combination.

The quest for celibacy is a worthy cause but in so far as it is done merely by dreaming up lofty aspirations, it is a blanket failure for the ascetic. If anything one should aspire for it in a realistic way in consideration of the lack of support by material nature and in nature's use of the sex drive for reproductive purposes.

There are two paths for celibacy. One is to have the aspiration and have no sexual partner. The other is to have it and have a sexual partner. In either the challenge is the same, even though externally it appears that the single ascetic has the advantage.

Neither has an edge when we consider celibacy as it relates to the subtle body. That body is free to indulge. It has no regard for social morality. On the astral planes, the celibate idea is irrelevant because the astral form can assume different dimensions simultaneously. It is not boxed in with one set of persons as the physical body is restricted.

Loneliness on the Celibate Path

A single or partnered ascetic, who aspires for celibacy has a lonely course to take. In either case, it is an individual examination with application of austerity to the subtle body. Regardless of physical indulgence or the lack of it, the subtle body must be monitored so that the ascetic can rate its indulgence.

Sexuality is only one facet of sensuality. In all respects, the sensual range of indulgence is vast with sex being an easy to identify and seemingly prominent feature.

Having a partner does not make the curtailment of sexuality or sensuality more difficult or easy. It is a challenge to those who are physically single or those who are partnered. Both must look aside from their physical performance and focus on bringing the subtle body to term.

Mystic Perception is Necessary

One who has no mystic perception cannot be successful in kundalini self-gender discovery. It is impossible to take the proper psychic actions if one does not have insight consciousness. However one may become trained so that one develops the vision. It does not matter if one is a partnered or not, if one has mystic perception and if one keeps developing it to improve accuracy, one could study this path and achieve it. One must be willing to break up the unity of the self. The core-self in particular must be segregated.

The so-called self is a composite consisting of a core-self, a sense of identity, an intellect, a kundalini with senses and memories. These are housed in a subtle body which is labeled as a self. It is not a cohesive reality because the core-self and its adjuncts have different frequency resonances. The core-self is such a high frequency that it cannot directly connect to the kundalini psychic lifeforce. The only adjunct which enjoys an intimate connection with the core-self is the sense of identity. This identity in turn has a close connection with the intellect, which in turn is intimate with the kundalini. The memories which are stored impressions of past circumstances also enjoys an intimate connection with the intellect. This is because the memories use kundalini sensation energy to write their information.

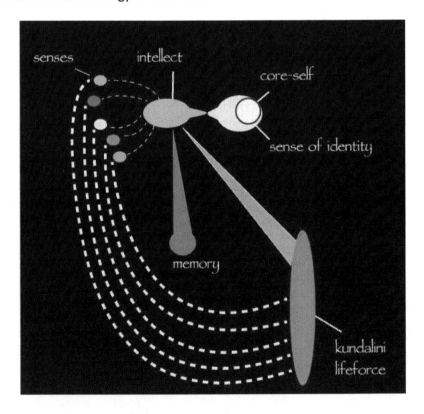

The senses are off-shoots of the kundalini psychic lifeforce but the senses are intimate with both the kundalini and the intellect. Each yogi must strive to perceive the core-self and its adjuncts as separate items in the psyche or self. A Yogi should stop mistaking the self or psyche as one cohesive reality. In practice however, in the social usage of the self, the yogi should comply with the convention which is to identity the self as one part-less reality. It does have parts but the yogi gains nothing by objecting to the social convention, even though during meditation and in the privacy of the mind, he should always be aware of the core-self as being distinct from its adjuncts.

Each Gender has Similar and Dissimilar Challenges

In the quest for control of the sensual energies, each gender has similar and dissimilar challenges. For each person of each gender it is unique. Ascetics should compare notes, hold productive discussions and study the successes and failures of each other. However it is a singular conquest, not a group effort.

Sorting the core-self from its adjuncts is a major accomplishment. After that there is much research to be done to realize the power of the core-self, its lack of control and the specific features of the adjuncts which the core-self cannot regulate.

If it is a fact that the core-self cannot control every bit of its energy which is used by the adjuncts, the question of how to reduce such energy intake becomes important. What would happen if the energy consumed, decreased to the minimum? What percentage of autonomy would that allow the core-self over the psyche?

There are general approaches to discovering self-gender which every ascetic of either sex may apply but there are specific remedies which one person must apply which would not be relevant to another yogi.

What is the gender of one ascetic? Is it male, female or neuter? Which gender should he or she adopt? That of the physical body?

That of the subtle form? That of the kundalini?

Reduction of Sensual Outreach

A yogi must see that the priority is reduction of sensual outreach, which includes sexual participation. As much as fate would allow, a yogi should by disinterest reduce all forms of sensual participation. This may begin with physical restriction and detachment but the real target is the subtle body. The psychic movements are the area in which the yogi should hammer out control.

The stretching out of any sense to anything in the physical or subtle environments should be curtailed. Every act no matter how minor and abstract should be catalogued.

The objective is to curtail the energy drainage from the core-self. The culprit is the kundalini which has the power to extract energy from the core-self. This energy absorption causes the core-self to be extrovert, to neglect itself and to remain unknown to itself.

Subtle Actions to Take

To grasp the sensuality and begin reducing its outreach, a yogi or yogini should do the following:

- Identify excess sensual outreach
- Note the joy of acquiring excess indulgence
- Manage feelings of helplessness in regards to excess indulgence
- Note the core-self's inability to reduce the influence of those who promote indulgence

Identify Excess Sensual Outreach

Any excessive sensual outreach should be realized by the ascetic. It does not matter if it is sexual indulgence or criticizing others. Even the smallest most insignificant sensual quest which is excessive is a danger to the ascetic. It is a mistake to focus only on the blatant breaches because these obvious vices are highlighted easily and targeted swiftly if one has effective methods of dealing with them. But these as well as the minor breaches have flip-back factors which when the ascetic is inattentive, will reassert with irresistible force.

Identification is necessary but it does not solve the problem of the core-self's forced participation in enjoying something which causes it to be drained of energy and to lose self-focus. The drainage of energy does not mean that the self becomes exhausted. It is a perpetual energy source. It is not exhaustion which is noted but rather extroversion with a lack of introspection.

Identification is the beginning of the process of determining what can be done to first reduce the outreach and then to find out if it is possible to eliminate it altogether. If it cannot be eliminated the self should consider relocating to an environment in which that outreach is totally absent.

Note the Joy of Acquiring Excess Indulgence

The yogi should after identifying an excessive outreach, note the joy he gets when indulging. How is this joy produced? What is the complex of energies which comprise that pleasure? Is the joy worth the negative aspect of the experience? Can the self get the joy and not lose insight simultaneously? If the pleasure must be had with the loss of the core-self's introspective ability, can that need for the involvement be removed from the psyche?

Manage Feelings of Helplessness in Regards to Excess Indulgence

Some outreaches are such powerful vices, that the ascetic after identifying with them is unable to curtail the behaviors. The ascetic feels helpless. At this stage some students turn away from asceticism. They abandon the practice due to frustration fatigue.

One who persists even after realizing that he is not powerful enough to upset an excessive behavior, does so because of being courageous and due to support from an advanced yogi. This person feels that even if he cannot rid the self of a destructive habit, still he should persist in the attempt even if it will render partial success.

One must manage the feeling of helplessness so that one can proceed and make progress in another area of pleasure regulation. In this respect small sensual outreaches are a great help to the yogi while a sensational one like sex desire is left as it is for the time being.

Note the Core-Self's Inability to Reduce
the Influence of Those who Promote Indulgence

An ascetic must note his inability to reduce the influence of people who encourage or induce him to indulge in excessive behaviors. By identifying these people even departed souls, he can plan how to ease from their association. He must admit to himself that he was open to their suggestions. He should find a way to avoid such persons. It is best that he not discuss the issue but should quietly move away from the influence.

Unlimited Variations of Sensual Appropriation

The psyche is capable of unlimited variations of sensual exploitation. However the tools used for procurement are the same. The pleasure extracted is similar even though the combinations vary considerably. Our concern in the practice of kundalini self-tantric is the inner content of an experience and the quest formation within the psyche which would result in the pursuit of an experience.

Once a pleasure is sensed, how does the self extract energy from the experience? Suppose the pleasure is derived from an object which is outside the psyche, how does the psyche experience inner sensations within itself? Conversely, suppose the pleasure is derived from an object within the psyche, how does the psyche realize that specific energy in contrast to its other sensations?

Sense Experience is a Composite

Sense experience is a composite of many different energies. Part of the way to undermine the self's irresistible attraction to it, is to discover the parts. Some of the mystery of any composite is dissolved as soon as one can see the individual parts and how they are combined as one unit.

The kundalini is involved because it provides the sensations which will flash here and there to compose the pleasurable or undesirable feelings. The memory may be involved because it will provide a registry of the event and will locate a previous reference to a similar occurrence. The intellect is involved because it will relate to the sense of identity its opinion about the sensations as to if they are irresistible or of little consequence. A particular sense, or some senses in concert, are involved. They will reach out to procure the experience. The core-self is involved because it will contribute energy to help energize the psyche which becomes the subject of the experience.

Besides this, if the object is inanimate, it will emit information by its mere presence. If the object is animate, it will emit information and produce sensations to represent what it desires to express in the environment.

Misunderstanding Sensuality

A yogi may begin this quest with a misunderstanding about sensual control; which is that one should absolutely control the senses. There are many ascetic groups which indulge in the fantasy of absolute sense control. If someone is discovered violating the precepts others will condemn that person as lacking sense control, as failing to control behaviors which are sense-motivated.

This bespeaks a religious or disciplinary sect which does not understand what sensuality is. In the first place it is unnatural for anyone to have absolute control of the senses. If we begin with the premise that the individual should control his or her senses absolutely, we start with a fallacy.

The individual is not supposed to have absolute control over anything, not even over his or her psyche. The individual must endeavor even for an understanding of the percentage of control he or she may have. Once the individual realizes the degree of control, he or she may strive to increase that percentage but there will never be a time when there is absolute control.

In fact control has to do with the psyche design and the environment in which the psyche functions. The question is not: Should I have absolute control?

The question is: Where could I have a format which interacts with an environment which always affords the core-self beneficial interactions without negative consequences.

For the time being, the ascetic should strive to get the most from this present situation but he or she should not waste valuable energy thinking about the impossible. Manage this as best as you can. Reduce the psychological expenditures of the kundalini as much as is possible. Be sure to research other dimensions in which the core-self is not subjected to negative returns.

Resentment from Lack of Sensual Participation

Sensual participation is of two types:
- Self-sensuality
- Social-sensuality

Self-sensuality is sensual self-indulgence which on the surface seems to be the individual indulging in sensual pleasure by himself or herself. On close examination there is no such thing as self-sensuality but from the angle of physical perception, there seems to be. Unless there is proof that no one else from any plane of existence interacted with the individual, it is not valid that the person is self-indulgent.

Departed ancestors living in the psyche may indulge from within the mind and emotions of the person. A relative who uses a physical body may send psychic inputs which cause indulgence.

Within the psyche any adjunct and the core self may interact to cause indulgence. When we say self-sensuality we need to define the components of the urges.

Social-sensuality is when there are obvious participants with the ascetic. These would be physical people who inspire, encourage, and participate in an experience of sensuality. This could be a thrilling indulgence or some other experience which has tiny bits of sensational experience only.

If the ascetic does not participate in a sensual experience, he or she may become the target of resentment either from others or even from one of the adjuncts. How to manage resentment energy? Can the ascetic ignore it safely?

Tantric Practice Failure

Tantric practice which means disciplines or participations between more than one person, for sexual or other reasons, is not part of kundalini self-tantric. However any information one may glean from tantric practice might serve as impetus to proceed with this very different self-tantric discipline.

Partner tantric is a mix of energies. These are difficult to sort. Just to figure one's self-gender is problematic and takes endless research and application. We could imagine the task for the complexity of partner-tantric. It is not about pleasure. It is not about sensation exploration. It is about the root of the gender, the breaking off from the kundalini gender displays to locate the essential singular core-self.

The upset in partner tantric is the relationship one would have with a deity or with two deities if each partner is connected to different spiritual root-persons. Mostly, partner-tantric is really kundalini-tantric practice or the exploration of the gender potential and expression of the kundalini psychic lifeforce. This is not core-self investigation.

The mistake of some tantric yogis is that they mistake the gender identity of the kundalini as that of the core-self. Nothing is further from the truth. The kundalini is not the core-self. Its preferences and expression are not those of the core. The misconception occurs because of the inability to hone in on the core-self in isolation to the kundalini's sensation arrays.

There are also advocates of partner tantric who feel that the partners experience soul-mate exchange. These opinions are erroneous because kundalini matching is not a core-self experience in the strict sense.

Hormone Accumulation and Expression Noted

The hormone system is a kundalini based operation. It is not a core-self presentation. The core-self is a perpetual energy-generating reality. That means that its energy is constant and is the same no matter what. It is not a production-and-utilization process like the hormone system of the kundalini.

A yogi should study hormone production and usage but with the distinction that it is a kundalini-sponsored production which is not the same as the core-self's radiance. The core-self for its part may be fooled into thinking that the ups and downs of the kundalini sensations are the core-self's fluctuations. Thus the core-self must endeavor for isolation and self-study so that it can sort itself from the kundalini and can know what is kundalini sponsored and what is core-self behavior.

Kundalini Gender Potential Realized

The kundalini's gender potential can be realized here and now but its actual spread and possibilities are realized by scanning through numerous past lives and seeing the projected growth of gender formats into future lives. Such insight is not possible except through acute mystic perception.

It is not sufficient to know the kundalini gender potential. The best approach is to research past lives in deep meditation and to see the potential development of future gender roles in lives to come. For one thing, even if one has the same gender over a series of lives, still the degree of masculinity and femininity in each life may vary considerably. This needs to be viewed and assessed to understand how the core is subjected to various gender identities.

How does the core segregate itself from these dramas? How is it to benefit from these experiences? What hints does it get about itself by being taunted by the kundalini's ever-changing formats?

The face of the kundalini is flexible and adaptable. How does it alter itself from one gender configuration to another?

The kundalini must bend and twist by the pressures which are applied to it by the particular environment in which it is manifested either as a subtle being or as a physio-psychic creature. What impact does this have on the core-self?

Core-Self as Stainless

The core-self is not the kundalini psychic lifeforce. The core-self is stainless. In this existence it has no gender variation. It did have, does have and will continue to have indirect experience of the kundalini's gender adaptations. These experiences are energy extractions where the sensual activity of the kundalini causes the core-self to release energy which the kundalini consumes. This is done indirectly through the sense of identity and the intellect.

This may feel as if the core-self becomes whatever gender the kundalini displays but actually that is not what happens. The core-self functions as a power supply only. This core is realized as a neutral genderless spiritual energy source. It is not influenced by the kundalini to render itself into a gender but its energy is compulsively extracted by the kundalini. That extraction causes a feedback impression which the core-self mistakes for itself.

In deep meditation, the core can realize that it is not the kundalini and that the feedback from the kundalini does not alter it to become what the kundalini fancies. This is the segregation from the influence of the kundalini such that the core-self can realize its stainless condition.

The analogy of the transparent diamond is applicable, where if it is in a rosy light, it will appear to be pinkish. In fact it is not pinkish. It remains as it is, transparent and clear. Only in deep meditation if the yogi can isolate the core-self from the adjuncts can it realize the stainless condition. So long as there is a feedback influence from the kundalini, the self is apt to mistake itself for the sensations which are produced in and enjoyed by the kundalini.

The self must reach a stage of transcendence where even when it is funding the activities of the kundalini, it still can discern itself as being stainless and unchanged. Imagine if a diamond even when it is in the presence of a rosy light realizes itself as being transparent, even though it looks rosy to the eye. The focus of the core-self on the energy which is drawn out from it needs to be relaxed so that such focus shifts to its radiance of perpetual energy. It should focus on its uninfluenced radiance not on the kundalini's use of the radiated energy. The obsession of the core-self with the kundalini's consumption of that radiated energy must be terminated if the self to understand itself in isolation (kaivalyam).

Simultaneous Identification and Disassociation

A yogi must master the art of simultaneous identification with and disassociation from the sensuous variations of the kundalini psychic lifeforce. Initially however that is not possible. The student should begin by practicing disassociation only. If he tries to identify he will increase the focus into the kundalini's theatrical performances, doing so to his detriment with inability to introvert the core-self.

Safe identification with the kundalini is done from an observational position whereby the energy which is compulsively drawn out of the core has within it an observational recorder. This allows that the pull of energy does not fracture the focus of the core-self so that it can simultaneously identify with and also dissociate from the experience. This is self-tantric operating deep within the psyche

To become proficient a yogi should astutely dissociate during meditation. Later, after he did that for a time, his expertise will feed over into all aspects of the life style, such that even when he is involved he can draw back the core and cause a reduction in its rendering energy to the kundalini. When the ascetic is proficient in that draw back procedure, when he does it internally even without anyone realizing, he should begin practicing so that during a sensual experience he takes an observational position which absorbs some of the energy which compulsively was drawn out of the core-self by the kundalini psyche life force.

During such practices, the intellect becomes indifferent to the kundalini. Instead of working against the core-self, the intellect becomes neutral or sides with it. This allows the self to use some of the energy which the kundalini extracts from the self, for purposes which benefit the self in terms of giving it psychic insight.

Subtle Body is a Kundalini Display

The subtle body is a kundalini display mechanism. It was created by the kundalini and is altered and maintained by it. The core-self has little to do with this. Pride in the physical body or the subtle one, indicates that the self misunderstands itself. Shame about the physical or subtle system indicates that the self does not know itself. It is neither to be praised nor blamed for the activities of the kundalini even though it is involved in energizing those behaviors.

The self must nonchalantly take responsibility for the activities of the kundalini but without having either pride or shame in the matter. Unless the self is the neutral observer of the sensations, it cannot act in a way which further isolates it and gives it the upper hand so that it can free itself to execute self-investigation. For discovering its gender, the core should leave aside the sensuous hunting ventures of the kundalini.

Kundalini ~ the Big Power

In this creation, the kundalini psychic lifeforce is the big power, not the core-self. The core is a small power in the psyche and as nature would have it, the core discovered itself as a subsidiary but necessary power-supply in the psyche.

What else can it do but try to gain some management control over how the kundalini extracts power from it. As it is the core does not have the power to totally remove itself from the reach of the kundalini. To gain authority it has to meditate using specific techniques which most core-selves are totally unaware of or have no access to. For that matter the majority of core-selves are not alert to the fact that they are stooges in the psyche. Most core-selves live a pretense existence feigning themselves as directors. The fact is however that the overseer is the kundalini.

If anything, the core-self will have to endeavor to segregate itself from the kundalini before it can understand that it is a power supply only. As nature would have it, the core is allowed to assume ignorance of its position as a victim. All the while it is being used for the operations which are drummed up by the kundalini for exploiting the various physical and psychic environments.

Intellect Serves Lifeforce

The intellect cannot be trusted. It serves the lifeforce such that instructions from the core-self are disobeyed if those suggestions do not support the kundalini's plans. The ascetic must by all means get insight into the operations of the kundalini. Without this experience, the core will have no prospect for segregating itself.

In the first place the intellect moves at the whim of the kundalini. This is how the psyche was originally designed. The core-self as it is has no chance of taking full control. It must first strengthen itself before it can attempt to take even a little more autonomy.

The kundalini designs sensations. These attract the intellect which become hypnotized or repulsed from them. The sense of identity focuses into the intellect and is subjected to the desirable or undesirable traumas. This results in energy being extracted from the core-self which makes it extrovert with excitement or depressive feelings.

Core-Self Relies on the Intellect

The core-self is for sure the highest principle in the psyche. And yet it is reliant on the intellect, which in turn is reliant on the kundalini lifeforce, which is reliant on the senses for rating the environments. Being superior, the core-self is not a completion unto itself. It must be assisted by the adjuncts to get information about the environments and their contents. This reliance causes the core to be subject to sordid and beneficial influences.

Freedom of the core-self from this reliance may come if the self can isolate itself, determine truthfully what it can and cannot exist without, and endeavor to free itself as much as is realistic. It would have to transfer to another environment in which its self does not have adjuncts which are of a lower frequency than itself and where what is in the environment is never detrimental to itself.

For the time being, however, the self should decrease its reliance on the adjuncts. If it can, it should act in a way which deceases the dependence, so that the negative consequences of that association are reduced.

Attraction between the Senses and Objects

The attraction between one sense and its desirable object is a real force in this creation. The core-self is not the sense which is attracted. Yet it feels the attraction as an energy withdrawal which powers the operation of the sense pursuing the object. To get to the realization about its gender identity, the core-self must segregate itself, so that a particular sense is unable to withdraw energy from the self for sensual operations which the core-self did not initiate.

In meditation, the core-self must study the mechanics of sensual acquisition. The core cannot recover its energies without first discovering how it is used and by which adjuncts. The self may find itself in an environment where the energy-draining adjuncts are not present but it will not remain in that place. It will transfer back to this place with memories of the transcendental experience.

The self should work to earn permanent transfer to the transcendental location. It can do so by detailed study of how its energy is appropriated by the adjuncts and how the adjuncts use the extracted energy. Deep meditation is the method for knowing this.

Ancestral Occupation

Ancestors do occupy the bodies of their descendants. First of all the body is not owned by the primary core-self within it. All persons who contributed to the upbringing of a body have rights into the life of that form. This means that at any time destiny may allow a contributor to use the body.

To ancestors who have an interest in the body of a descendent, there are two uses of the body:
- To complete physical actions
- To derive an embryo

A departed ancestor who wants to do something physical may use the body of a descendant to complete that act. People with only physical vision will know that the act was done by the descendant but in fact, the motivation for the act came from the departed soul. The descendant may not realize this but may think that he or she committed the act. This happens because movements in the mind are mostly identified as being psychic acts of the primary core-self in the body.

A departed ancestor who requires an embryo may sexually motivate the body of a descendant to take lust-actions which result in a pregnancy, either in the body of the descendant if she is a woman or in the body of someone else if the descendant is of male gender. It is possible that a descendant who is so motivated may inspire another descendant, or someone who is not related, to act for the development of the pregnancy.

Besides its adjuncts, the core-self must contend with ancestral influences which may force the psyche to complete contrary desires. However understanding that the body is a joint enterprise, with ancestors having shares in its potential, a yogi should not be disheartened when ancestors take command of the body and cause it function in an undesirable way.

Plan to Migrate

A plan to migrate to a dimension in which the core-self can be its gender without being muffled by the kundalini lifeforce, should be figured by the yogi. The exception is however that from the present location, the yogi has no authority to create that plan of escape. Even though one can easily descend from a higher plane, the reverse does not apply because one cannot plan to ascend using features of a lower place.

Unless the yogi can develop higher features in the lower place, he has no foothold from which to launch the ascent. This is cause for alarm. This requires deep planning. This is beyond wishful thinking and hope. The level of the core-self is there but the core-self still does not experience itself in a corresponding environment. Instead it finds itself in an environment which suits the kundalini lifeforce. There are some related verses in the Bhagavad Gita:

श्रीभगवानुवाच

काम एष क्रोध एष

रजोगुणसमुद्भवः।

महाशनो महापाप्मा

विद्ध्येनमिह वैरिणम् ॥ ३.३७॥

śrībhagavānuvāca
kāma eṣa krodha eṣa
rajoguṇasamudbhavaḥ
mahāśano mahāpāpmā
viddhyenamiha vairiṇam (3.37)

śri bhagavān — the Blessed Lord; uvāca — said; kāma — craving; eṣa — this; krodha — anger; eṣa — this; rajoguṇasamudbhavaḥ = rajo (rajaḥ) — passion + guṇa — emotion + samudbhavaḥ — source; mahāśano (mahāśanaḥ) = mahā — great + aśana — consuming power; mahāpāpmā = mahā — much + pāpmā — damage; viddhyenam = viddhi — recognize + enam — this; iha — in this case; vairiṇam — enemy

The Blessed Lord said: This force is craving. This power is anger. The passionate emotion is the source. It has a great consuming power and does much damage. Recognize it as the enemy in this case. (Bhagavad Gita 3.37)

धूमेनाव्रियते वह्निर्

यथादर्शो मलेन च ।

यथोल्बेनावृतो गर्भस्

तथा तेनेदमावृतम् ॥ ३.३८॥

dhūmenāvriyate vahnir
yathādarśo malena ca
yatholbenāvṛto garbhas
tathā tenedamāvṛtam (3.38)

dhūmenāvriyate = dhūmena — by smoke + āvriyate — is obscured; vahnir = vahniḥ — the sacrificial fire; yathā — similarly; 'darśo = ādarśaḥ — mirror; malena — with dust; ca — and; yatholbenāvṛto = yatholbenāvṛtaḥ = yatho (yatha) — similarly + ulbena — by skin + āvṛtaḥ — is covered;

garbhaḥ — embryo; tathā — so; tenedam = tena — by this + idam — this; āvṛtam — is blocked

As the sacrificial fire is obscured by smoke, and similarly as a mirror is shrouded by dust or as an embryo is covered by skin, so a man's insight is blocked by the passionate energy. (Bhagavad Gita 3.38)

इन्द्रियाणि मनो बुद्धिर्

अस्याधिष्ठानमुच्यते ।

एतैर्विमोहयत्येष

ज्ञानमावृत्य देहिनम् ॥ ३.४० ॥

indriyāṇi mano buddhir
asyādhiṣṭhānamucyate
etairvimohayatyeṣa
jñānamāvṛtya dehinam (3.40)

indriyāṇi — the senses; mano = manaḥ — the mind; buddhir = buddhiḥ — the intelligence; asyādhiṣṭhānam = asya — if this + adhiṣṭhānam — warehouse; ucyate — it is authoritatively stated; etair = etaiḥ — with these; vimohayatyeṣa = vimohayaty (vimohayati) — confuses + eṣa — this; jñānam — insight; āvṛtya — is shrouded; dehinam — embodied soul

It is authoritatively stated that the senses, the mind and the intelligence are the combined warehouse of the passionate enemy. By these faculties, the lusty power confuses the embodied soul, shrouding his insight. (Bhagavad Gita 3.40)

Lifeforce Monitoring

The core-self should monitor the activities of the life force. It must do this by being aware of the energy which the lifeforce extracts from the core. Even though the core-self is a perpetual energy-producing reality that does not mean that it is comfortable with the energy extraction from itself.

For one thing, the extraction takes place involuntarily, which means that usually the core-self is exploited. In considering different sensuous operations, the core-self should curtail the energy expenditures which are inefficient for the self.

Sensation Interpretation

The sensation interpretation system which we are familiar with was not designed by the core-self. In fact, currently in this body, that system was discovered in the infantile stage of the body. Most human beings during their life time may not make the effort to inquire into the format of enjoyment and suffering. As the psyche is, it is not designed to render sensible information about the formation of the interpretation as to why one experience is enjoyable and another, or even the same experience at another time, is afflicting.

The design is that one or more senses make contact with a matching object and report to the lifeforce about the contact. The lifeforce in turn shares this information with the intellect which rates the experience to a memory which is presented to it. When it matches the experience to the memory, the intellect forms a conclusion, which is arrested by the sense of identity. This identity-sense informs the core-self but with a decisive energy, whereby the core-self accepts the opinion of the sense of identity and gives approval to the idea.

If the intellect and the sense of identity interprets that the experience is enjoyable, the core welcomes it. If it is assumed as afflicting, the core makes an effort to shy away from it. The effort may or may not be successful. That depends on the kundalini's attachment to the experience. It does not matter if an experience is enjoyable or afflicting, if the kundalini is unable to rip itself away from the experience, the self will endure the sensations which arise.

The flow of this communication is taxing to the core but if the self has the idea that the experience is enjoyable, it feels justified in giving energy to the experience, while if it finds that the experience is afflicting, it feels uneasy about the event. If it likes the experience, this increases its consent which results in an increased flow of energy from the core to the kundalini. If it detests the experience, an effort is made to reduce the flow of energy to the kundalini. That effort may or may not be effective because the kundalini may be resistant to the mood of the core.

Fault of the Core-Self

In the matter of power consumption, much of the energy required to operate the psyche is generated by the kundalini itself. However some power must come from the core-self. Without this power, the kundalini could be deactivated and the psyche of individual would vanish in the nick of time. The contact between the kundalini and the core-self is what produces the psyche in the first place. Hence if they are fully disconnected for any reason, the psyche would no longer be.

The fault of the core-self is that it has a preference for the experiences which the kundalini and the intellect interpret as enjoyable. This prejudice comes with an energy which deactivates the insight of the core, such that regardless of if an experience is positive or negative, the core loses its ability to regulate the flow of energy from itself to the kundalini. This causes the core to function as a willing or unwilling power-supply.

By detachment from all the kundalini's experiences, the core-self through that segregation gets free of its fault with the result that it develops the insight required to monitor and regulate the flow of its power to the kundalini.

Celibate Practice is Valuable

Celibate practice is valuable but the yogi should be realistic and not feel that the physical body is his possession. He should figure in the contributions of the ancestors who made services for its upbringing. A miscalculation about this could be fatal in the sense that the yogi's progress could be erased completely by some jig of material nature which causes him or her to enter a destiny in which celibacy or any other type of sense control is just not possible.

It is a bad idea to go up against material nature's creative powers. In the long term the limited selves cannot individually or collectively challenge material nature.

Even though celibacy is a valuable practice, it should be done with reservations and with open-mindedness and readiness to yield control of the physical and subtle body to non-celibate demands. Deep inside the yogi should maintain the celibate stance, knowing fully well that the psyche is not his for the taking. It is a shared enterprise. Whosoever has rights in its usage does not have to comply with the yogi's celibate aims. The ascetic should keep his percentage of the psyche in a celibate condition if he can. He should always bear in mind, that whatever belongs to the ancestors is not for his dictation.

When a yogi is free from the consequential energies which are due to his body because of ancestral influence, he can aim for full celibacy. This may occur before his physical body dies but usually it happens hereafter when the yogi becomes a siddha. Then his subtle body sheds the ancestral concerns and becomes free from their influence.

Lifeforce Must be assisted

The core-self must study how the lifeforce operates, how it procures energy, how it consumes energy and how it manages the psyche singlehandedly. After completing that insight, the core-self should assist the lifeforce in routine tasks. The self should closely monitor the food intake of the body. Physical food has a subtle counterpart which influences the preferences of the lifeforce.

The core-self should not continue under the influence of the sensations. The self should take itself to task for making the lifeforce a more efficient energy consumer. This will free the core-self to introspect and develop more insight consciousness, where it can better monitor its energy contribution and protect itself from wanton out-focus.

The practice of kundalini yoga should be mastered so that the kundalini becomes a more efficient operator and remains on the highest level of consciousness which is possible for it.

Chapter 22
Core-Self Segregated

In all aspects of yoga and yoga tantra, it is necessarily for the yogi to have insight about the subtle body. Those who ignore this requirement and who feel that they can jump from physical perception to spiritual vision without integrating and upgrading the subtle body, will fail to permanently integrate to higher planes.

The subtle body must be dissected so that the yogi understands its composites. There are details but understanding the subtle body begins with understanding that there a mind; there are emotions; there is random energy which in its present form cannot be tagged as either sensations or thinking constructions.

What is the Mind?

The definition for mind varies from to person. In this publication, mind is defined as the container which is felt as the head of the subtle body. When I use the term psyche, I mean the entire subtle form which includes the head. The psyche is the complete container which is the subtle body. The mind is the head of the form. This head is regarded separately because thinking and imaging takes place there. The core-self, sense of identity and intellect are located in the head as well. This is in contrast to the rest of the subtle body (psyche), which consists of its neck, trunk and limbs. In the neck and trunk there are memories, a kundalini lifeforce, emotions and random energy.

Ordinarily the intellect is regarding as the thinking/imaging faculty. Ordinarily it is not regarded as a subtle organ. In this publication however it is defined as such. The emotions occur mostly in the subtle chest but they spread in other parts of the psyche even into the head.

The lifeforce, kundalini, is usually located in the lower back part of the trunk. This feature is hard to detect except as sexual pleasure expression in the genitals. A yogi can however arouse this kundalini by doing breath-infusion. Then he gets definite perception of it. In the meantime until there is insight, a yogi realizes the kundalini as sensation feelings in the psyche. The most acute of these is the sex pleasure feelings.

Physical System is Revelatory

The physical body can be a source of accurate information about the subtle form. That depends on the intentions of the person's physical actions. If the idea is to focus on physical reality, what will happen is that subtle sensations will be used for defining physical-ness. This will not help us in yoga practice. Instead of using subtle energy to map the physical body and world, one should use the subtle force to focus back into the subtle and define that. Physical reality should help us to map the subtle. This is done by checking the contours of sensations.

A yogi must learn how to be physical while gaining subtle insight. The subtle leans on the physical. It requires the physical to complete some motivations. Still, the subtle should learn about itself through its use of the physical.

Suppression of Sensations

Austerity means the denial, suppression and elimination of sensations. It does not matter what it is, if it is sexual pleasure or simply flavor pleasure. It all concerns the denial, suppression and elimination of sensations.

An ascetic must discover if it is possible to permanently eliminate some or all sensations. He must define for himself, and he must do so realistically, as to what sensations he should deny, suppress or eliminate. Denial means that while the sensation is exhibited, the ascetic denies himself the feeling of it. This is a psychological process. Most attempts in denial end in failure because the individual may not have the power to stop the feelings.

To suppress a sensation, the yogi must have a willpower which is recognized and respected by the sensation energies such that on command the sensations cease their bombardment and become quelled.

To eliminate a sensation permanently, the ascetic must deactivate the mechanism which generates the sensation. He must first discover the mechanism. He must study it. He must know its source. He must get into position to upset it.

Social In-Focus

A yogi should curb social interest and still function socially in an efficient way. The up-front close-up social world is the one in the psyche, where the relationship between the core-self and its adjuncts must be inspected. Whatever is there as mandatory social focus should be internalized so that the sense of identity, the intellect, the kundalini lifeforce, its senses, and the memories, are reviewed and monitored. Their relationship each to the other and each to the core-self results in a community which is supervised by the core.

In terms of marriage and loyalty between partners, the first marriage, and it is a monogamist moral one, is between the core-self and the sense of identity which surrounds the core. The core cannot do anything. It cannot make a move or attempt any interest or perception unless it does so through the sense of identity. This identity energy surrounds the core spherically. So long as the self is present in this psychic creation, it cannot release itself from the sense of identity. It cannot achieve a divorce. This is a marriage under lock-down with the core being in a forced morality where it cannot bind itself directly to any other adjunct.

As a jealous woman presents herself as the only wife of a man, where she effectively screens out any other woman, so the sense of identity cordons the core-self and does not allow it to fuse itself directly to any other adjunct.

All the same even though the core-self is captive in that forced unity, the sense of identity maintains one outside relationship, one of deep love and kinship with the intellect. With itself wrapped around the core-self, the sense of identity also protrudes and touches the intellect in a relationship which is lusty.

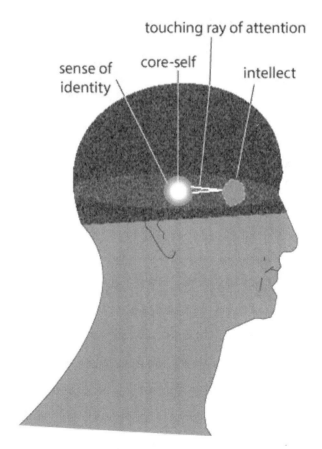

The love between the sense of identity and the intellect is such that the intellect is lovelorn when it disconnected from the sense of identity. It feels as if it does not exist when it is disconnected. For that matter it literally disappears from view until the sense of identity reaches out to it, bringing it to life again.

The intellect needs the sense of identity's interest but once the intellect is enlivened by contact with the identity, the intellect reaches out to absorb the influence of the lifeforce, the senses and the memories. The intellect takes energies from these, configures impressions and expresses these to the sense of identity, which in turn shows these to the core-self.

This is the community of the self, a supposed unity, operating like members of a family with social relationships which are to be reviewed, monitored and rearranged so that the core-self's autonomy would be increased.

Partnership Focus

To discover the core-self's gender, one has to abandon the search for the perfect partner. It is a pursuit which is perpetual but it must be left aside nevertheless. The idea of finding a soul mate is terribly flawed because it is based on a need of the kundalini psychic life-force. We have to realize that most of our productive and non-productive efforts are sponsored by the kundalini and is not serviceable for the core.

A yogi must sort the core-self from the kundalini so that he knows which is which. He will have to permit many kundalini operations. He will have to agree with fulfilling many of the kundalinis desires which are serviced by fate. But all the same he must distinguish the core's desires from those of the kundalini.

So long as the self is in this creation, it will have to service the conveyor belt of desires which are produced in the kundalini and which the psychic environment detects, resists or accommodates. Thus the yogi must be practical and service the kundalini while simultaneously disowning its operations as not being the drama of the core.

The discovery of a perfect or near-perfect partner on this side of the existential divine, in this realm of the psychic and physical material nature, has some value but it is a kundalini operation. The core-self cannot discover full-blown spiritual relationships in this environment. This does not mean that the ascetic should reluctantly service fate-enforced liaisons with perfect or near-perfect partners, but while doing so he should not identify the relationships and their pleasant or unpleasant interactions as being displays of the core.

Assistance Required

An ascetic must get assistance from more advanced yogis. The ascetic will discover some techniques but not all. Some must be acquired from great yogis who pioneered methods before. The two factors of personal effort and assistance from advanced teachers, should be applied step by step.

In this practice there is no room for only personal effort. All the same there is no room for assistance only. Both must work side by side for success. The objective is to get a foothold within the psyche for observing the core-self and its relationship with the adjuncts. This results in a clear segregation in which the core-self can analyze itself and determine what it is linked to. The influences which the core-self absorb should be cataloged. The attempt should be made to decrease the amount of energy which flows from the core-self to an adjunct. This conserved energy should flow back into the core, as that would result in increased insight and more independence.

If a behavior is complex, the core should sort the components and their contributions. It may have to compel an adjunct to cease an influence over another adjunct. Or it may have to do austerities to develop the power to compel an adjunct to act or not to act in a certain way.

If the self does not have an effective method of restraining an adjunct, it may have to get a process from an advanced yogi. It can then apply that process for the desired effect. Overall this is a painstaking, time consuming redesign of the psyche.

Self-Discovery Motive

Self-discovery of any feature of the self or psyche, is itself the motive for the investigation. However self-discovery merely for curiosity sake, is not sufficient to complete this study. One should be inspired by a yoga-guru or by a deity who wants the student to move to a higher dimension.

If the yoga guru or deity desires that one should be promoted to a higher environment that would require changes in the psyche, so that it gravitates to that higher world. Hence the authority would render assistance which with one's efforts may bring success. This is a push-and-pull operation with the student pushing himself upwards while the authority pulls the student upward. These conjoint actions are vital for success.

Kundalini's Program

The kundalini has a program which is based on its responsive and conductive energies. It manufactured the psyche which houses the core-self and its adjuncts. The kundalini is a gender display apparatus which is capable of expressing a variety of gender configurations. The core-self must become familiar with the operations of the kundalini even though the knowledge is no insight into the core.

It is difficult for the core-self to objectify itself. However if it investigates the kundalini psychic lifeforce, it will begin to develop the abstract insight which is needed to investigate the core. Reduction in the power used by the kundalini is vital because that causes conservation of energy in the core-self which in turns, awards deep introspective clarity.

Sensual Prominence

The priority of most humans is sensual access to the physical and subtle environments. This is a reasonable proposition because the physical and subtle bodies are dominated by the conclusions reached from sensual information. The language of the kundalini is sensuality. The kundalini reads sensations and replies to what it perceives through sensations.

The core-self for its part has the convention of accepting the sensual outlay of the kundalini as itself. That is not the core but until that self can segregate itself, observe and come to terms with the influence of the kundalini, it cannot determine itself.

The core-self is not devoid of senses. The core-self has sensuality. However presently it has neutral sensation energies which do not have the variety of display which is expressed by the kundalini. At this point in time, the core is like a bird with plumage of a single color, while the kundalini is a multicolored bird of paradise. It is for this reason that the core is hypnotized by the kundalini. In association with the kundalini, there is a giving and taking of energy between the core and the kundalini such that the core apparently adopts the kundalini's coloration. Thus it mistakes the moods of the kundalini as its feelings.

The core-self must discover itself by itself, as a featureless, colorless, mood-less reality which is higher than the intellect and the kundalini. It must reorient itself to itself. It must train itself to be satisfied with itself, without the variety of energy expressions which are displayed by the kundalini.

Path for Loners

The venture for self-gender discovery is a single person path. There is no feature in it for partnership. However the student must take help from more advanced entities and from deities. The social relationship with the teacher does not matter. The help is granted by the teacher regardless. The student applies the method in meditation. On occasion, the teacher enters the psyche of the student and teaches techniques from within the mind. The teacher takes a miniature subtle form to do this or transmits the method in an idea format into the mind of the student.

A student must be serious enough to venture this path all by himself or herself. It is not a group effort. Status in society does not help with this process. It is internal only, between the core-self and its adjuncts.

Hints from the Subtle Body

A yogi should take hints from the subtle body regarding the possibility of the spiritual form. However the yogi should not think that these hints are the spiritual situation. The mistake ascetics make is that they sometime mistake experiences with the subtle body for spiritual facts. Anything which happens on this side of the existential divine, on this side of the causal energy, is mundane. We differentiate between physical mundane and psychic mundane but in the final analysis both are mundane even though the psychic energy is superior. The subtle body is not spiritual. The indications of it, the lessons we can learn from it, are indirectly indicative of the spiritual body, but it is still not the spiritual form. To get information about the spiritual form, one has to pass through a neutrality energy and then wait and see what develops on the other side, the spiritual reality.

One recurring hint we get from the subtle body, which could assist us in being interested in the spiritual side, is that of social relationship. How does social relationship form? Can a man be a father without having a child? Can a man be a lover without having a partner?

Relationship is vital to gender expression. It invokes the functioning and completion of it. From this and without a definite idea, we may assume that on the spiritual side, there will be relationship-fitted bodies. As a stretch fabric tightly hugs and assumes the contour of a form, so we can assume that the format of the spiritual body will adjust according to the social proximity it finds itself to be in on the spiritual side. This leaves the possibilities wide open, but not to speculation, only to being transferred so that one can discover how one will fit into the spiritual environment one discovers oneself to be in when and if one is transferred to a spiritual dimension.

Environmental Adaptability

Physical existence has within it hints about subtle existence. The subtle body experience gives hints about the possibility of a spiritual form. Because the physical form is created on the basis of the subtle one, there are many correlations between the two levels. Some experiences of one are so similar to the experiences of the other. The subtle body however does not give us a mirror record of the spiritual body but still there are hints.

In the subtle world there are heavenly and hellish situations just as there are in the physical existence. These however cause enjoyment or affliction according to the type of physical or subtle body used. For instance in the rainy season a person with an aquatic body, a reptile, is not inconvenienced but many who have mammal bodies are put to peril.

In the subtle world one experiences enjoyable or hellish existences, according to the location and the body used in that place. Once the writer went to one hellish location where many men and women used subtle forms. We travelled barefooted on a road. It was very uncomfortable. There was no way to turn around and no way out. Everyone was compelled to move on. Some could hardly find the way due to having diseases in the subtle body. Some were blind but they were forced to move on by the threat of guards. Others hobbled along because their feet were diseased with sores and blisters.

At a certain point along the way, we entered a building. We went down a staircase into the planet. On either side we saw women and men indulging in sexual intercourse but we could not leave the stairway or stop moving to relate to them. There was a high wall and even though we could see the indulgers we could not go over. The indulgers were intoxicated by a drug. We kept moving. After some time the stairs began to rise. We were again on an open road which was surrounded by a swamp. There were men up ahead carrying huge boulders. They strained to lift these. Even though the men were some one hundred feet ahead of us, we never could reach them. It seems that as we got closer, the distance remained the same. After this my subtle body was released from that place. I returned to my physical body on earth.

This experience shows that in each of the astral dimensions, one has to use a particular version of the astral form which is suitable to that place. Such a form develops spontaneously as soon as one finds oneself to be in that domain. Whatever happens there continues after one leaves that place.

In the physical and astral existences there are both pleasant and detestable experiences but in the spiritual environment there is only pleasant aspects. According to the environment, one will have a body which suits the place.

Subtle Body Reproduction

The subtle body does not reproduce through sexual intercourse but it does so indirectly when it creates for itself a physical form. Under certain circumstances, the subtle body will attract to itself materials from the physical existence. With these it will create a lifeform. This is how creation begins. After that the lifeform with the help of other subtle bodies, creates new lifeforms through reproduction.

Due to the fact that the conditions of physical matter are ever changing, a subtle body can only create a physical system for itself when matter is in a conducive molecular format. Because matter does not remain in that condition forever, the physical forms created initially by direct attraction of physical molecules to subtle bodies, developed a reproductive ability to create other bodies. These other forms create in their reproductive organs molecular conditions whereby other subtle people can create for themselves physical bodies. This we know as a pregnancy.

A being must be manifested as a subtle form before it can manifest as a physical body but the subtle body cannot reproduce through sexual means. That is done by the physical system which the subtle body produced. A subtle body can, however, cause other subtle beings to arise merely by desire. These newly created subtle bodies transit from other subtle realms or are manifested from energy on the causal plane.

In the subtle existence, sexual involvement is for pleasure only but even so the participants might become attracted to physical reproduction. That interest would cause such subtle people to develop physical forms from which progeny could be produced.

Child forms do appear in the subtle world but they are not produced by sexual indulgence. They are not formed from embryonic development. Their appearance in the subtle existence is based on expressions of the entities who have subtle parental interest towards them.

All of this has nothing to do with spiritual existence but it does give us a hint of what may happen in a spiritual universe. Because the spiritual body is all-attentive in every part, having a child body or an adult body does not have the significance it carries in the physical world. In a spiritual body, sheer pleasure of the highest type possible is present in every part. There is no part which is pleasure-insensitive.

Abandon Interest in Kundalini Gender

For kundalini self-tantric the yogi must abandon interest in sexual intercourse. This is because sexual intercourse as we are familiar with it pertains to the kundalini psychic lifeforce and not to the core-self. All types of sensuality of the kundalini pertain to the needs, development and expression of the kundalini and not to the core-self.

This does not mean that the psyche is only a core-self mechanism. It is not that. In fact the psyche was generated by the kundalini psychic lifeforce. It was designed by that adjunct, not by the core-self. Hence we can assume that this psyche will continue serving the needs of the kundalini no matter what one does or aspires for. This is why the ascetic needs a practical method which takes into account the kundalini's plans and the isolated core-self condition which is separate but which is not the only expression which the body will manifest.

The yogi must abandon the concerns of the kundalini psychic lifeforce and yet he must realize that the lifeforce will continue its operations regardless. It is just that the core-self should be segregated so that it does not identify any of the kundalini's behaviors as its actions.

Certainly, the core-self gained companionship and servitude from the kundalini lifeforce but at the cost of distraction, at the cost of not having an interest in itself.

Actually it does not matter if the affiliation with kundalini was worth it or not. What is relevant is that the core-self should segregated itself and develop interest in itself by retracting itself from the kundalini's influence. It cannot cease every activity of the kundalini, which means that it must fund a certain set of the kundalini behaviors regardless of whether these action discourage self-interest or not. But still the core-self must retract itself as much as possible and push on to segregate itself and realize itself by itself, turning away from the demands of the kundalini and its allied adjuncts, which are the intellect, senses, and memory.

The remaining adjunct, the sense-of-identity, cannot be shed by the core self until it transits completely out of the psychic material nature. The segregated core-self must live with this sense-of-identity but it is a neutral energy when the core-self is withdrawn from the other adjuncts. Hence it does not frustrate core-self integration.

Yogis who have the opportunity to shut down the kundalini operations completely in meditation, can get a full focus on self-inquiry, otherwise for the time being, a yogi must realize the core-self and simultaneously experience the adventures of the kundalini. That is a complex achievement because while the kundalini pursues its operations, it extracts energy from the core-self which in turn causes the self to have split interests. However if the yogi does not get the opportunity to have full segregation from the kundalini, he must by all means do his best to withhold the majority of his interest for the core-self. This will render him the maximum self-focus for the time being and will promote more insight.

Gender Maturity Benefits

A yogi must access gender maturity benefits as well as gender minority privileges. The young adult status of any body is the peak of its development. All through the growth and deterioration of the body there are privileges and benefits as well as denials and downsides. The range of it however is produced by the kundalini psychic lifeforce and not by the core-self.

A study must be made about the investment of energy by the core-self. It must realize its interest and figure how it is held to identify the kundalini's developments as its own. Does the core-self lack self-development where it has to tag along with the kundalini and parry behind that lifeforce's developments, like a starving beggar who follows a sumptuously-fed wealthy man.

Realizing itself as being sexless in this creation, as being without gender definition, the core self can learn how to be satisfied with its neutral status instead of following behind the kundalini like a scavenger tailing a powerful predator to get the scraps it leaves behind.

The core-self is not developing in this creation. It is the kundalini which does so. The core-self may takes hints about development by observing the behavior of the kundalini. The self should turn away from the possibilities of the kundalini, while retreating into its neutral feature. It should realize an environment in which it may directly participate and develop without having to mimic the kundalini.

Study the Least and Most Energy-Consuming Behaviors

Even though the core-self is not the kundalini, the self is still tasked with understanding the kundalini behaviors. The knowledge of this by meditative insight is absolutely essential if the self is to curtail interest in the kundalini's affairs.

The self should know which sensations are the most taxing and which are median or the least. It should know how it is forcibly attracted to certain behaviors and how it is induced or forced to contribute to these.

In many instances, the self, even though it might have insight into the ways and means of a behavior, will still not have the power to stop the action but it should, even then, study the occurrence and make the effort to withdraw some interest from the sensations. From within the psyche, the core-self should always be busy sorting itself from the adjuncts and rating its energy contribution to a circumstance. It should know of its weakness for being involved in pleasant or unpleasant experiences.

Relative Power of the Core-Self

For gender discovery, a yogi must accept and understand his position in this creation as a relative non-absolute being with limited power to thwart the extensive mundane energy. There is no question of the yogi being unlimited or absolute in any way. Everything hinges on time and circumstance. With this understanding a yogi must be prepared to achieve or not achieve on the basis of opportunities provided by the physical and psychic material nature.

The aspiration is that the core-self will be segregated from its adjuncts permanently but that cannot happen unless it is facilitated by fate. In the meantime, the yogi must do his best to segregate from the adjuncts. He should not resent if there is a lack of opportunity. Providence owes him no favors. That is what he should know. A bird in a cage should wait patiently for the door to open. It should ever be hopeful about this even though it knows that such an incidence is hardly likely.

Continuation of Nature's Behaviors

There will be a continuation of nature's behaviors. An ascetic cannot put an end to nature's development. What we see before us is the result of millions of years of activity in the present manifestation as well as billions of years of activity from previous creations from which this one emerged. There is absolutely no way that a limited being can thwart any of this in a meaningful way. Perhaps superficially a yogi can make a minor adjustment but that is all.

Since the physical and subtle bodies are part of the material nature, their behaviors must be in compliance but it allows that a yogi can make small adjustments here and there. Eventually however the core-self will have to become totally segregated to function as a spiritual reality in an all-spiritual environment. Otherwise whatever will be will be according to the progressive alteration of nature.

Extraction of the Core

Every effort should be made to extract the core from the influence of its adjuncts. This will meet with partial success only, at least until the self can exit from the physical and psychic realms of material nature. As human beings take baths even though they again become unclean, so the ascetic must make repeated efforts to extract the self from the influences and to constantly curtail and reduce as much of the interest of the core-self which goes to sponsor the kundalini adventures.

It is an ongoing achievement which is never-ending so long as the self is in this situation. The difference between a yogi and others is that the yogi makes the effort and reduces the interest in the kundalini's activities. The activities are a continuum but for the yogi there is a reduction no matter how small. For others it is an ever-increasing participation with no realization that the core-self misidentifies with the adjuncts. Yogi or no yogi, everyone has to sponsor some kundalini activities. That is mandatory. The yogi realizes this and takes steps to retract some interest.

Shift Focus to the Subtle Plane

It is vital that for this practice, a yogi should shift focus to the subtle plane. Whatever happens in the physical existence including whatever austerity or yoga practice one does, should be done with a subtle objective as the aim. What we know for sure is that the physical body has a short lifespan. Whatever will be left as the subtle being is the objective. Thus it makes sense that the yogi should focus on that remnant self. Self in this usage means the composite psyche which one has now which is a physical and subtle body in combination. At death, we know that the physical body will be off-limits as a self or person. The subtle will continue but not all of it. Whatever in it was reliant on the physical for support will fade away, be altered or will remain with disfigurement or shrinkage.

The focus should be on the remnant of the subtle form which will persists after the physical system is terminated. A yogi should, day after day, always switch focus to the psychic plane. This should continue to happen to thwart the kundalini's continual effort to make the physical its priority.

Religious Affiliation

Religious affiliation has little to do with the success of an ascetic. It is the information about techniques, the effective practice done and the assistance from advanced teachers which determines if one ascetic will progress and another will fail. Declarations about religious or institutional loyalty is not the issue. The discovery of self-gender is a bold venture which has inner drive and assistance from great yogins as its motivation.

The argument about who is God, or about whose God is the best, has no place in this effort. Ultimately it is the strength of the ascetic and his link to some great yogins which will cause success. It does not matter if someone is theistic or atheistic, if that person does the inner research into self-gender and sorts the kundalini, he or she will realize the core-self. For that matter an atheist who is serious in this research may accept instructions from a theist great yogin. The converse is possible as well where a theistic student learns meditation techniques from an atheistic great yogi.

Physical Habits Monitored

A yogi must monitor every physical habit which his body executes so that he can log the amount of inefficiency involved in the kundalini operations. Little by little he should curb the behaviors which drain energy from the core-self without rendering for it some insight. In fact those experiences which dull insight should be monitored closely to discover ways of eliminating or curtailing them.

Sensual research may not be productive to insight. A yogi must determine when sensual participation is not insightful. For instance in sex indulgence, there is much sensual research done by the kundalini in terms of cataloging various types of pleasure sensations and yet that is not insightful in terms of the core-self's dolling out energy to sponsor the activity. Someone may indulge in sex frequently and have absolutely zero insight into the core-self and how it is related to the adjuncts or how the pleasure of the experience is formulated and operated in the psyche.

The more pleasure there is in an experience, the less insight there may be for the core-self as its objectivity may be compromised by the experience. This does not have to be so. A yogi can gain insight even in the most pleasurable or blissful experience, even in sexual indulgence but to do so he has to develop the segregation of the core-self even when it is involved in pleasure activities.

The difficulty with objectivity is experienced even during the spiritual practice of kundalini arousal through the spine into the brain. That is not a sexual activity, and still an ascetic may have difficulty maintaining an objective view. Many students become lost during such high experiences, just as they would during sex indulgence.

When one notes that a behavior is mandatory, that one cannot prevent it, one should take steps to extract from it one's sincere interest. In that case the energy from the core-self will continue to sponsor the activity but with less reinforcement.

The unwanted but compulsory behaviors should be studied. Methods should be implemented to curtail and bring them to a closure. No one needs to dictate to a yogi which habits are counterproductive. The yogi will discover these or will be inspired to realize these. He does not need moral stipulations and group prejudices to assist in curbing these. It does not concern social pressure. It is a total inside-the-psyche regulation between the core-self and its adjuncts. They are the community.

Sensual Preference

The kundalini designed the sensual preferences of the body according to the evolutionary indication of the particular species. It was not designed for the core-self's development of insight. The core-self can execute an investigation into its identity but to do so it must segregate itself from the adjuncts. When this is achieved insight develops. That allows the core to pin down kundalini operations which deprive the self of insight.

With this development, the yogi can recognize the sensual activities which are in the interest of the core. The core may suggest these preferences but the kundalini may disagree with the ideas. The core may then study how to enforce its decisions.

This will result in a power struggle in which the core may become marginalized by the kundalini and its allies; the intellect, senses and memories. The core-self will then realize how little control it has over the psyche. It could then seek the aid of an internally-accomplished yoga guru and/or deity. It is a sad day for the core-self when it begins to understand its predicament of having very little power over the psyche. It is a glad day as well.

Sexual Sensuality Control

Sexual sensuality control was earmarked as a major achievement for yogis. This was known as brahmacharya or celibate behavior. The idea was that if someone was oriented away from sexual interest before sexual maturity, that person may continue that perspective even after adulthood. Sex being a highlight pleasure is considered to be a distraction. The evidence is that once a person has access to it, he or she cannot resist. It becomes the focus of that person's life.

However, when we consider that the psyche is not the core-self, the social behavior of the person is not the behavior of the core-self. It is for the most part the conduct of the kundalini psychic lifeforce. Reform and conquest of the kundalini is not directly the mastery of the core-self over the psyche. For core-self-discovery, the interest of the self must be inverted back into the core self, withdrawn from the compliant or non-compliant kundalini. So long as the psyche continues to exist, there will be deviations of the kundalini. This is due to the fact that for survival certain unwanted behaviors must continue.

Sexual sensuality control is a major achievement in the annals of austerity. Nevertheless, it is not core-self-discovery. Efficient use of the energy of the kundalini is required before one can increase the insight of the core-self but all the same focus on the core-self is a different austerity.

Kundalini Subtle Body Sensations

At first a yogi does a study of the kundalini operations in the physical system. This is an achievement which has kundalini arousal in the physical body as a highlight of it. However, once this becomes a regular behavior, where the kundalini rises through the spine into the brain, the yogi should ardently shift his attention to the subtle body.

A wakeful physical body has the subtle body interspaced in it. In that condition, a physical experience is a subtle one as well. However, during the sleeping stages of the physical system and during the astral projection of the subtle form the yogi should study the subtle body all by itself. The operation of the kundalini in the subtle body when the physical system is sleeping is a separate observation. A yogi should complete that study as soon as he can, and before death of the physical form.

As nature would have it, while the physical body lives, the kundalini remains stationed in the physical form at the muladhar base chakra at the bottom of the spine. Even when the astral body is displaced out of the physical form during astral projections, the kundalini remains primarily in the physical system. This means that astral experiences are sponsored by energy projected from the kundalini into the displaced astral system. This is problematic because it makes recall of astral experiences to be sporadic and irregular.

A yogi should work in the psyche so that this recall becomes precise and regular. He must know how to manage his lifestyle on the physical side, so that the kundalini reserves energy to operate memory and decisiveness in astral encounters. This will allow the yogi to know the ins and outs of the subtle form, and to experience various high level astral planes even while using a physical form. Such a yogi would have astral experiences during the life of the physical body which usually one cannot have until after death of the body.

Causal Plane Research

Of the three general levels of existence within the psychic material nature, the causal plane is the most abstract. It is the one in which a core-self could get a more comprehensive view regarding its neutrality to whatever exists in the other two planes, which are the physical and subtle.

In the causal zone, one uses a causal body which is not a body in the traditional sense. It does not have limbs and senses. It does not engage in activities except perhaps to be observational of the energy which surrounds it.

The causal body is not a body. It is a state of awareness with slight observational ability and with slight objectivity which permits the self to know that it exist in slight contrast to the energies on the causal plane. On the causal level the self is surrounded by its sense of identity. It has no intellect, kundalini, senses or memory.

A yogi should go there in meditation. He should remain there for a time and garnish from the experience what the core-self is without its adjuncts except for the sense of identity, which surrounds the self in the causal zone.

Opinion

On an astral level, before its publication, Srila Yogeshwarananda, one of the author's gurus, read the manuscript. He gave this review:

If Krishna is the Supreme Lord in fact, that still does not relieve the puny selves of self-realization in terms of their internal conflict with adjuncts. The responsibility for sorting the adjuncts and gaining autonomy of the psyche still rests with the limited selves.

Since it takes into account sexual affairs, this book is a milestone in the literature about yoga. Previously we omitted that by requiring that students be brahmacharis, celibates with no sexual access and relational complications. I applaud this publication.

Index

sexual arousal,
fulfillment, 109
monk's, 98
sexual dormancy, 10
sexual energy,
composite 103
route, 193
sexual expression, 95
sexual fluids, ascent, 157
sexual intercourse,
astral, 54-55;
distraction, 112;
electrical event, 166;
female approach, 205
harasses the species, 127;
inspection of, 112;
liability, 109;
nature urge, 24;
negative aspects, 204;
purpose, 21;
supervised, 92;
termination, 108;
sexual life, spiritual world, 240
sexual potency reservoir, 238
sexual tantra, 72
sexual tendencies, cosmetic, 97
sexual urge, as a person, 18
sexual utility, 112
shaktipat, 244
shame, 309
Shankaracharya lineage, 22
shareholder, 160
shares of ancestor, 107
ship captain, 72
Shiva, 22
shock-sensation, 105
Shudyuman, 218
sickly woman, 265
siddha, 107, 131
signature mentality, 119
silver spoon, 152
singular conquest, 301
Sita, 45
sleep, 203
social adjustment 113

social conventions, 49
social involvement, departure, 101
social power, 24, 58
social property, 112
social relationship, 170
social seniority, 265
social services, 166
social-sensuality, 305
sociology, supernatural, 222
soul-mate, 306, 320
sound, consumable, 39
spark-like entity, 242
specialness, 141
species survival, 214
sperm, docking, 112
sphincter muscle, 76, 297
spices, 198
spinach, 39
spinal kundalini, 194
spiritual body, sensations, 84
spiritual form, Krishna, 241
spiritual perception, 323
spiritual world, sexual life, 240
spoon, 152
status, 115
stimulation, 27, 90
stimuli, access, 73
stop-gap, 156
stress energy, 35
stress release, 42
stretch fabric, 323
student, unique, 52
subconscious, urge, 110
subtle body,
adapter, 233
compliant, 10
components, 117
details, 114
dormant sex desire, 28
flexible, 213
frequency, 244
highest frequency, 244
hungry, 79
insight necessary, 317

About the Author

Michael Beloved (Yogi *Madhvāchārya)* took his current body in 1951 in Guyana. In 1965, while living in Trinidad, he instinctively began doing yoga postures and tried to make sense of the supernatural side of life.

Later in 1970, in the Philippines, he approached a Martial Arts Master named Arthur Beverford. He explained to the teacher that he was seeking a yoga instructor. Mr. Beverford identified himself as an advanced disciple of *Śrī* Rishi Singh Gherwal, an Ashtanga Yoga master.

Beverford taught the traditional Ashtanga Yoga with stress on postures, attentive breathing and brow chakra centering meditation.   In 1972, Michael entered the Denver, Colorado Ashram of *kundalini* yoga Master *Śrī* Harbhajan Singh. There he took instruction in bhastrika pranayama and its application to yoga postures. He was supervised mostly by Yogi Bhajan's disciple named Prem Kaur.

In 1979 Michael formally entered the disciplic succession of the Brahmā - Madhava-Gaudiya Sampradaya through *Swāmī* Kirtanananda, who was a prominent sannyasi disciple of the Great Vaishnava Authority *Śrī Swāmī* Bhaktivedanta Prabhupada, the exponent of devotion to Sri Krishna.

However, yoga has a mystic side to it, thus Michael took training and teaching empowerment from several spiritual masters of different aspects of spiritual development. This is consistent with *Śrī* Krishna's advice to Arjuna in the *Bhagavad Gītā*:

Most of the instructions Michael received were given in the astral world. On that side of existence, his most prominent teachers were *Śrī Swāmī* Shivananda of Rishikesh, Yogiraj *Swāmī* Vishnudevananda, *Śrī Bābāji Mahasaya* - the master of the masters of *Kriyā* Yoga, *Śrīla* Yogeshwarananda of Gangotri - the master of the masters of *Rāj* Yoga (spiritual clarity), and Siddha *Swāmī* Nityananda the Brahmā Yoga authority.

The course for kundalini yoga using pranayama breath-infusion was detailed by Michael in the book *Kundalini Hatha Yoga Pradipika*. This current book is an exposition of the gender-discovery of the core-self. It shows how to progress from kundalini mastery to core-self-discovery.

Michael's preliminary books relating to this topic are *Meditation Pictorial*, *Meditation Expertise*, and *Meditation ~ Sense Faculty* (co-author). Every technique (kriya) mentioned was tested by him during pranayama breath-infusion and samyama deep meditation practice.

This is a result of over forty years of meditation practice with astute subtle observations intending to share the methods and experiences. The information is published freely with no intention of forming an institution or hogtying anyone as a disciple.

Publications

English Series

Bhagavad Gita English

Anu Gita English

Markandeya Samasya English

Yoga Sutras English

Hatha Yoga Pradipika English

Uddhava Gita English

  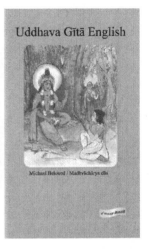

These are in 21ˢᵗ Century English, very precise and exacting. Many Sanskrit words which were considered untranslatable into a Western language are rendered in precise, expressive and modern English.

Three of these books are instructions from Krishna. **In Bhagavad Gita English** *and* **Anu Gita English**, *the instructions were for Arjuna. In the* **Uddhava Gita English,** *it was for Uddhava. Bhagavad Gita and Anu Gita are extracted from the Mahabharata. Uddhava Gita was extracted from the 11ᵗʰ Canto of the Srimad Bhagavatam (Bhagavata Purana). One of these books, the* **Markandeya Samasya English** *is about Krishna, as described by Yogi Markandeya, who survived the cosmic collapse and reached a divine child in whose transcendental body, the collapsed world was existing.*

Two of this series are the syllabus about yoga practice. The Yoga Sutras of Patanjali is elaboration about ashtanga yoga. Hatha Yoga Pradipika English, is the detailed information about asana postures, pranayama breath infusion, energy compression, naad sound resonance and advanced meditation. The Sanskrit author is Swatmarama Mahayogin.

My suggestion is that you read **Bhagavad Gita English**, *the* **Anu Gita English, the Markandeya Samasya English,** *the* **Yoga Sutras English,** *the* **Hatha Yoga Pradipika** *and lastly the* **Uddhava Gita English**, *which is complicated and detailed.*

For each of these books we have at least one commentary, which is published separately. Thus your particular interest can be researched further in the commentaries.

The smallest of these commentaries and perhaps the simplest is the one for the Anu Gita. We published its commentary as the _Anu Gita Explained_. The Bhagavad Gita explanations were published in three distinct targeted commentaries. The first is _Bhagavad Gita Explained_, which sheds lights on how people in the time of Krishna and Arjuna regarded the information and applied it. Bhagavad Gita is an exposition of the application of yoga practice to cultural activities, which is known in the Sanskrit language as karma yoga.

Interestingly, Bhagavad Gita was spoken on a battlefield just before one of the greatest battles in the ancient world. A warrior, Arjuna, lost his wits and had no idea that he could apply his training in yoga to political dealings. Krishna, his charioteer, lectured on the spur of the moment to give Arjuna the skill of using yoga proficiency in cultural dealings including how to deal with corrupt officials on a battlefield.

The second Gita commentary is the _Kriya Yoga Bhagavad Gita_. This clears the air about Krishna's information on the science of kriya yoga, showing that its techniques are clearly described for anyone who takes the time to read Bhagavad Gita. Kriya yoga concerns the battlefield which is the psyche of the living being. The internal war and the mental and emotional forces which are hostile to self-realization are dealt with in the kriya yoga practice.

The third commentary is the _Brahma Yoga Bhagavad Gita_. This shows what Krishna had to say outright and what he hinted about which concerns the brahma yoga practice, a mystic process for those who mastered kriya yoga.

There is one commentary for the **Markandeya Samasya English**. The title of that publication is _Krishna Cosmic Body_.

There are two commentaries to the Yoga Sutras. One is the _Yoga Sutras of Patanjali_ and the other is the _Meditation Expertise_. These give detailed explanations of ashtanga Yoga.

The commentary of Hatha Yoga Pradipika is titled _Kundalini Hatha Yoga Pradipika_.

For the Uddhava Gita, we published the <u>Uddhava Gita Explained</u>. This is a large book and requires concentration and study for integration of the information. Of the books which deal with transcendental topics, my opinion is that the discourse between Krishna and Uddhava has the complete information about the realities in existence. This book is the one which removes massive existential ignorance.

Meditation Series

<u>Meditation Pictorial</u>

<u>Meditation Expertise</u>

<u>Core-Self Discovery</u>

<u>Meditation Sense Faculty</u>

  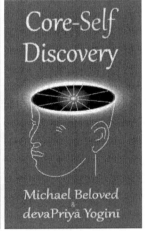

The specialty of these books is the mind diagrams which profusely illustrate what is written. This shows exactly what one has to do mentally to develop and then sustain a meditation practice.

In the **Meditation Pictorial**, one is shown how to develop psychic insight, a feature without which meditation is imagination and visualization, without any mystic experience per se.

In the **Meditation Expertise**, one is shown how to corral one's practice to bring it in line with the classic syllabus of yoga which Patanjali lays out as the ashtanga yoga eight-staged practice.

In **Core-Self Discovery**, (co-authored with devaPriya Yogini) one is taken though the course of pratyahar sensual energy withdrawal which is the 5th stage of yoga in the Patanjali ashtanga eight-process complete system of yoga practice. These events lead to the discovery of a core-self which is surrounded by psychic organs in the head of the subtle body. This product has a DVD component.

Meditation ~ Sense Faculty (co-authored with devaPriya Yogini) is a detailed tutorial with profuse diagrams showing what actions to take in the subtle body to investigate the senses faculties. The meditator must first establish the location and function of the observing self. That self must be screened from the thoughts and ideas which usually hypnotize it.

These books are profusely illustrated with mind diagrams showing the components of psychic consciousness and the inner design of the subtle body.

Explained Series

Bhagavad Gita Explained

Uddhava Gita Explained

Anu Gita Explained

The specialty of these books is that they are free of missionary intentions, cult tactics and philosophical distortion. Instead of using these books to add credence to a philosophy, meditation process, belief or plea for followers, I spread the information out so that a reader can look through this literature and freely take or leave anything as desired.

When Krishna stressed himself as God, I stated that. When Krishna laid no claims for supremacy, I showed that. The reader is left to form an independent opinion about the validity of the information and the credibility of Krishna.

There is a difference in the discourse with Arjuna in the Bhagavad Gita and the one with Uddhava in the Uddhava Gita. In fact these two books may appear to contradict each other. In the Bhagavad Gita, Krishna pressured Arjuna to complete social duties. In the Uddhava Gita, Krishna insisted that Uddhava should abandon the same.

The Anu Gita is not as popular as the Bhagavad Gita but it is the conclusion of that text. Anu means what is to follow, what proceeds. In this discourse, an anxious Arjuna request that Krishna should repeat the Bhagavad Gita and again show His supernatural and divine forms.

However Krishna refuses to do so and chastises Arjuna for being a disappointment in forgetting what was revealed. Krishna then cited a celestial yogi, a near-perfected being, who explained the process of transmigration in vivid detail.

Commentaries

Yoga Sutras of Patanjali

Meditation Expertise

Krishna Cosmic Body

Anu Gita Explained

Bhagavad Gita Explained

Kriya Yoga Bhagavad Gita

Brahma Yoga Bhagavad Gita

Uddhava Gita Explained

Kundalini Hatha Yoga Pradipika

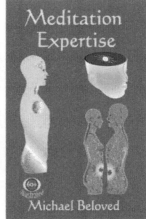
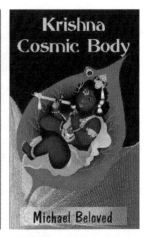

Yoga Sutras of Patanjali *is the globally acclaimed text book of yoga. This has detailed expositions of yoga techniques. Many kriya techniques are vividly described in the commentary.*

Meditation Expertise is an analysis and application of the Yoga Sutras. This book is loaded with illustrations and has detailed explanations of secretive advanced meditation techniques which are called kriyas in the Sanskrit language.

Krishna Cosmic Body is a narrative commentary on the Markandeya Samasya portion of the Aranyaka Parva of the Mahabharata. This is the detailed description of the dissolution of the world, as experienced by the great yogin Markandeya who transcended the cosmic deity, Brahma, and reached Brahma's source who is the divine infant, Krishna.

Anu Gita Explained is a detailed explanation of how we endure many material bodies in the course of transmigrating through various life-forms. This is a discourse between Krishna and Arjuna. Arjuna requested of Krishna a display of the Universal Form and a repeat narration of the Bhagavad Gita but Krishna declined and explained what a siddha perfected being told the Yadu family about the sequence of existences one endures and the systematic flow of those lives at the convenience of material nature.

Bhagavad Gita Explained shows what was said in the Gita without religious overtones and sectarian biases.

Kriya Yoga Bhagavad Gita shows the instructions for those who are doing kriya yoga.

Brahma Yoga Bhagavad Gita shows the instructions for those who are doing brahma yoga.

Uddhava Gita Explained shows the instructions to Uddhava which are more advanced than the ones given to Arjuna.

Bhagavad Gita is an instruction for applying the expertise of yoga in the cultural field. This is why the process taught to Arjuna is called karma yoga which means karma + yoga or cultural activities done with yogic insight.

Uddhava Gita is an instruction for apply the expertise of yoga to attaining spiritual status. This is why it is explains jnana yoga and bhakti yoga in detail. Jnana yoga is using mystic skill for knowing the spiritual part of existence. Bhakti yoga is for developing affectionate relationships with divine beings.

Karma yoga is for negotiating the social concerns in the material world. It is inferior to bhakti yoga which concerns negotiating the social concerns in the spiritual world.

This world has a social environment. The spiritual world has one too.

Currently, Uddhava Gita is the most advanced and informative spiritual book on the planet. There is nothing anywhere which is superior to it or which goes into so much detail as it. It verified that historically Krishna is the most advanced human being to ever have left literary instructions on this planet. Even Patanjali Yoga Sutras which I translated and gave an application for in my book, **Meditation Expertise***, does not go as far as the Uddhava Gita.*

Some of the information of these two books is identical but while the Yoga Sutras are concerned with the personal spiritual emancipation (kaivalyam) of the individual spirits, the Uddhava Gita explains that and also explains the situations in the spiritual universes.

Bhagavad Gita is from the Mahabharata *which is the history of the Pandavas. Arjuna, the student of the Gita, is one of the Pandavas brothers. He was in a social hassle and did not know how to apply yoga expertise to solve it. On the battlefield, Krishna gave him a crash-course on yogic social interactions.*

Uddhava Gita is from the Srimad Bhagavatam (Bhagavata Purana), *which is a history of the incarnations of Krishna. Uddhava was a relative of Krishna. He was concerned about the situation of the deaths of many of his relatives but Krishna diverted Uddhava's attention to the practice of yoga for the purpose of successfully migrating to the spiritual environment.*

Kundalini Hatha Yoga Pradipika *is the commentary for the Hatha Yoga Pradipika of Swatmarama Mahayogin. This is the detailed process about asana posture, pranayama breath infusion, complex compressions of energy, naad sound resonance intonement and advanced meditation practice.*

This is the singular book with all the techniques of how to reform and redesign the subtle body so that it does not have the tendency for physical life forms and for it to attain the status of a siddha.

These books are based on the author's experiences in meditation, yoga practice and participation in spiritual groups:

Specialty

Spiritual Master

sex you!

Sleep Paralysis

Astral Projection

Masturbation Psychic Details

In **Spiritual Master**, *Michael draws from experience with gurus or with their senior students. His contact with astral gurus is rated. He walks you through the avenue of gurus showing what you should do and what you should not do, so as to gain proficiency in whatever area of spirituality the guru has proficiency.*

sex you! *is a masterpiece about the adventures of an individual spirit's passage through the parents' psyches. The conversion of a departed soul into a sexual urge is described. The transit from the afterlife to residency in the emotions of the parents is detailed. This is about sex and you. Learn about how much of you comprises the romantic energy of your would-be parents!*

Sleep Paralysis *clears misconceptions so that one can see what sleep paralysis is and what frightening astral experience occurs while the paralysis is being experienced. This disempowerment has great value in giving you confidence that you can and do exist even if you are unable to operate the physical body. The implication is that one can exist apart from and will survive the loss of the material form.*

Astral Projection *details experiences Michael had even in childhood, where he assumed incorrectly that everyone was astrally conversant. He discusses the life force psychic mechanism which operates the sleep-wake cycle of the physical form, and which budgets energy into the separated astral form which determines if the individual will have dream recall or no objective awareness during the projections. Astral travel happens on every occasion when the physical body sleeps. What* is missing in awareness is the observer status while the astral body is separated.

Masturbation Psychic Details *is a surprise presentation which relates what happens on the psychic plane during a masturbation event. This does not tackle moral issues or even addictions but shows the involvement of memory and the sure but hidden subconscious mind which operates many features of the psyche irrespective of the desire or approval of the self-conscious personality.*

Online Resources

Email:	*michaelbelovedbooks@gmail.com*
	axisnexus@gmail.com
Website:	*michaelbeloved.com*
Forum:	*inselfyoga.com*
Posters:	*zazzle.com/inself*

Made in the USA
Columbia, SC
22 December 2024

50507797R00200